P9-CMY-025

THE RIPON PAPERS 1963-1968

Edited By
Lee W. Huebner & Thomas E. Petri

THE NATIONAL PRESS, INC.
128 C STREET NORTHEAST
WASHINGTON, D. C. 20002

Library of Congress Card No. 68-8699

Manufactured in the United States of America
McGregor & Werner, Inc.

Contents

INTRODUCTION AND ACKNOWLEDGMENTS

Each chapter of *The Ripon Papers* was originally issued by the Ripon Society as a position paper or appeared as an article in the Society's monthly magazine, the Ripon FORUM. Each paper had its genisus with one or two individuals in the organization who took the lead in formulating an idea and then researching it and writing their conclusions. After the initial drafting is completed a paper is circulated among the Society's National Governing Board, chapter members and individuals of competence outside the organization before being returned to the original authors for final drafting. By employing this process we have sought to realize the advantages of individual creativity and verve as well as securing the benefits of outside criticism and group judgment.

And now for some well earned expressions of appreciation. First to John S. Saloma, III, the first President of the Ripon Society. He guided the group through its first years and is responsible for inspiring many of the papers here collected. While not themselves writing material, Christopher T. Bayley, John R. Price, Peter J. Wallison, Emil A. Frankel, W. Stuart Parsons, Robert D. Behn, Ralph B. Earle, Jr. and a number of others made important contributions.

John R. Topping, William Wessels, J. Eugene Marans, John R. Lazarek, William H. Linder, Elliot Richardson, Bruce K. Chapman, Christopher W. Beal, Howard A. Reiter, Michael A. Christian, Robert H. Donaldson and Robert Dickson Crane actually wrote the various chapters of this book, as did Josiah Lee Auspitz, the Editor of the Ripon FORUM, where much here collected first appeared. To him we owe a special gratitude.

Thomas E. Petri
Lee W. Huebner

PART ONE
TOWARD A NEW REPUBLICANISM

CHAPTER 1
A CALL TO EXCELLENCE IN LEADERSHIP

an open letter to the new generation of Republicans

The first public statement of the Ripon Society was written in the weeks following the assassination of President John F. Kennedy. It was distributed to Republican leaders on January 6, 1964, as a new session of the Congress convened and as the 1964 Presidential campaign officially began.

The Washington STAR typified editorial reaction when it greeted the Society as "a new voice in the land, . . . a voice that ought to be heeded." And General Eisenhower wrote: "I am delighted that the Ripon Society is doing its best to concentrate some attention on those concepts that are truly the foundation of our Party."

The statement is reproduced here much as it appeared then, for the expressions of the early 1960's have not lost their relevance as the end of the decade approaches. Ripon's sense of the deficiencies of the Johnson-Humphrey administration, for example, is largely unchanged from 1964. So is its assessment of the dangers of over-simplistic conservatism and of the opportunities for a renewed Republicanism. Now, as then, the nation's mood is grim; fresh national tragedies give special urgency to America's search for excellence in leadership.

– Editors

For a moment a great Republic stood still. Everywhere men reacted first in disbelief and horror, then in anger and shame, and then in more measured thought and silence. The President is dead. A nation is in mourning.

History provides us with few such occasions to pause and reflect upon the state of our society and the course of its politics. While we yet sorrow, so must we seize this moment before our thoughts slip away to be lost in the noise of "life as usual."

It is in this context that we have chosen to speak. We speak as a group of young Republicans to that generation which must bear the responsibility for guiding our party and our country over the coming decades. We speak for a point of view in the Republican Party that has too long been silent.

The Republican Party today faces not only an election but a decision. Shall it become an effective instrument to lead this nation in the last third of the twentieth century? Shall it emerge from the current flux of American politics as the new majority party? Or shall it leave the government of the nation to a party born in the 1930's which appears unable to meet the challenge of a radically new environment?

We should like to approach this decision from three aspects – the strategy for achieving a new Republican consensus, the nature of a Republican philosophy appropriate to our times, and the qualities of excellence required in our leadership.

TOWARD A NEW REPUBLICAN CONSENSUS

Recent election results indicate that there is no clear political consensus in the country. We are perhaps at one of those points in our political history when a new majority is about to emerge.

American politics has been by and large one-party politics. A single party has been dominant for considerable periods of our past history – the party of Thomas Jefferson, the party of Abraham Lincoln, and most recently the party of Franklin Roosevelt. Each of these great parties emerged during a period of revolution in political ideas and was based upon a new majority consensus.

The Roosevelt coalition of the 1930's is still the majority party in this country. But its loyalties are fading, its base is eroding, and its dynamism has been exhausted. FDR forged his great coalition of the urban minorities, trade unions, "liberal" intellectuals, farmers, and the Democratic South with a program to meet the economic distress of the depression years. Accordingly, the Democratic party of today looks *back* to 1932 and 1936 and has never quite been able to escape the dialogue of domestic politics from that period. In a real sense the Democratic coalition of the 1930's, dedicated to the preservation of its economic and social gains since the Great Depression has become the "stand-pat" party of today.

At the time of his death, John F. Kennedy was attempting to rebuild the Roosevelt coalition – to infuse it with the idealism of a new generation that found the political issues of the depression years increasingly irrelevant. He was seeking to lift the Democratic party to a broader international concern. But fate deprived him of that opportunity – and fate also delivered control of his party to a leader far closer to the era of Roosevelt than to his own. Lyndon Johnson tried to put Roosevelt's coalition back together once again. Trained as an apprentice of the New Deal; representing the Southern wing of his party with its decidedly regional orientation; inclined by temperament to national rather than international concerns; will he not be a "prisoner of the past?" While the nation may admire his knowledge of political power and his ability to manipulate it, Lyndon Johnson is not likely to fire the hearts and minds of Americans. At best, his will be an administration of "continuity." And so will any Democratic administration which does not take cognizance of the radically transformed nature of American politics.

If the Democratic party, bound to the cliches and fears of past history, is incapable of providing the forward-looking leadership this country needs, the Republican party must. There are at least two courses open to the party – the strategy of the right and the strategy of the center. We feel strongly that the center strategy is the only responsible choice the party can take.

The strategy of the right is a strategy for consolidating a minority position. It is an effort to build a coalition of all who are opposed to something. As an "anti-" movement it has been singularly devoid of positive programs for political action. The size and enthusiasm of the conservative movement should not be discounted, however. It represents a major discontent with the current state of our politics, and, properly channeled, it could serve as a powerful constructive force. But the fact remains that the strategy of the right, based as it is on a platform of negativism, can provide neither the Republican party with an effective majority nor the American people with responsible leadership.

The strategy of the right should be rejected for another basic reason. It is potentially divisive. Just as Disraeli warned the British Conservative party a century ago of the dangers of the "two Englands," so would we speak out against a party realignment of the small states of the West and South against the urban centers of America – or any similar realignment that would pit American against American on the basis of distrust or suspicion. We must purge our politics of that rancor, violence, and extremism that would divide us. In the spirit of Lincoln, we must emphasize those goals and ideals which we hold in common as a people:

> *With malice toward none; with charity for all; with firmness in the right, as God gives us to see the right, let us strive to finish the work we are in; to bind up the nation's wounds; . . . – to do all which may achieve and cherish a just and lasting peace among ourselves, and with all nations.*

We believe that the future of our party lies not in extremism, but in moderation. The moderate course offers the Republican party the best chance to build a durable majority position in American politics. This is the direction the party must take if it is to win the confidence of the "new Americans" who are not at home in the politics of another generation: the new middle classes of the suburbs of the North and West – who have left the Democratic cities but have not yet found a home in the Republican party; the young college graduates and professional men and women of our great university centers – more concerned with "opportunity" that "security;" the moderates of the new South – who represent the hope for peaceful racial adjustment and who are insulted by a racist appeal more fitting another generation. These and others like them hold the key to the future of our politics.

Since 1960 John F. Kennedy had moved to preempt the political center. Republican moderates for the most part remained silent. Now the very transfer of power means that the center is once again contestable. We believe that the Republican party should accept the challenge to fight for the middle ground of American politics. The party that will not acknowledge this political fact of life and courageously enter the contest for power does not merit and cannot possibly win the majority support of the American people.

Must the Republican party then adopt Kennedy-New Frontier programs to compete for the center? No. Such a course would be wrong and it would smack so obviously of "political opportunism" as to insure its defeat. The Republican appeal should be rooted in the party's own rich history and current strengths. As Republicans, we must prove to the American people that our party, unbeholden to the hostages of a faded past, is a more flexible instrument for the governing of this great nation and for the realization of dignity at home and around the world.

TOWARD A MATURE REPUBLICAN PHILOSOPHY

A Republican philosophy capable of capturing the imagination of the American people must have at least three attributes. It must be oriented toward the solution of the major problems of our era – it must be "pragmatic" in emphasis. It must also be "moderate" in its methods – concerned more with the complexities of the means toward a solution than with a simplistic view of the ends. And finally, it must marry these attributes of pragmatism and moderation with a passion to get on with the tasks at hand.

* * * * *

First, our philosophy must be oriented toward the solution of problems. The image of "negativism" that has too frequently been attached to our party must be dispelled. The new generation in American politics is looking for a party that is able to grasp the problems of the last third of the twentieth century and able to devise meaningful solutions to them. We note only the most salient: the legitimate aspirations of the Negro in the northern cities, as well as in the South; the human adjustments to the process of automation in industry and in business; the phenomenon of the megalopolis with the attendant problems in housing, transportation and community services; the emphasis of quality in our educational system, our health services, and our cultural services in general.

The Democratic party will have solutions or purported solutions to all these domestic problems. But does it have the imagination demanded by the new world we face? Or will its answers merely be retreads of the "New Deal," more of the same, more indiscriminate massive federal spending, more government participation in the economic and social life of the nation and of the individual?

If our times demand new vision and new solutions on the domestic scene, how much greater is the need on the international front. The greatest challenge this nation will face in 1970, 1975 and 1980 will most likely be decisions in its foreign policy. Merely "to continue" our foreign policy will not be enough. The American President must now serve as "the first statesman of the world." He must set new directions in foreign policy, shape new relationships with Europe, pioneer new means of weapon control, understand the diffusion of power within the Communist bloc. All of this will demand the finest qualities of statesmanship, of political engineering, of shrewd bargaining and adjustment of which our nation is capable. The Republican party has produced a proud lineage of pragmatic statesmen since Lincoln. It is our hope that once again it will provide the leadership to meet the occasion.

* * * * *

While our philosophy and our program must be pragmatic so must it be moderate. Simply to define the problems is not to solve them. The moderate recognizes that there are a variety of means available to him, but that there are no simple unambiguous ends. He recognizes hundreds of desirable social goals where the extremist may see only a few. Moreover, the moderate realizes that ends not only compete with one another, but that they are inextricably related to the means adopted for their pursuit. The moderate chooses the center – the middle road – not because it is half way between left and right. He is more than a non-extremist. He takes this course since it offers him the greatest possibility for constructive achievement.

In contrast, the extremist rejects the complexity of the moderate's world. His is a state of mind that insists on dividing reality into two antithetical halves. The gray is resolved into black and white. Men are either good or evil. Policies are either Communist or anti-Communist. It is understandable that the incredible complexity and mounting frustrations of our world will cause men to seek one right answer – the simple solution. The moderate cries out that such solutions do not exist, but his would appear to be a thankless task. Who will reward him for telling them their dreams can never be? It is not surprising that the doctrinaire has always reserved his greatest scorn for the pragmatist and not for his opposite number. The moderate poses the greatest danger to the extremist because he holds the truth that there is no simple "truth" which will answer all his questions with ease.

Moderation is not a full-blown philosophy proclaiming the answers to all our problems. It is, rather, a point of view, a plea for political sophistication, for a certain skepticism to total solutions. The moderate has the audacity to be adaptable. The Republican moderate approaches these problems from a more conservative perspective, the Democratic moderate from a more liberal one. The fact that we may meet on common ground is not "me-tooism." It is time to put away the tired old notion that to be "real Republicans" we must be as different as possible from our opponents! There is no more sense in that view than in the idea that we must be for isolationism, prohibition, or free love because our opponents are not. It is time we examined the merits of a solution in itself rather than set our policy simply in terms of the position the Democratic party may have taken.

* * * * *

But can the moderate produce the image of conviction and dedication that has been so much a part of the attraction of extremists throughout history? Is the "flaming moderate" just a joke, or is he a viable political actor? Can we be emotional about a politics so pluralistic, so relative, so limited in its range of available maneuver? Perhaps we share the too abundant enthusiasm of youth but we feel that we not only can – we must. We must show our world that our emotion can be aroused by a purpose more noble and a challenge more universal than the cries of an irresponsible extremism. Tempered with an honest uncertainty we must be ever willing to enter upon yet another great crusade. We must learn to be as excited about openmindedness as we once were about final answers, as dedicated to partial solutions as we have been to panaceas. We must engage life as we find it, boldly and courageously, with the conviction that if we and reason endure we shall surely succeed – and with the knowledge that the greatest sin is not to have fought at all.

TOWARD EXCELLENCE IN REPUBLICAN LEADERSHIP

The Republican party must not only define a new strategy and a positive program but it must now find the men who can forge a new national party; men who can renew the great progressive Republican tradition; men who possess the qualities of excellence that we should be the first to see as "the Kennedy legacy."

As Republicans we have often disagreed with programs of the New Frontier. As members of the responsible opposition we have been critical of the Kennedy administration's performance. But as Americans and as members of a generation still younger than his, there was something in John F. Kennedy that we admired. It would be petty to ignore this, dishonest to deny that we look for no lesser qualities in the future leadership of our own party.

John F. Kennedy brought to the Presidency a perspective of the years ahead. His vision of America and its role in the world was not simply the product of youth, of the "new generation of Americans" to whom the torch had been passed. It was derived from those qualities of mind and spirit that comprise his legacy to us: his sense of imagination and inquisitiveness, his subtle and keen intelligence, his awareness of the ultimate judgment of history, his courage to affirm life, his love for the art of politics, his respect for excellence. Robert Frost had spoken of his era as an "age of poetry and power."

Kennedy brought to the Presidency a style and a zest that challenged the idealism and won the enthusiasm of our generation.

Republicans protested with candor that there was too much style and not enough substance to his policies. Fate denied us a full judgment on that question. The merits of the man and his leadership will long be debated, but there are lessons in his life and death that we cannot completely escape. We have witnessed a change in the mood of American politics. After Kennedy there can be no turning back to the old conceptions of America. There can be no turning away from the expectations of greatness that he succeeded in imparting.

To all thinking Republicans the meaning of November 22nd, 1963, should be clear. The Republican party now has a challenge to seek in its future leadership those qualities of vision, intellectual force, humaneness and courage that Americans saw and admired in John F. Kennedy, not in a specious effort to fall heir to his mantle, but because our times demand no lesser greatness. Our party should make the call to excellence in leadership virtually the center of its campaign platform for 1964 and for the years to come. The Republican party should call America's finest young leaders into the political arena. It should advance its talented younger leadership *now* to positions of responsibility within the national Republican party and the Congress. Great government requires great men in government. In a complex age, when truth is relative and total solutions elusive we can do no more than pledge the very best qualities of mind and soul to the endless battle for human dignity. And we dare do no less at every level of social activity, from the presidency to the town selectman.

The moderates of the Republican party have too long been silent. None of us can shirk the responsibility for our past lethargy. All of us must now respond to the need for forceful leadership. The moderate progressive elements of the Republican party must strive to change the tone and the content of American political debate. The continued silence of those who should now seek to lead disserves our party and nation alike.

The question has often been asked, "Where does one find 'fiery moderates'?" Recent events show only too clearly how much we need such men. If we cannot find them, let us become them.

CHAPTER 2
A DECLARATION OF CONSCIENCE FROM RIPON, WISCONSIN – JULY 4, 1964

The most important domestic issue of the early and mid-1960's was the legal guarantee of civil rights. Ripon members helped to prepare state and federal legislation in this field and, in two public papers in 1964, called on the Republican party to assume its traditional leadership in this important field. The first was a research paper prepared for the Critical Issues Council of the Republican Citizens Committee and entitled REPUBLICANS AND CIVIL RIGHTS: A CONTINUING COMMITMENT. The second was a statement issued on Independence Day, 1964, from the small white school house in Ripon, Wisconsin, where the Republican party was born. It sounded a moralistic note which has come to dominate the new politics of the late 1960's, a call for the GOP to return to the Lincolnean tradition which the pursuit of "a southern strategy" in the Presidential campaign of 1964 threatened to violate.

– Editors

It began here on a wintry night in March, 1854. Fifty-three men – Free Soilers, Whigs, dissident Democrats, and others – declared that they would break their party-ties and unite in opposing the extension of slavery to the free territories. Their declaration signed by candle light marked the beginning of the anti-Nebraska movement – the political storm set off by the bill that repealed the Compromises of 1820 and 1850, the "nefarious" Kansas-Nebraska Act. The men at Ripon preferred to be called Republicans.

The nation has seen nothing quite like those years between 1854 and 1860 – either before or since. It was without a doubt the greatest grass-roots movement in our turbulent political history. It was a spontaneous movement. It swept state conventions first in Michigan, and then in Indiana, Ohio, Wisconsin, and Vermont. By 1856 the new Republican party had polled 33 percent of the popular vote; by 1860 it had projected into the Presidency a man who would leave an indelible imprint on both the young party and the divided nation.

It was a moderate coalition, avoiding the elements of fanaticism and hatred that sought to capture its center – the Abolitionists and the Know-Nothings. It had no answer to the problem of slavery itself but it had a common cause in stopping its extension. It found unity in "free soil and free men."

The movement was already well underway when a tall, angular, young lawyer from central Illinois emerged from political retirement in the summer of 1854. His words were soon to set the moral tone of the voice of protest that was sweeping the land.

> *This declared indifference . . . for the spread of slavery I cannot but hate. I hate it because it deprives our republican example of its just influence in the world; enables the enemies of free institutions with plausibility to taunt us as hypocrites; causes the real friends of freedom to doubt our sincerity; and especially because it forces so many good men among ourselves into an open war with the very fundamental principles of civil liberties, criticising the Declaration of Independence, and insisting that there is no right principle of action but self-interest.*

The men who launched this crusade could not foresee the consequences of their action but they could not abide indifference. Soon the Union was riven, the irrepressible conflict joined, and men hurled into the maelstrom of steel and smoke. They came from the prairies of Illinois, the rolling hills of Pennsylvania, the quiet villages of New England – the proud regiments of the Union Army. And they died at Chancellorsville, Bull Run, and Gettysburg. In moments of despair it was "Mr. Lincoln's war." At first it was a war to preserve the Union but irreversibly and inevitably it led to the question that had been avoided so long – the future of slavery and of the American Negro.

When renominated by his party, just one hundred years ago this summer, Lincoln had already begun to think ahead toward the course the nation must take upon the resolution of the terrible conflict.

"The purposes of the Almighty are perfect, and must prevail . . . Surely He intends some great good to follow this mighty convulsion which no mortal could make, and no mortal could stay."

The union Lincoln had saved and the party he had led were deprived of his genius at that fateful juncture of our history. We cannot know what great good might have come from his policy of moderation and reconciliation. We have still to solve the problems that he left unanswered.

But the loyalties that formed in those years, that bound the Republican party to the Union and to Lincoln have endured for more than a century. In the mountains of Tennessee, North Carolina, Kentucky; in the new states of the great midwest; in the towns and rocky countryside of Vermont and Maine men knew what it meant to be a Republican. Lincoln gave his party over six decades of virtually uninterrupted political power. And they acted decisively to enforce those principles on which the Republican party claimed to rest. They gave our Constitution those perfecting amendments that have since been a bulwark in the defense and enlargement of our civil rights and liberties. They left us a heritage – the heritage of a great political party.

* * * * *

Today America stands at another point of great moral and physical crisis. The Kansas and Nebraska of 1854 are to be found in the Birmingham, Saint Augustine, and Philadelphia, Mississippi of 1964. Once again the conscience of America – and especially young America – has been struck. Once again a voice of protest is sweeping the land. The Negro, who has waited patiently for a century since emancipation, is now making his demands on American society. They are, by and large, reasonable and rightful demands.

As Americans, we have mutely watched the brutal subjugation and twisted justice that have denied him his basic Constitutional rights. We have been silent to the injustices of segregated schools and public facilities. We have practiced a cruel hypocrisy in segregated housing and unequal educational and employment opportunities. Our indifferences and inaction have brought us to the edge of new crisis.

Civil rights legislation is one hopeful response. But we must recognize that this legislation is long overdue and that regardless of its merits it alone cannot resolve our current crisis.

Now as never before Republicans should seek leadership in the example of Lincoln – leadership motivated by his strong moral commitment, tempered by his compassion and understanding, guided by his quiet wisdom and sense of moderation.

* * * * *

Today the Republican party faces its greatest internal crisis since its founding one hundred and ten years ago. It must choose within the next two weeks whether or not it will embrace a candidate who has by his actions in the Congress and by his silence in the face of national crisis disqualified himself to be the leader of the party of Lincoln. It must choose whether or not to adopt a strategy that must inevitably exploit the "white backlash" to the civil rights movement in the South and in the suburbs of the North.

Can the Republican party turn its back on the principles and ideals which gave it birth? Can Republicans sacrifice the conscience of their party to the conscience of a "conservative"? At this hour of national need can the Republican party repudiate the vision of Lincoln? Can any man who calls himself a Republican permit this deed to take place?

We are told that we must make this sacrifice for the "conservative" principles of our party. There is no "conservative" tradition in our party – only a "Republican" tradition – born in Ripon, shaped by Lincoln – a Republican tradition which grew out of moral crisis, out of a struggle and hopes that were uniquely *American.* If we are true conservatives we will preserve that which is most noble and worthy in our heritage. We will reinterpret the principles that gave meaning to Republicanism a century ago which still hold meaning for our nation at this hour.

Where is the conscience of the Republican party? As a young generation of Republicans and Americans we feel shocked and betrayed by what we have been forced to witness – the sight of a great political party about to violate its own moral basis. For lonely months there was only one voice in our party that had the courage to speak out in unmistakable terms. At the eleventh hour others have taken up the cause. But even now there is silence . . . a silence that must rend the very soul of Republicanism. A silence in the great states of the Union that were so much a part of the groundswell of those years in the 1850's, that have given the Republican party so many of its finest statesmen and leaders . . . a silence in Illinois . . . a silence in Ohio . . . a silence in Wisconsin.

* * * * *

We speak today so the world will know that there is not a stillness at Ripon. We speak so that men will know the conscience of a great party is not dead. We speak as the heirs of Lincoln – unwilling to surrender our Republican inheritance in him – unable to escape the implications of his legacy.

Our party may pay little heed to what we say here today. The protest at Ripon 110 years ago did not stop the passage of the Kansas-Nebraska bill. But of one thing we can be sure.

The spirit that gave birth to Republicanism is still alive in the land today. The moral force of free men seeking moderate solutions to great crises survives. It will live to give birth to another Ripon. It will fire the conscience of men long after our present confusion and turmoil is forgotten. It will outlive the pitiable men who were unequal to its challenge or who denied its existence.

We are proud today to declare our allegiance to the men of Ripon. We are proud, as they were, to be called Republicans. We are confident that we shall yet have the future we are determined not to relinquish.

CHAPTER 3
THE YOUNG AMERICANS
a message for the Grand Old Party

Ripon member William E. Wessels summarized the organization's growing concern with a political generation gap in this editorial. It appeared in March of 1966, at a time when the political importance of the generational revolution was just beginning to be understood.

– Editors

The United States is entering a new political era. By the late 1960's at least half of the American people will be under 25. By the mid 70's, a third of the population will be in school and education will cost more than defense. Americans voting for the first time in the next election will have no personal knowledge of the Korean War, World War II, or the long agony of the Thirties. To them, the debate over social and economic issues which has dominated American politics ever since Franklin Roosevelt first made canes rattle in clubrooms more than thirty years ago, will seem about as stimulating as Calvin Coolidge dozing over national affairs after a New England boiled dinner. The new voters will have to choose between the last of the New Dealers, presiding skillfully – if somewhat unhappily – over this increasingly noisy revolution, and someone brave enough to say he *can do more* to improve the quality of American life. Both candidates will have to preach political morality at home and abroad to appeal to a very powerful new voting bloc, the educated young – impatient for change and ready to act to get it.

In 1960, John Kennedy's youth, flair and intelligence made enough people feel like risking a little security to discover their potential. By 1964, with the missile crisis, the Test Ban Treaty, the March on Washington, and Dallas behind them, Americans seemed primarily concerned with our moral stature at home and abroad. Senator Goldwater talked about "crime in the streets" and restoring a proper moral climate but we were still pragmatic enough to prefer working for an improved if not a great society to returning to a golden age that never was in search of the "whole man." But in his otherwise disastrous acceptance speech, he captured something of the mood of the United States. Still recovering from November 22, 1963 and richer than ever before, Americans *were* looking "beyond material wealth to the inner meaning of their lives."

A poll taken shortly before the election showed an almost total preoccupation with how others viewed us and our obvious failure to guarantee justice and equal opportunities for all Americans. When asked what they considered our most important problem, 51 percent replied international affairs and 38 percent the racial question. Only 4 percent said unemployment and 3 percent the cost of living.

In October, 1964, Max Ways interpreted the President's poverty program as an "appeal to a spiritual discontent among many of the neo-poor who regard continued poverty as an aesthetic blot upon an affluent society." It was no longer a confrontation of Republican haves and Democratic have nots. To the dwindling, unhappy few in the clubrooms Nelson Rockefeller was just as much a "traitor to his class" as Franklin Roosevelt at his egalitarian worst but most people had money and time enough to be concerned about the failures of our society.

Out of this troubled affluence has come a new, politically "aware" generation. Often maligned for their activist fringe, they are skeptical, pragmatic and better-educated than their parents. Encouraged by the Civil Rights movement and the too brief Kennedy experience, they combine a deep sense of the lingering injustice in American life with a willingness to act and, if necessary, go to jail for their beliefs. After the "silent generation" of the 50's, they come as something of a shock to their troubled elders.

When the new voters leave school and move into the rapidly expanding suburbs, their views will probably shift to the center. They won't, however, fit neatly into Nelson Rockefeller's mainstream or Lyndon Johnson's consensus. They will still care about foreign affairs, Civil Rights, and the elimination of poverty but any candidate they vote for will have to be fresh, well educated, and full of good ideas about education and how to make our cities livable.

It is difficult to say how much President Kennedy meant to young people. The first "young" President since Theodore Roosevelt, he was certainly the first to make them feel like a part of the country. A recent NEWSWEEK poll of teenagers found that 58 percent considered him a "great" President. Although Abraham Lincoln ran a respectable second, George Washington, and Lyndon Johnson, ran very far behind. In spite of the "cult of personality" that has been created about him, they see a troubled pragmatist like themselves who took chances for what he believed in and, by creating the Peace Corps, gave them a chance to make something other than a military contribution to society.

The same poll indicates that we are moving further and further away from the relative complacency of the Eisenhower era. Fifty-eight percent of those interviewed considered "avoiding war" our most important problem and, sixteen percent, the elimination of racial discrimination. Most striking of all was the survey of that most personal of all liberal dilemmas, the Negro next door.

"Nearly half" of the parents interviewed in an earlier poll said they would object to Negroes living next door but only "*just over a quarter*" of their children had similar objections.

A thirteen-year-old Iowa farm boy thinks "It's a shame to let the poor go so low. But now that they're there, what do we do about it? It isn't always the person's fault." A New York prep-school boy tutors on Saturday because he "sort of felt" he "should." A fourteen-year old Houston girl works as a nurse's aide and is trying to learn sign language to help deaf students. Already acting out of a vaguely-defined but unmistakable social conscience, they are part of the most enlightened and responsible generation in our history.

We have a long and healthy tradition of dissent, witness Anne Hutchinson, Roger Williams, John Peter Zenger and, of course, Henry Thoreau. Abraham Lincoln spent only one term in Congress because he opposed the Mexican War. We have had young activists before. Eighteen-year old Alexander Hamilton and some of his fellow King's College (Columbia) students forced their Tory president to leave the country. He also led the mob which pulled down King George's statue and melted it into bullets. Before the Civil War, Oberlin College students ran an underground railroad. Two of them died in southern jails.

If the activists of the 60's have traceable roots, they are in the Civil Rights movement. Since Martin Luther King's successful boycott of the segregated buses in Montgomery, Alabama, and the first "sit-in" at a Greensboro, North Carolina, lunch counter, thousands of students have joined organizations which usually have only two things in common: a refusal to accept their parents' excuses for the world as it is, and an almost evangelistic sense of their mission to reform society. Since 1960, student organizations – especially of the self-styled "new left" have multiplied so rapidly that many people would no doubt prefer to dismiss them as so much alphabet soup. It is easy to be put off by such well-publicized folly as blood drives for the Viet Cong, Joan Baez's school for non-violence, and the Berkeley Vietnam Day Committee's attempts to stop troop trains. Such engaging personalities as Barry McGuire and Mr.Robert Zimmerman Dylan of Duluth do little to win the sympathies of anyone untrustworthy enough to be over thirty.

But genuine accomplishment and strength of conviction cannot be ignored. Burning a draft card in the face of severe penalties requires more than a little courage. Whatever its shortcomings, Y.A.F. provided many of the hard-eyed conservatives who cleared (some would say "bulldozed") the path for Senator Goldwater's nomination. Since it was founded in 1961 by a Yale freshman, the Northern Student Movement has supplied books and tutors for Negro school children and sent many of its members to live and work in Northern ghettos. The struggle of the Civil Rights movement now bears a measure of federal sanctity but students continue to work in voter education and registration, risking the anger of the nightriders who do not agree with Senator Dirksen that the time has come. Perhaps one of the most important voices of progress in the South could be the SOUTHERN COURIER, an Alabama newspaper founded in the summer of 1965 by members of the Harvard CRIMSON and staffed by white and Negro reporters who battle Negro suspicion and white hostility for $20 a week.

It is already clear that education will replace the welfare state as our most important domestic political issue. Mountains of "baby-boom" statistics show that, within the next five to eight years, the number of college students will increase fifty percent. The school population will jump from 68 million in 1965, to 77 million in 1970 and 103 million in 1985. Teachers are already our biggest single occupational group but the number of teachers per student will continue to decline. Programmed instruction and team-teaching will have to fill the gap but a machine, however efficient, cannot teach values or generate intellectual excitement. "Meaning" is still our greatest educational problem and a poor boy, white or Negro, in a big city high school has a hard time finding it.

As a freshman he will probably have to go to an annex which is usually older and shabbier than the parent school. His English teacher may assign THE LADY OF THE LAKE or A MIDSUMMER NIGHT'S DREAM but he may never have seen a lake and all that a summer night evokes for him is the smell of hot tar and uncollected garbage and the wail of a police car. If he wants to play football he may have to practice in a hard-topped school yard or a parking lot. If he goes out for winter track, he will probably practice in school corridors and compete in drafty armories. He is used to fifteen-year old textbooks, teachers who have long since quit trying and give half their classes "study periods," and staggered twenty-minute lunches in which he may eat off emergency counters on the basement corridor wall because he can't find a seat in the cafeteria.

He sees a thousand 19th-century variations of *mens sana in corpore sana* on the walls and he can't help thinking that the head-master who quotes this is a phoney. If he wakes up in his senior year and decides he wants to go to college, he may have to spend a year in a special prep school to learn all they didn't teach him in the previous four. Used to short cuts, he read CLASSIC COMICS for his book reports in high school and now he reads the CLIFF'S NOTES on CATCHER IN THE RYE. If he was a faithful memorizer and made it into college, his freshman composition teacher quickly informs him of his barbarous English and at mid-year the Dean may tell him he never learned to study.

The costs of providing even this kind of education will continue to rise. But clearly we cannot continue to provide this squalid preparation for a modern and increasingly technical society. The quality of life and the quality of education are linked too closely to permit one to flounder in pursuit of the other. The parents of the near future will not condone the continuation of the brand of education they were exposed to, and the GOP must be prepared to meet this dissatisfaction with clear and practical remedies. Court-inspired reapportionment will bring new and powerful representation to the cities and their suburbs, handing to the groups most likely to be most concerned about education the means with which to accomplish their objectives.

Obviously federal money will be needed for education and yet neither party has really offered any workable long-range plan that will get enough money to the cities and states and minimize federal control. Revenue sharing on a "no strings" basis could be a big part of the answer.

A NEW GENERATION

Both parties must readjust to appeal to the best educated, most affluent generation in our history. If the Republican Party wants to survive it cannot continue deploring the encroachment of big government while offering no solution to the growing problems of our cities. What Peter Drucker calls the new "Technical-managerial class" will live in giant urban belts stretching from Boston to Washington, Milwaukee to Detroit, and San Francisco to San Diego. They will require clean air and water, efficient public transportation and quality education for their children. The number of young volunteers in Mr. Lindsay's campaign should have convinced our custodial leadership of this by now. We cannot continue to fight reapportionment and allow rural minorities to strangle the cities and still expect to become a truly major party again. Only one out of four Americans will admit to being a Republican now. If we keep on trotting out the same tired horses – no matter what colors they may wear for the race – Republicans may become as rare as the buffalo.

A seventeen-year old California girl talks about legalizing marijuana and homosexuality, works for a high school branch of the University of California's Vietnam Day Committee, and marches on induction centers whenever the opportunity presents itself. She did, however, spend a summer working with Negro children. If only she can manage to leaven her hysteria with accomplishment, then we can still be a "great society."

Once we were the children of God, set down in the wilderness, surrounded by what we thought were "devils", but determined to build a new society. We leveled the wilderness and conquered the devils and now we bear half the world's burdens on our shoulders. If our party is to survive, it must be a source of strength, not opposition, to the young shoulders which will bear the burdens of the future.

CHAPTER 4
SOUTHERN REPUBLICANISM AND THE NEW SOUTH

SOUTHERN REPUBLICANISM AND THE NEW SOUTH was written by Ripon members John C. Topping, Jr., John R. Lazarek, and William H. Linder after a summer of extensive travel and interviewing in the South. The project was initiated and financed by Republicans for Progress and was published in the fall of 1966. The discussion which follows served as an introduction to the 129 page analysis, most of which was given to detailed state by state and even county by county examination. The general conclusions, as summarized here, are still valid and important.

– Editors

The 1964 elections in the South produced a dramatic turnabout in Republican fortunes. In no place other than the South did the Republican Party gain anything from the Goldwater candidacy; yet in no other region is the Republican Party likely to suffer greater long-term losses. Until 1964, Republican growth in the South was centered in the urban and suburban communities, which enjoyed an atmosphere of more racial moderation, higher educational attainment and greater economic prosperity than the less advanced areas of the region. Meanwhile, the Deep South, the stronghold of white supremacy, generally maintained strong Democratic allegiances. But in 1964 the Republican Party carried all five states of the Deep South, and failed to carry a single other Southern state. The Goldwater campaign strategists had boasted that their so-called Southern Strategy would produce a solid Republican South. Instead, Senator Goldwater carried only 47 of 128 electoral votes in the South; Dwight D. Eisenhower did better in both 1952 and 1956.

The Goldwater Southern Strategy of 1964 was a deliberate attempt to trade away Republican strength among the rapidly growing Negro and moderate white electorates of the South in return for the support of dissatisfied segregationist Democrats. The failure of the Goldwater strategy to make its predicted strong showing in the South was due in large measure to the unexpectedly rapid emergence of those forces the Goldwater strategy ignored, the Southern Negro and the racially moderate urban white. While the Goldwater strategy failed to improve on previous Republican presidential showings, it did produce a radical redistribution of Republican strength. As the highly astute political analyst Samuel Lubell noted:

Of the 507 Southern counties which Goldwater won 233 had never gone Republican before. The five Deep South states he carried are a measure of the depth of support for a separatist racial policy. But all of the more urbanized Southern states responded to much the same voting influences that were so evident in the North and West. Their support for Johnson can be taken as a gauge of the degree of progress that has been made in unifying the South with the rest of the nation.

The revolutionary nature of the Goldwater candidacy is readily apparent upon comparison of the county by county returns in the 1960 and 1964 presidential elections. Republican losses were most dramatic in the large cities of the South, such as Dallas, Fort Worth, Houston, Atlanta, Memphis, Charlotte, and Richmond. Goldwater gains were strongest in those areas of the South with a large, but almost wholly disenfranchised, Negro population.

The tenuous nature of the Goldwater gains was soon underscored by the passage of the Voting Rights Act of 1965, which will produce its most significant impact in the Black Belt and other rural segregationist strongholds of the Deep South. In many rural counties Negroes will soon constitute either a voting majority or a minority substantial enough to exercise a balance of power role. Meanwhile, the progressive character of Southern urban politics is becoming more firmly established. Thousands of Negroes have been added to the voting rolls in Houston, New Orleans, Atlanta, and Birmingham since the 1964 election. The urban Negro vote in most Southern states will soon exercise a political wallop which cannot be ignored by any political party seriously intent on winning presidential elections.

The future alignments of Southern politics will depend heavily upon the type of Southern strategy which the Republican party pursues. If Republican leaders tacitly consent to President Johnson's campaign to consolidate the overwhelming majority of the new Negro electorate in the Democratic party, a genuine competitive two party system may never be realized in most areas of the South. Yet, if the Republican party re-fashions the strategy employed during its growth in the South from 1952 to 1960, it may again be able to ally itself with the forces of change working to build a New South. Republican strength in the South, unlike party strength in the North, has been greatest in urban areas. GOP organizations in many Southern cities are considerably more professional and better manned than the rival Democratic organizations. Southern Republican parties may secure the most rapid Republican big city breakthroughs by adding to their organizational strength a committment to reforms desired by urban voters of both races.

SOUTHERN REPUBLICAN GROWTH FROM 1952 TO NOW

The face of Southern politics has been reshaped during the past two decades by three revolutions – the rapid urbanization and industrialization of the South, the emergence of the Southern Negro as a meaningful participant in the politics of the region, and the growth of an aggressive, competitive second party. The magnitude of the Republican Revolution has been most dramatically displayed in presidential voting. The 11 states of the former Confederacy maintained unbroken Democratic allegiance in the five presidential elections from 1932 to 1948. Yet, in the four elections from 1952 to 1964 every Southern state except Arkansas and North Carolina has supported a Republican presidential nominee at least once. Shortly before the 1952 elections a leading Southern political observer noted:

> *To many citizens of the South, a Republican is a curiosity. They may have heard about the Negro undertaker who goes to Republican conventions, or the eccentric railroad official who came from Ohio; but a genuine, breathing Republican is a rarity in most of the counties of the region.*

Yet, today throughout the South in small towns as well as large cities there are vocal and aggressive Republican organizations. Where once Republicans hid their allegiances for fear of suffering social stigma or economic loss, youthful, exuberant Republican volunteers are seeking energetically to proselytize their Democratic friends and associates. Two Republican Senators and seventeen Republican Representatives from states of the former Confederacy sit in Congress. Republican breakthroughs at the presidential and congressional level are now beginning to be matched at the local level. Moreover, the Republican party has grown throughout the South during a decade in which it has had difficulty holding its own in the rest of the country. The factors that have encouraged the growth of the Republican party in all areas of the South include:

1. *The growth of a large class of young business and professional persons.* Since World War II, the relocation of many Northern industries in the low-wage and natural resource-rich areas of the South has accelerated the rate of Southern industrial expansion. Many managerial and technical personnel who have come from the North with these industries have retained their original Republican allegiances. In Forida and North Carolina immigrants from Northern states constitute a large portion of the organization Republicans; in Arkansas Northern transplant Winthrop Rockefeller has spearheaded the creation of an effective Republican party. The major impetus for Republican growth, however, has been supplied by native Southerners who are entering the burgeoning business and professional classes.

2. *The nationalization of Southern politics.* For most of the last century the South has maintained a distinct regional political identity. A Southerner could maintain his identity as a Southern Democrat without agreeing with the programs of the non-Southern wing of his party. Yet, as Southern insularity has been reduced by the region's exposure to network television, the national press, and other forces tending to produce national unification, the Southern voter has been exposed to the same two party influences which tug at voters in the North. The Southerner working in a large national business corporation is now receptive to the same Republican attractions as his Northern colleagues. Furthermore, the growth of labor and other forces which support the policies of the national party has sometimes tended to push Southern Democratic office holders closer to the liberal posture of the National Democratic Party. In turn, business and financial elements which have formerly enjoyed hegemony in the conservative local Democratic parties have begun increasingly to shift into Republican activity.

3. *The vulnerability of rusty Democratic "machines" to attack by aggressive Republican organizations.* In most areas of the South which are just beginning to experience two party competition there is really no Democratic "organization". Democratic strength has rested largely on tradition; Democratic organizations have tended to center around candidates rather than "party". Emergent Southern Republican parties have emphasized organization out of necessity; furthermore, the presence of a large number of aggressive young converts in the Republican apparatus has given muscle to the organization's activities. Many Democratic candidates have discovered in recent elections that their Republican opponents can count on much better election day organizations than the old-fashioned Democratic courthouse machine can provide. In some areas of the South the existence of strong Republican organizations has helped solve a recurrent party problem – the recruitment of well-known candidates. With increasing frequency, prominent Democrats, assured they would have the support of the Republican election machinery behind them, have agreed to run as Republicans.

4. *The opportunity for early advancement in the Republican Party.* Possessing few incumbents of their own, Southern Republicans can offer capable political aspirants nominations much more quickly than the Democrats can. A survey of the seventeen Republican members of the House underscores the youth emphasis among Southern Republicans. Five Southern Republican Congressmen are under forty, while thirteen of the seventeen are under fifty.

5. *White Southern resentment against the liberal economic and civil rights policies of the Kennedy and Johnson Administrations.* President Kennedy's stock with Southern whites plummeted in late 1962 when he dispatched thousands of Federal troops to enforce integration of the University of Mississippi. President Johnson's subsequent expansion of his predecessor's civil rights commit-

ment further fanned the fury of segregationist Southern Democrats. The growing disaffection of white Democrats from the party of their forebearers coincided closely with the rise of the Goldwater Movement within the Republican Party. But the attraction of these former Dixiecrats to the GOP was accompanied by losses among many moderate whites and Negroes who had begun to support the Republican Party during the Eisenhower era. These losses were dramatically underscored in the 1964 presidental election.

And what will be the effects of this Republican growth in the South?

First, a reduction of Southern Congressional seniority; the source of the tremendous strength of Southern Democrats in Congress. The presence of a rival party organization intent on winning elections should pose much more of a threat to an incumbent Democratic Congressman than the possibility of a Democratic primary challenge has normally offered. The sacrifice of generations of Congressional seniority made by Alabamians who sent five freshman Republicans to Washington may be a foretaste of a trend which will considerably diminish Southern power in Congress.

Second, a considerable expansion of political interest and involvement throughout the South. Since 1948 a drastic increase has occurred in voting participation in general elections in every Southern state. As campaigns are contested more vigorously, rival party organizations will certainly seek to recruit the support of previously apathetic portions of the electorate.

Third, enhancement of the power of the growing Negro electorate. The growth of a two party system is quite conducive to the increase of Negro political influence. Negroes can be a swing vote *both* in party primaries and in general elections. Thus, at two stages in a closely contested election Negro political leaders will have consirable bargaining power. In states of the North such as Illinois, New York, Michigan, and Pennsylvania which enjoy strong two party ststems, Negroes, who number about ten percent of the population, enjoy a strong balance of power position. In the South where Negroes normally form a much larger portion of the population, the development of a competitive two party system should help create a situation conducive to Negro political gains.

The 1964 Presidential campaign drew segregationist Democrats by the thousands into the Republican column. This switch-over was most dramatically symbolized by the defection of South Carolina's segregationist Democratic Senator Strom Thurmond to the Republican Party. Although the 1964 elections in the South demonstrated to all but the dullest observers that race would not be a profitable long-term basis for Southern Republicanism, Congressional Republicans in early 1965 welcomed Albert Watson, a defecting segregationist South Carolina Democratic Congressman, to their ranks. When Watson resigned his seat in order to secure a vote of confidence from his constituency, the Republican Congressional Committee rushed forward with lavish financing for his special election candidacy. Rather than chiding Watson for the blatantly racist character of his campaign, Republican Congressional leaders hailed his re-election as another breakthrough in the struggle to build a two-party South. This short-sighted response of Republican leaders was given considerable attention by the Negro press. Perhaps the most spectacular breakthrough in the effort to trade the Republican birthright for a bowl of segregationist pottage was scored by freshman Congressman William Dickinson of Montgomery, Alabama. On the floor of the House Dickinson delivered speeches alleging widespread sexual immorality and drunkenness by members of the clergy on the 1965 Selma to Montgomery march. Dickison's wild charges were refuted by a predominantly Republican interfaith team of clergy and laymen. Nevertheless, Dickinson's reckless attempt to appeal to racists in his constituency caused the Republican Party considerable damage throughout the nation in the Negro community, in the civil rights movement, among the clergy, and on the campus.

THE REPUBLICAN NATIONAL IMAGE

Even disregarding the huge Negro voting potential, there are several crucial reasons why the Republican Party cannot afford to acquire a lily-white tag. Probably no movement has gained more widespread support from college students than the Negro drive for full citizenship. Economic conservatives and liberals on the campuses find themselves in agreement on the desirability of effecting a full integration of the Negro in American life. Moreover, the overwhelming mass of national opinion leaders in the clergy, the press and among intellectuals are strongly committed to the Negro Revolution. If the Republican Party appears indifferent or hostile to the Negro plight, it can expect to alienate a substantial number of those who shape the opinions of the electorate. It also would lose many of its brightest potential candidates.

CHAPTER 5
CAN WE BRIDGE THE IDEOLOGICAL GAP?

This Ripon editorial attempted to explore possible grounds for the reconciliation of "liberal" and "conservative" Republicans in June of 1967.

– Editors

Across the country these days at party rallies and conventions and banquets, Republicans have been continually exhorted to remember that in "unity" lies their salvation. What is often missed in these pleas is an answer to the question: "Unity for what?" "Unity on what terms?" "Unity to what purpose?" As one reporter remarked after one such harmony-oriented rally: "Everyone's afraid to mention issues!"

The Ripon Society believes that meaningful unity requires that issues be mentioned, that these questions be answered. For issues, not personalities, are what really obstruct or create party harmony in the long run. There can be no effective *rapprochement* based merely on an empty call for cooperation or a candidates good looks. Nor does such a strategy attract Republican votes. People in politics and people who vote are just not that shallow.

Unhappily issues, particularly positive initiatives, are not popular topics at party gatherings. Many are afraid that a candid discussion of ideology will expose differences too wide for compromise. There is a real and often understandable temptation to sweep issues under the rug, to see that splits are papered over and the delicate balance of factions maintained.

We believe that the Republican party can do better than this. Where real divisions exist the party is strong enough to frankly acknowledge its internal differences rather than letting the call to unity be a public shield behind which factions maneuver. And where agreement is possible, and we believe there are important areas where it is, that agreement will be stronger and more productive if it is based on a full understanding of its ideological foundations.

Accordingly we suggest that the party begin to at least talk more objectively and more candidly about its internal divisions. If we are trying to span an intra-party gulf, then let us first map its outlines. In what area is it widest? where does it narrow? Where can it most effectively be bridged? This statement is intended as a contribution to that discussion.

To many, the issues of the 1964 convention already seem distant. The platform debate, it will be remembered, centered on extremism, civil rights in public accommodations, and the proposal for giving the NATO commander control over nuclear weapons. None preoccupy us presently, though the basic differences underlying each have by no means disappeared.

One reason the extremism issue has been somewhat muffled is the behavior of the 1964 candidate. Senator Goldwater asserted after the election that he had not seen the Romney plank on extremism or he would have backed it. He did back nearly identical wording when it was approved by the Republican Coordinating Committee in 1965 and today, in Arizona, Goldwater is himself struggling against the John Birch Society. Extremism, at least in the pursuit of Goldwater, may be a vice, after all. Like other conservatives who have come under the radicals' guns (Karl Mundt and Milton Young are recent examples), Goldwater is no longer sanguine about the dark passions that pound in some of the old hearts that "knew he was right."

The extremists are still around, of course, and the party will again be tempted to compromise with them. But the Republican will to resist extremists is a little stronger now, and there is always the happy possibility the extremists will desert the GOP for Governor Wallace and other non-Republicans who solicit their support.

A similar pattern emerges in the second area, that of civil rights, where important guarantees have now been written into law. There remains, however, an important civil rights division in the party. The Southern Strategy and the lure of the backlash still prevent the party from making a wholehearted shift toward an aggressive metropolitan and minority group appeal. Yet some GOP rightists and moderates have at least renewed their dialogue on the parry role in civil rights, a dialogue interrupted about 1962. Moreover, many Republicans from both camps are going one step farther, arguing that legal protections *alone* will never better the lot of Negroes in America sufficiently, that something more is needed. They thus focus on fundamental questions of ghetto life and the psychology of individual improvement. Here are opportunities for creative and unified Republican initiatives. The muting of the Democratic commitment makes it all the more imperative that Republicans take advantage of these opportunities.

The third issue, that of the NATO commander's prerogatives, is not presently an important factor in party struggles, though the general question could be raised again by Vietnam. Its importance three years ago resulted because it was the focus of the nuclear irresponsibility fear, one which arose out of Senator Goldwater's peculiarly careless rhetoric. But it also was intra-party shorthand for a more fundamental and lasting party split – that between "confrontation" and *"detente"* – between those who emphasize military intervention as the most useful of American policies and those who believe our strongest weapon is peaceful economic competition. One strategy may not preclude the other (each international situation calls for a unique response), but the party does presently divide on the matter of priorities and emphasis. The Morton-Dirksen confrontation of early 1967 on East-West *rapprochement* is just one manifestation of this division. In Vietnam, those Republicans who see salvation in increased force will disagree with increasing sharpness from moderates who emphasize the desirability of negotiations and the dangers of war with China.

It is true that the desire of progressives to promote more foreign aid through private channels often divides them from liberal Democrats and allies them with conservatives. However, prospects for united GOP initiatives seem most promising in domestic affairs.

They are particularly promising in new areas of concern which had not received significant attention three years ago. Life goes on and our world changes with astonishing speed. Remarkably, since 1964, the party's ideological factions have been surprising each other with agreement on a number of issues that are relatively new. We would list eight examples of issues and programs where wide ranging Republican agreement seems to be developing:

1. Opposition to the conduct and administration of many poverty programs, support for "structural-economic" alternatives and complements and for programs like the Prouty-Curtis Human Investment Act.

2. Enthusiasm for expanding home ownership among the poor through programs like the Percy plan, a proposal which boasts backing from all 35 GOP Senators.

3. Wide support for the principle of federal revenue sharing with the states and localities, and for its corollary, progressive and innovative government on the state and local level.

4. Wide and growing recognition of the inequity and inefficiency of the present draft. A preference is emerging for an all-voluntary military, a program consistent with the libertarian position of a Taft and a Vandenberg, and now the program of Senator Goldwater, Senator Hatfield, and the Ripon Society.

5. Growing moderate and libertarian support for replacement of the dehumanizing and wasteful "Welfare State" with an "Opportunity State" based in large part on a Negative Income Tax.

6. Agreement on the need for more problem solving by volunteer organizations as a complement to and in some cases a replacement for governmental or even business efforts. Both our leaders and our laws create a climate which encourages such volunteer responsibility. A Republican President could demonstrate and inspire such a new attitude, and otherwise foster more reflection upon and more public recognition for the potential of the independent sector.

7. Party-wide recognition of the problem of de-personalized government and its impact upon the way a citizen perceives his rights and powers and responsibilities. This problem is understood more clearly than it was, and the proposed solutions – neighborhood mayors, ombudsmen, and so on – are growing ever more specific. Senator Scott has presented one outline of the matter in his introduction to the Ripon Society's recent book, *From Disaster to Distinction.*

8. A recognition by conservatives and progressives alike of the growing burden of educational costs and the consequent inability of private colleges to maintain their relative standing in the total educational picture. Many Republicans see an answer to these and associated programs through direct federal aid to college students, (either through tax credits or outright grants) as a way of stimulating private education while avoiding governmental controls.

All of these issues and programs represent positive attempts to deal with the dehumanizing or inefficient consequences of centralized power. But on each of the above issues, many conservative and progressive Republicans agree. Interestingly, they do not attract support from all in either camp, which raises the question of how much the conservative-liberal definitions explain. It is curious, for example, that a proposal like the volunteer army has received precious little support *or even attention* from the party's Congressional leadership, despite its endorsement by the 1964 platform.

Certainly sensitive progressives need not celebrate party leaders just because they call themselves "moderates" when they seduously avoid creative stands on one major issue after another. Nor need they castigate all conservatives when some conservative thinkers contribute to their own political guidance. *If there is an ideological split between progressives and conservatives, then there is also a real split between those who want to use principles to solve public problems and those who do not. The rightist obstructionists and moderate do-nothings are together in the latter camp and their number is legion.*

Thus in one respect, thoughtful progressives may have more in common with their counterparts on the right than with the personality cultists of all factions, the superficial many for whom the final mark of all that is good is its ephemeral popularity. And certainly those from either wing who seek new answers to perplexing problems will make a greater contribution than those whose ultimate litmus test is "Where did you stand on Goldwater?" or "What do you think of Rockefeller?" Ripon's ideological premises may not be those of a libertarian-conservative like Milton Friedman, let alone a traditionalist-conservative like William Buckley (and it's time we learned to distinguish the two varieties), but we can at least grant that some intellectuals on the right are thinking.

If we find that in some areas their thinking and ours coincide, greater is the chance for bringing the rest of the party around to the position in question.

Consequently, we submit that there is a need for greater intra-party examination of where Republicans stand on issues. The hope for some common ground which is expressed in the list cited earlier is only a hope. Such hopes have been held in the past, but they have faded in the lights of personal campaigns. This present expression may not survive the political fires ahead; to become a reality it needs encouragement from all points of view within the GOP. But it must be given substance in a positive manner, not in compromising differences, not in seeking a lowest common denominator by chopping off the sharp corners and offensive edges from factional positions. *What the party needs today is a quest for ideological consensus based on a common search by all segments for new and bold programs which need no such whittling down.* There are many opportunities for such agreement, particularly on the domestic scene. The way to realize them is for serious thinkers on all sides to sit down independent of political motivations and begin intensive and honest communication with one another.

Increased communication can clear up misunderstanding as to where we differ. Clearly there are important – perhaps fundamental – differences, but it will hurt no one to examine them, and it may increase the respect of each side for the views of the other. On the other hand, communication will help the party to better appreciate the extent of its common ground.

The Ripon Society would submit this proposal as a first step toward such a goal, a preliminary step to the writing of a national platform. Let a committee of Republican thinkers not identified with current political campaigns gather to *seek some unity through creativity rather than through mere accommodation.* Let it be small enough to prevent posturing and let it represent a broad cross-section of ideological viewpoints. Rather than calling on active politicans, let it bring together thinkers of the right and left (writers, scholars, representatives of idea-oriented groups like the Ripon Society). Too often such people who could help the party to appreciate the overall application of its philosophy have been relegated to the periphery of politics, when as in British and European life they should be utilized at the very center of action. The Coordinating Committee or the Congressional leadership could sponsor such meetings, which should be private and involve no formal votes. The goal would be educational not political. The mandate would *not* be to write a compromise program for the party. That starts at the wrong end and accomplishes nothing. Instead let such a committee seek first to understand and better articulate areas of disagreement, second to probe for coinciding objectives, and finally to propose ways in which a unified, creative program might be realized.

Let it be perfectly clear that the Republican split will not be healed by means of the project suggested here. No single party in a two-party system will ever be perfectly harmonious, and the current GOP split is more serious than most. But the proposal is a start, and the differences will never be diminished if they are not confronted. Because both parties are necessarily coalitions, and because coalitions thrive best when a common cause motivates its member factions, such a conversation could help the Republican party. At the very least it would improve the level of intra-party debate.

In January of 1967 Barry Goldwater was sent a copy of the Ripon Society's paper on the draft. In his reply he said, "Some time it might be to the mutual advantage of all Republicans to sit down and explore in detail just how close this party is together and how drastically separated the opposition has become." Later (in correspondence with a member) he explained that while he thought it a good idea for the "liberals" and the "conservatives" to get together "to find out where their thinking is different," he felt "the real effort of unity must come from the so-called liberal side." This proposal represents such an effort.

In this regard, it is useful to consider the problem of the Republican Party's "national image". There can be little question that the actions of a Republican Party in one state may influence the electoral success of a Republican Party in another state. If the Republican Party is to win elections in California, Ohio, Illinois, New York, and Michigan, it cannot afford the albatross of staunchly segregationist fraternal parties in the Deep South. Those who take a laissez-faire attitude toward this situation and argue that each state party should have absolute policy discretion in its operation ignore the crucial interdependence which all fifty state parties share.

The defection to the GOP of Dixiecrat politicians who have become uncomfortable in the Democratic Party because of their disagreement with its civil rights views is an embarrassment which the Republican Party has only recently experienced. Some argue that since the Democratic Party has had, and still does have, a large segregationist wing in Congress and yet has won elections, the Republican Party can afford to accept a few of these same segregationists on its side of the aisle. Such a "pragmatic" argument overlooks the realities of the Republican position. Although the Democratic Party has for generations possessed a large segregationist wing in Congress, it has also in modern times enjoyed a powerful pro-civil rights Northern wing. In the past two years the National Democratic Party has finally dropped its position of ambivalence on race to support firmly the principle of an open nationwide party. It would be remarkably short-sighted for the Republican Party to adopt the Democratic strategy of ambivalence just as that party is discarding its obsolete posture.

With the growth of a revitalized Republican Party, many areas of the South are experiencing the first real taste of party competition which they have had in this century. In these circumstances, if a party polarization were to occur along racial lines, a lily-white Southern state party would be much more of an embarrassment to its party nationally than has been the case in one party states. While the Democratic parties of the South have hardly been sympathetic to Negro aspirations, they have not had to outdo any opposing party in their championing of segregationist views. Although it is evident that an adoption of a "white man's party" stance by the Southern GOP would have catastrophic consequences for the Republican Party, strong forces are at work in a number of Southern state parties, particularly those of South Carolina and Alabama, to establish the Republican Party on a white-only basis. It is imperative that national Republican leaders and well-intentioned party leaders in these states act decisively to stem this tragic tide.

The surest means of insuring that Southern state parties will not be committed either explicitly or implicitly to anti-Negro policies is through increased activity by Negroes in Southern Republican organizations. But it should be recognized that any program to secure meaningful Negro participation in Southern Republican activities possesses a partially revolutionary aspect and will be stoutly resisted. Almost to a man, the Negro Republican can be expected to support progressive Republicans in efforts against the ultra-right. In addition, the presence and activity of Negroes in the Republican Party will enable the party to avoid becoming a lily-white haven for rabid segregationist Democrats who may be uncomfortable at the expected mass arrival of Negroes into Democratic primaries.

Moral and political considerations demand that the Republican Party guarantee that the Southern Negro will feel welcome and comfortable in the party which was founded to resist the spread of Negro slavery.

A CRISIS OF CONSCIENCE

"Is our party the party of Lincoln or the party of Thurmond?" many Republicans asked themselves in the fall of 1964 as they watched their party marching through Dixie in a presidential campaign all too reminiscent of the Dixiecrat effort of 1948. The defection of Southern Democratic Senator Strom Thurmond to the Republican Party at the height of the Goldwater presidential campaign served to increase the disgust of many Republicans with their party's apparent repudiation of the principles of advancing Negro rights upon which it was founded. Thurmond, who had headed the 1948 States' Rights archsegregationist Presidential ticket and who had since carved out a niche for himself as the most outspoken spokesman for white supremacy in the United States Senate, seemed a curious addition to a party which had almost singlehandedly ended slavery and passed the Thirteenth, Fourteenth, and Fifteenth Amendments.

Perhaps the most disturbing aspect for the Republican future of this sudden attraction of Thurmond and other segregationists to its ranks was the incredibly unfortunate timing. Just as this nation was undergoing the second great moral revolution in its history – the Negro drive for full acceptance in the mid-twentieth century as first class American citizens – the Republican

Party appeared to be pandering to those elements in the South intent on turning back the clock of history. While the powerful Republican leader in the Senate, Everett McKinley Dirksen of Illinois pleaded for the passage of the civil rights bill, the Republican Party went on in its 1964 San Francisco Convention to choose as its presidential nominee one of a handful of non-Southern Republican members of Congress who had opposed the 1964 Civil Rights Act.

At that moment both great American political parties stood at a crossroads in history. The young Democratic President, while affirming his sympathy for Negro aspirations, nevertheless refused to send a civil rights bill to Congress, despite the urgings of members of Congress of both parties. He sought instead by a gradualist approach to assuage Negro demands without alienating the Southern Democratic base which had provided his electoral margin in 1960. This striving for political consensus finally broke down in the streets of Birmingham. There the tough police of Birmingham Public Safety Commissioner Eugene "Bull" Connor (now Democratic National Committeeman for Alabama) shocked the national conscience by their manhandling of Negro demonstrators. The pictures of Negroes having their clothes ripped off by high-pressure water hoses, of police dogs turned on youth, and of police hurling Negro women to the ground, raised a moral outcry throughout the nation which the politically sensitive Kennedy brothers could not ignore. Having been exposed to considerable criticism by the civil rights movement for his delay, President Kennedy finally sent a civil rights bill to Congress. The relatively pallid initial Administration-drafted bill was beefed up considerably by the bipartisan Congressional civil rights bloc before its enactment in June 1964.

THE REPUBLICAN RESPONSE TO THE NEGRO REVOLUTION

Many Republican legislators showed an early appreciation of the moral and historical significance of the Negro freedom movement. One group of Republicans in Congress, typified by men such as Senators Javits, Keating, Case, and Scott and Congressmen Lindsay, Curtis, and Mathias sought constantly to pressure the Democratic President to make good on his 1960 campaign promises to send civil rights legislation to Congress immediately after he assumed office. The choice argued for by Republican progressives was one in which Republican gains in the South would be led to the growth of a moderate white elecorate and to the securing of voting power by the mostly disenfranchised Negro. The progressives could point to the remarkable Eisenhower vote totals in 1956 in the Southern Negro community (e.g. 71 percent in Richmond) and to the large Nixon vote in 1960 in Southern Negro precincts. The young Southern middle class, intellectuals, and Negroes, all of whom had grown disenchanted with a hereditary one party system, would, it was argued, be natural adherents of the revitalized Southern Republican parties. Indeed, it was the relatively liberal Repubican National Chairman Meade Alcorn of Connecticut who in 1957 initiated Operation Dixie, the Republican National Committee's crash program to break ground in the South. Until 1960 Republican growth in the South had been most prominent in the urban areas, as envisioned by the progressives.

However, soon after the 1960 elections it became clear that the Republican Parties in the South were rejecting the path proposed by the Republican progressives. In part this was due to the failure of the progressives to articulate any coherent program for moderate growth. All too often expressions of horror made by Republican moderates at the possibility of an emergent Southern anti-civil rights wing were unaccompanied by any alternative proposals. As the moderates failed to press their case, the militantly right-wing views espoused by those such as Senator Goldwater and Texas' newly elected, articulate Senator Tower soon gained ascendancy in most of the Republican organizations of the South. The economically fairly conservative Southern organization Republicans had a natural affinity for the views of the Republican right. Moreover, as the events of 1962 and 1963 increasingly alienated white Democrats from the National Democratic Party, Southern Republican leaders glimpsed an opportunity for a major Republican breakthrough in the South. With only a few exceptions Republican candidates did not try to "outrace" their Democratic opponents. Instead they generally espoused a hard-line conservatism and opposition to the Administration in Washington. Without overtly mentioning race, this appeal could, nevertheless, attract those Democratic segregationists whose alienation from their national party was largely due to its racial policies. Meanwhile, very little effort was expended by most Southern Republican parties to attract the growing Negro vote to the Republican fold. Thus in a calculus of defeat rarely matched in politics, the party which had suffered the stigma in the south of being the "Black" Republican Party while most Negroes lacked the franchise chose to ignore the Negro just as he was beginning to acquire political power.

The assassination of President Kennedy wrought considerable change in the whole equation of Southern politics. First, to Southern Negroes, as to many Americans elsewhere, John Fitzgerald Kennedy became enshrined as a martyr, revered more in death than he had been admired in life. Second, the assassination itself and all the trauma which the nation underwent at seeing such a vigorous young President plucked from its midst served to produce a cooling off period in the South in which the white hysteria (so strongly anti-Kennedy) could subside. Third, Lyndon Baines Johnson, the second Southerner in a century to occupy the White House, enjoyed at the outset incredibly strong support among white Southerners. While Lyndon Johnson's support among white Southerners was to diminish rapidly as he came to identify himself more closely with the Negro drive for equality than John Kennedy ever had, his Southern heritage nevertheless gave him powerful assistance in holding the states of the Old Confederacy against a Republican onslaught.

THE POLITICAL ARRIVAL OF THE AMERICAN NEGRO

To many American Negroes the 1964 Presidential campaign became a fight for survival, a test of whether the gains they had made since the historic 1954 school desegregation decision were to be snatched away. The Negro answer to the Goldwater challenge and to the much vaunted "white backlash" was the "blacklash" – the steady trodding of millions of Negro Americans to the polls. Garnering anywhere from ninety to one hundred percent of the Negro vote in various areas throughout the country, Lyndon Johnson received greater support from the Negro community than any previous presidential candidate had ever received from any ethnic group. This Negro support was instrumental in carrying a number of Southern states for the Texan, and it also proved decisive in the defeat of a number of Republican Congressional candidates in the South and North alike. The large pro-Democratic Negro vote was instrumental in costing the GOP four senate seats it might otherwise have picked up (two in Tennessee, one in Ohio, and one in Nevada).

It is ironic but evidently true that the Goldwater nomination of 1964 was to serve as the greatest boost to Negro political power in America in this century. The apparent gravity of the Goldwater challenge was sufficient to move many previously apathetic Negroes to their first participation in the electoral process. In view of the exhilaration which so many felt at the election's demonstration of Negro voting power, it is unlikely that future elections will witness any substantial drop in Negro voting participation. To some degree the Voting Rights Act of 1965 may be viewed as a by-product of the 1964 election. And while the long-term effects of the Voting Rights Act are still a matter of speculation, it is becoming increasingly clear that the political structure of the Deep South will eventually be transformed. Although American Negroes number about 11 percent of the total U.S. population, they constitute a much larger percentage of the eligible voting age population in most of the Southern states.

It would seem an exercise in sheer madness for Southern Republicans to write off the Negro vote. While a Wallace-style appeal to lower class whites on racial grounds might reap short-term dividends, such a strategy would have catastrophic long-term implications for the Republican Party both in the South and in the nation. Race cannot indefinitely remain an issue; once the fears of white working men that they will lose their jobs to Negroes are not realized and once other scare stories are found to be just that, other factors such as economic interest will play a more powerful role in determining the electoral behavior of such persons. Moreover, the Negro, as the one who has experienced discrimination, is likeliest to have the longest political memory. Thus, after race has ceased to be a crucial issue with Southern whites, Negroes may still remember which party years before tried to block their advance. Consequently, Republican blundering on this issue could have a price which will be paid in costly installments over the next several generations.

Population trends could hardly give comfort to those who advocate ignoring or deliberately sacrificing the Negro voter. Because of the higher birthrates prevailing among American Negroes approximately one out of every seven youths under fifteen is a Negro. To write off such a portion of the pool of future voters would require an exercise in folly rarely witnessed in politics.

FACTORS PREVENTING NEGRO INVOLVEMENT IN THE SOUTHERN REPUBLICAN PARTIES

Probably the strongest factor inhibiting Negro involvement in the Republican parties of the South is the impression held by Negroes that local white Republicans are unsympathetic or hostile to their aspirations. The Goldwater campaign seared into the minds of many Negroes a distrust of the Republican Party much more intense than most whites realize. One Southern Negro Republican leader proclaimed, "There is no meeting ground of Goldwaterism and Lincolnism, there is only a meeting ground of Goldwaterism and Jeff Davisism. If we are to have any success with the Negro voter, we must prove to the Negro that the Goldwater idea isn't predominant in the Republican Party." Another long time Republican Negro leader, a distinguished Nashville attorney, sadly remarked "Negroes now are ashamed to stand up and say they are Republicans. The few who still are Republicans are quiet about it."

Just as important as the Goldwater crusade in dampening Negro enthusiasm for the Republican Party is the militantly conservative stance of so many Southern Republican organizations. This upper-middle-class-oriented conservatism often shows a complete unconcern for the problems of the poor among whom the Southern Negro bulks so heavily. Furthermore, to many Negroes the word "conservatism" has acquired a connotation as a synonym for racism. If the fair minded Southern Republican conservative is to make his views relevant to the Negro, he must prove the sincerity of his conviction in the effectiveness of decentralized government and voluntary action by private groups by engaging himself in such activities beneficial to Negro citizens.

One factor plaguing the Republican Party in the South and throughout the nation is the extremely high popularity of the last two Democratic Presidents with the Negro man on the street. This, however, is not an insurmountable obstacle as GOP successes with Negro voters in cities like Louisville and New York have demonstrated.

The Louisville election results point out the value of conscientious and fair administration of local government as a means of winning the esteem of Negroes who have been dissatisfied with the treatment they have received from administrations of the Democratic Party. The very fact that the great majority of segregationist Southern government officials are Democrats provides an opening which the Republican Party can exploit. However, the Republican Party's out of power status constitutes a major weakness in campaigns in the South as well as in the big cities of the North. When President Eisenhower left the White House the sole patronage source of many Southern Republican organizations dried up. Many fairly strong Southern Negro Republican organizations in such cities as Atlanta, New Orleans, and Memphis rapidly lost strength following Kennedy's accession to the White House. In addition to providing patronage, control of important political offices provides the party in power with a very practical attraction to disadvantaged minority groups. Arthur J. Chapital, executive secretary of the New Orleans branch of the NAACP explained, "This state is Democratic. These are the people you want the most control of."

Associated with the Republican Party's out party status is its handicap in attracting ambitious and capable young Negroes into active participation in party activities. The paucity of patronage-wielding offices in GOP hands is only one problem. In addition, because of the currently low repute of the GOP in the Negro community, Negro Republican candidates labor under a disadvantage in races against Negro Democrats in predominantly Negro districts. This problem was evidenced in the 1965 elections to the Georgia state legislature from Atlanta. Six Negro Democrats (among them Julian Bond) were elected from predominantly Negro districts. Two were unopposed, while four beat Negro Republican opponents by margins ranging from 5 to 2 to 10 to 1. Several of the Negro Republicans were extremely well qualified; one was an Atlanta University dean. It may be even more difficult to recruit candidates of this caliber in the future.

Compounding the many weaknesses of the Republican Party in its search for Negro support is the absolute ineffectiveness of the national party's minorities program. In all of our interviews with Negro political leaders and rank-and-file voters in the South we discovered no evidence of communication from the Republican National Committee to them. The well-financed Operation Dixie effort was plainly geared to economically very conservative whites and made no pretense of appealing in a meaningful way to Southern Negroes. While the National Committee, as it began increasingly to follow the so-called Southern Strategy, stepped up its support of the Southern Division, it gutted its very undermanned Minorities Division.

Any reshaping of the national Republican minorities effort must contend with a number of severely limiting factors. Among these are 1) the shortage of capable Negro Republican political professionals 2) the preponderance of existing Negro Republican talent in the older business and professional classes at a time when the young civil rights activists are beginning to assume Negro political leadership 3) the lack of much Republican appeal to the youthful new Negro leadership generation 4) the inability of the Republican Party to offer ambitious young Negroes significant prospects of success in bids from primarily Negro districts 5) the Republican party's out-of-power-status – and consequent inability to offer necessary patronage – in those areas in which the great majority of Negro Americans live, the South and the big cities 6) the almost total lack of communication between leaders of the republican National Committee and the civil rights leadership and 7) the failure of the Republican Party when out of power to offer a "cause" to excite the Negro idealism which has been so clearly displayed in the Negro freedom movement.

The Republican Party does, however, possess several assets in any effort to create an effective Republican minorities effort. These include 1) the vulnerability of the Democratic Party to attack because of the actions of many of its Southern officeholders, 2) the existence of strong minorities programs on the state and local level in such places as Pennsylvania, New York, and Louisville, 3) the presence of some very prominent Negro leaders in the Republican Party and 4) the existence of the National Negro Republican Assembly, founded by independent-thinking Negro delegates and alternates to the 1964 San Francisco Convention, which provides the only existing framework for the articulation of Negro Republican opinion.

THE POLITICS OF TOMORROW

If the Republican Party is to re-establish any meaningful influence in the Negro community, it must act dramatically. It must make plain that thinking Republican conservatism does not and will not tolerate any denial of equal opportunity to any American because of his race or creed. Such a stance by the national party will inevitably produce the withdrawal of certain ultrasegregationists from party activity. But a trade of the backing of a few extreme racists for a large share of the political support of the rapidly growing Negro and moderate white electorate will ultimately prove highly beneficial to the Republican Party in the Deep South and elsewhere.

But it is not enough merely for the Republican Party to reaffirm that it is "the party of Lincoln"; the Party must make clear that it is moving now to meet the problems which will confront the Negro and the nation in the 1970's. Negro Americans, Mexican Americans and Puerto Ricans will not join the Republican Party in substantial numbers until that party has shown to them that it cares about their living conditions, their jobs, their physical safety, the quality and character of the education their children receive, and the respect which each of them is accorded as an individual human being.

All too frequently Republican rhetoric is phrased in terms of "getting the Negro vote"; thus it often seems, as one Southern Negro leader declared, that "They want our votes, they don't want us." If this misconception is to be dispelled, Republican leaders and rank-and-file must redouble their efforts to secure through private action as well as through local, state, and national governments a better life for all citizens.

Finally, the Republican Party must seize the initiative from the Democratic Party in the fight to build a better South. Once it has cleaned its own house of racists, the Republican Party can demand that the Democratic Party do likewise immediately. The Republican Party can point to the presence of "Bull" Connor, George Wallace, Orval Faubus, James Eastland, Allen Ellender, and other ardent segregationists in the Southern Democracy. By running candidates committed to the betterment of both races against Democratic segregationists, the Republican Party can demonstrate that it has the greater commitment to building a New South.

The forces of change transforming Southern Society have produced an improvement in the regional political climate with a rapidity which would have appeared unattainable to even the most optimistic political observers of the 1950's. There can be little doubt that the feudal, race-baiting politics of past decades is nearly at an end.

Yet, well before the passage of the Voting Rights Act of 1965, it was already clear that a New South was emerging politically. In 1964 the normally solid Southern anti-civil rights front was breached slightly as a handful of Southern Congressmen lined up behind the 1964 Civil Rights Bill. Significantly, all 12 Southern and Border State Congressmen who voted for the Civil Rights Bill were re-elected. Congressman Ross Bass of Tennessee who had supported the civil rights legislation defeated Governor Frank Clement in the Democratic primary for the U.S. Senate seat formerly held by Estes Kefauver. Bass' victory margin in the Democratic primary and in the subsequent general election against a strong Republican opponent was supplied by the heavy Negro support he received.

The 1964 election results, by destroying the myth that all eleven Southern states were a solid anti-civil rights political bloc, triggered latent impulses of many practical Southern politicians toward racial moderation. This shift in sentiment was most dramatically underscored during the House debates on the voting rights legislation when Democratic Whip Hale Boggs of New Orleans beseeched his colleagues to support the Administration-backed bill. Boggs, a superbly political man, could appreciate the significance of Negro voting power. In 1964 although Boggs had voted against the Civil Rights

Bill, Negro voters provided his victory margin over his right wing Republican opponent. In the House vote on passage of the Administration-backed Voting Rights Bill 23 Congressmen from states of the old Confederacy supported the bill.

A number of pragmatic Southern Democratic Governors and Senators who have in the past shamelessly used race as a political issue are now trying feverishly to shed their former images. Governor Orval Faubus of Arkansas, a superb opportunist who gained international notoriety in 1957 in Little Rock as the defender of segregated education, has attempted for the last year to curry Negro support by promises of fair state hiring practices. Faubus' decision not to run for a seventh term as governor was undoubtedly conditioned in part by the remarkable increase in Negro registration in Arkansas since 1964. Faubus' Republican opponent, Winthrop Rockefeller, carried the preponderance of the Negro vote in 1964 while running a strong gubernatorial race. A candidate for governor in the 1966 election, Rockefeller seemed the likely beneficiary of this new Negro vote. Rather than face the prospect of being mowed down by the strengthened Republican coalition, Faubus is entering temporary retirement. Tennessee's Governor Frank Clement, whose opposition to the 1964 Civil Rights Act contributed mightily to the strong Negro support which his 1964 senatorial primary opponent Ross Bass received, has been furiously mending fences with the Negro community in the last year and a half, appointing Negro judges and a number of middle echelon Negro state employees. Another more surprising convert to racial moderation is Georgia Senator Herman Talmadge. As governor of Georgia and then as U.S. Senator, Talmadge has engaged in a considerable amount of race-baiting. Yet in early 1966 Talmadge spoke before a predominantly Negro men's club in Atlanta and was accorded a very friendly reception.

The new political moderation of the South, however, is not merely a reaction to Negro voting power. The racial attitudes of white Southerners have changed considerably over the last decade. Undoubtedly the national news media, particularly television, have done much to influence Southern attitudes. The strong commitment in recent years of so many church organizations to the cause of racial justice has certainly influenced some religiously conscious white Southerners. The emergence of a younger generation of community leaders less firmly imbued with traditional prejudices has facilitated community acceptance of a new pattern of race relations. Economic factors have also played a role in the reshaping of white attitudes. The reluctance of outside industry to relocate in an area of probable racial turmoil has encouraged many growth-conscious Southern businessmen to work toward the achievement of racial progress. Finally, it is quite likely that since race played such a comparatively major role in the 1964 Presidential campaign, the result was seen by many as a national mandate in favor of Negro advancement. In view of the failure of the much vaunted white backlash to materialize in any substantial way outside the South, the will of many white Southerners to resist the Negro drive for equality has dissolved. Whatever their personal feelings, many Southern whites now are willing to acquiesce in what they regard as inevitable.

Beside the growing climate of racial moderation, there has arisen an increasing demand by Southerners for an upgrading of their local and state governmental services. For most of the last century the South has trailed woefully behind the rest of the nation in governmental services such as public education. The one-party political system which has predominated in the South for generations has been particularly conducive to the suppression of political reformism. The devices of Negro disenfranchisement which have accompanied the one party system have often served to disqualify poor whites as well as Negroes. With such groups removed from the political arena, a politics of stagnation could easily reign. In this atmosphere wealthy landowners and businessmen could combine with the parochial middle class small town residents to prevent gains which would benefit the Negro or "the white trash." Now, however, the Negro and the poor are gaining political power in most of the South. Furthermore, the thriving Southern business community seems increasingly imbued with the spirit of civic improvement, realizing that the inadequacy of state services has been detrimental not only to Negroes and poor whites but also to the growing Southern middle class. Thus, the young Southern business or professional person is increasingly likely to be an advocate of local political reform.

The Republican Party as the out party throughout the South can establish itself as the bearer of the torch of reform. The tremendous backlog of unmet state needs should provide Southern Republicans with much fuel for progressive, program-oriented campaigns. The Republican Party can and must demand better education, better health facilities, and fairer enforcement of the law, as the Republican Party in Arkansas has done. The growth potential of this stance was demonstrated in the 1964 Arkansas gubernatorial campaign between Republican Winthrop Rockefeller and Democrat Orval Faubus. Rockefeller carried 43 percent of the total vote but ran strongest in the areas of the state which enjoyed higher educational levels and higher percentages of white collar workers. Since educational levels in Arkansas and elsewhere in the South are likely to continue to rise, Republican programs which appeal most strongly to the educated, white collar voter should enjoy increasingly favorable reception. The success of the reform-oriented Rockefeller campaign in attracting support from the expanding sectors of the electorate bolsters the argument for similar campaigns to build the Republican Party throughout the South.

RECOMMENDATIONS

In order that the Republican Party realize its potential as a strong party promoting progress for all Americans, in the South and throughout the nation, we recommend specifically:

1. *That the Republican National Committee require any state party possessing a segregation or discriminatory clause in its party platform or rules to repeal this provision without delay.* According to the 1964 Platform of the Mississippi Republican Party: "We feel that in the field of racial relations that Mississippi has its own distinct problem that can best be handled at the state level without outside interference. To this end, we feel segregation of the races is absolutely essential to harmonious racial relations and the continued progress of both races in the State of Mississippi."

Accordng to Article III of the by-laws of the Mississippi Republican Party: "Membership of the Party shall consist of all persons who are qualified electors under the laws of the State of Mississippi, and who are in accord with the statement of principles of the Party, which principles shall have been declared by the State Convention of this Party."

In order to meet the requirements for Mississippi Republican Party membership which are set out in Article III, a Mississippi citizen would have to be in accord with the pro-segregation stand of the party platform. Such a requirement would, if applied, ban all advocates of integration and practically all Negroes from participation. Ironically, the only Negroes who even in theory could meet this requirement for Republican membership would probably be Black Muslims or adherents of other separatist Black Nationalist groups. There is absolutely no reason why the Republican Party should allow such a flagrantly discriminatory provision to go unchallenged. A National Committee resolution requiring elimination of such discriminatory provisions would both remove an ugly stain from the Republican record of fighting racism, and strengthen the hand of fair-minded Southern Republicans in a showdown with racists in their party ranks.

The repeal of pro-segregation clauses in Republican platforms has taken a new urgency now that the Alabama Democratic Party has finally voted to remove the "White Supremacy" label from its ballot emblem.

2. *That the Republican National Committee adopt procedures to achieve a prompt termination of any racial discrimination which exists in Republican facilities anywhere in the nation.* To this end we urge that the Republican National Committee enact rules requiring that all state and local parties pledge to tolerate no racial or religious discrimination in any of their activities. In order to insure that these pledges are honored we urge that the Republican National Committee appoint an ethical standards committee of prominent Republicans active in human relations, religious, or civic affairs to investigate any

party organizations accused of maintaining discriminatory practices. Should the ethical standards committee find that a state party organization was maintaining discriminatory practices the National Committee would then place that party on probation and take away its votes on any official national party committees. If the discriminatory party persists in its practices, the Republican National Committee should strip that state organization of any official recognition as a Republican body.

3. *That national, state and local Republican parties make a concerted effort in those states with party registration to register a significant portion of the new Negro registrants as Republicans.* Where local Republican organizations decline to encourage Negroes to register as Republicans because of fear that the party's ideological tone will be affected, Republican citizens organizations should set up their own voting registration campaigns. In most cases, however, such campaigns could be carried out by forward-looking official Republican organizations. Yet, identifying Negroes with a Republican Party moving into a new racial climate in the South is not merely a job for Republican organizations, official and volunteer. It is also the task of church and civil rights groups to encourage Negro participation in *both* major political parties, particularly the Republican Party which is standing at a new political crossroads.

In a number of Southern states in which Republican strength is quite limited, this coalition could nominate as the Republican candidate, a person strongly committed to fight racial injustice. Somewhat over 300,000 Negroes remain unregistered in Louisiana. If only a fraction of these rapidly registering voters were to sign up in the Republican column, they would have very strong voting power within the Republican Party. Their strength within the much larger Democratic Party would be much less significant. Negro leaders in Louisiana, aware of the possibility of securing a progressive stance within the Republican Party of their state, have given consideration to the possible encouragement of such voter registration. The same should be true in other areas of the Deep South in which Republican strength is minuscule and in which Negroes make up the bulk of the unregistered voter pool.

4. *The reactivation of the Minorities Division of the Republican National Committee under the leadership of a vigorous Negro Republican on excellent terms with the civil rights leadership.* Sufficient funds would be provided to the Minorities Division to allow it to have several staff men in the field at all times, some of whom would be stationed in the South. At least one staffer of Spanish-American descent should be employed to encourage Republican contact with the nation's growing Latin-American communities. The Minorities Division should consider publication of a monthly magazine on the order of SOUTHERN CHALLENGE, the magazine of the former Operation Dixie. However, its ideological content would be vastly different. The new chairman of the Minorities Division should be someone who will attempt to secure cordial

relations between the Republican National Committee and the leaders of the National Negro Republican Assembly.

5. *That a Conference on the Republican party and Human Rights be held in the South under the auspices either of the Republican National Committee or of interested Republican citizens groups.*

6. *That the Republican Congressional leadership announce publicly that the Republican Party will welcome any Democratic defector to the Republican side as long as the convert will state his agreement with the cardinal Republican principle of equal opportunity for all Americans whatever their race.*

7. *That Republicans undertake a major effort to carry their views to Southern Negro campuses and to human rights organizations, to church groups and press associations.* The action of Charles Percy in speaking before the Mississippi Council on Human Relations despite the objections of former Mississippi Republican Chairman Wirt Yerger set an example for other Republicans to follow.

8. *That Southern Republican Parties nominate capable Negroes for office in predominantly non-Negro areas.* In many cases given the disadvantage a Republican Negro suffers in a race against a Negro Democrat in a non-white district, this may be the best way to elect a Negro Republican. In recent municipal elections in Atlanta, Q. V. Williamson, a Negro Republican, was elected alderman over a white Democrat. The Atlanta election, however, was officially nonpartisan. At-large elections in many Southern cities will provide the Republican Party with an opportunity to elect Negro candidates.

9. *That the Republican Co-ordinating Committee appoint a task force on the Republican party and the New South.* This committee would survey the changes rapidly underway in the American South and would attempt to develop Republican approaches to problems which will confront Southern Negroes and whites in the next decade. The Republican Party could then map out a vital role for itself as a builder of a bright new future for the states of the former Confederacy.

10. *That Southern Republican moderates undertake the publication of a monthly newsletter which would be circulated to forward looking Republicans throughout the South.* The lack of communication among Southern moderates and between them and their brethren elsewhere in the nation has been continually evident during the course of the Southern Study. This absence of contacts with moderates elsewhere has produced a strong sense of isolation and despair which has caused many moderate Southern Republicans to withdraw from active Republican participation. Some progressives who in the 1950's saw the Republican Party as the best hope for surmounting the politics of race have recently joined the Democratic Party which has captured the torch of progress in much of the South. Such actions as the dropping by the Alabama Democratic Party of its White Supremacy motto have had a real impact upon Southern moderates of both races. Meanwhile, during the past several years

thousands of the most reactionary Democrats have flooded the Southern Republican parties, inevitably influencing the tone of the parties. Official state and local party publications with few exceptions propagate a staunchly right wing viewpoint highly unsympathetic to the civil rights cause.

Thus, the Southern Republican moderate or progressive is faced with a crisis of party identification. No longer able to see his beliefs reflected in local party action he may just give up the fight or he may actually leave the party. The Southern Republican moderate desperately needs some assurance that he is not fighting alone. One way in which this could be provided would be through the publication and distribution of a monthly Southern Moderate Republican newsletter.

This newsletter could serve to reinforce the convictions of many presently discouraged Southern Republicans. It might also help to galvanize moderates into common political action within their states and region. The newsletter could make Southern moderates aware of the presence of allies in other areas of the South and of the activity of national progressive Republican organizations.

The publication should be prepared for a white and Negro readership. No party publication of significant circulation is designed for a Negro audience. Southern Negroes, Republican or Democrat, receive no communication from moderate Republicans, yet they are exposed to a steady barrage of publications and television appearances publicizing the pro-civil rights activities of the Democratic Administration. The Southern newsletter could fill this void. It might also serve as a means of linking white Republican progressives together with Negroes for common political action.

11. *That the Republican Party refuse national party financial or technical assistance to Republican candidates for Gubernatorial, Senatorial, Congressional, or local office if these candidates wage racist campaigns or allow racism to be used in their behalf by campaign supporters.* Senator Thruston Morton of Kentucky, Chairman of the Republican Senatorial Campaign Committee, has indicated that this committee will cut off funds to segregationists running as Republican Senatorial candidates. The Republican National Committee and the Republican Congressional Committee should both follow the path outlined by Senator Morton. Racist propaganda can do nothing to advance the long term interests of the Republican Party or the nation. Yet, unfortunately, in a few campaigns this propaganda has been employed on behalf of Republican candidates.

The time is short for the Republican Party to cast itself as the party of Southern reform. If the Republican Party chooses instead to campaign by going to the right of James Eastland or Allen Ellender, it will have only itself to thank for its continuing weakness in coming decades. The enhanced power of the cities through legislative reapportionment and the enfranchisement of a huge number of Negro citizens will start to reshape dramatically the face of

Deep South politics. The Republican Party must respond to the challenge of change in the South by stepping forward boldly and offering Southerners of all races hope for a new tomorrow. Timidity today will mean irrelevancy tomorrow.

CHAPTER 6
THE COURAGE TO EMBRACE TOMORROW

the "New Politics" and a new Republican Party

FROM DISASTER TO DISTINCTION, the first Ripon Society book, was published in September of 1966. Thomas E. Petri was the general editor. Richard Rovere, writing in the NEW YORKER magazine described the contents as "some of the boldest political thinking being done anywhere." A syndicated editorial which appeared in newspapers in all sections of the country suggested that "the political center is so firmly defended, that if voters will read Ripon's book, it could have a real impact on the elections next month. The San Francisco EXAMINER AND CHRONICLE called it "an unsparing and refreshingly honest analysis of the state of Republican politics."

The selection which follows originally appeared as Chapter Five of that book, following a detailed analysis of the 1964 presidential campaign, the impact of the election on the party at all governmental levels, and the failure of moderate Republicans, between 1964 and 1966, to bring their party "home again." "Where do we go from here?" the authors asked. "The Courage to Embrace Tomorrow" presented some of their answers – and the answers are still relevant.

– Editor

The Presidential election of 1964 and its aftermath have obscured one central fact: *America stands on the verge of an exciting new era of politics.* Events are fast outracing the leaders of both major parties. A new order is coming in American politics – based upon a new generation and continued growth and concentration of population. By 1975, the politics of today will be almost unrecognizable – in style, in vocabulary, and in substance. But few politicians have yet begun to explore the changes which lie ahead. How will the new politics affect the two-party system? What issues will dominate? Who will lead the new order? And what impact will these changes have on the lives of every American?

Few would pretend to answer these questions. Only a handful of political seers have begun to examine the political scene of tomorrow. They include scholars and journalists on the edge of contemporary politics – men like pollster and writer Samuel Lubbell, management consultant Peter Drucker, and FORTUNE magazine author Max Ways. In this essay we shall suggest some new ideas that may provide the raw materials for the new politics. And we shall look at their implications for a new Republican party and a winning Republican strategy.

THE PASSING OF THE OLD ERA: THE CRUMBLING POLITICAL EDIFICE

The mood of American politics in 1966 has a strange unreality about it. Republican "rebuilding" has begun to restore a sense of "politics as usual." But when we compare our political parties with virtually any other organization or institution in American society, we see how deceptive appearance is. By almost any standard of measurement our political parties and their leadership show the greatest lag in adjustment to change. American business and industry is rapidly adjusting to the revolution in data processing and automation. The entrepreneurial skills of the private sector are meeting the challenges of new, affluent and expanding markets. The situation today is the reverse of that which existed at the beginning of this century, when a great flood of national legislation was necessary to force American business to update its methods. The oldest institutions of the republic – the universities and the churches are experiencing an unprecedented ferment of innovation and reform.

In the political sphere a combination of fate and circumstance has somehow held back the forces of change. The Johnson consensus masks revolutionary change, change that was foreshadowed in the Kennedy years. In the early 1960s, the young Democratic President represented something new in American politics. The words of his inaugural address cut across the lines of party and spoke to a new and yet untried political force. "Let the word go forth from this time and place, to friend and foe alike, that the torch has been passed to a new generation of Americans . . ." We in the Ripon Society, and young Americans generally, remember the challenge of this call. Yet today that torch burns only at an Arlington grave, for today no man and no party carries the torch of our generation.

This was the tragedy of 1964 and it is the shame of our current politics. In 1964 what might have been a great debate became for the American people a grand detour. For the Republican party it was a dead end. The overbearing presence of a dominant political personality now prolongs our distraction from the politics of tomorrow. And the Republican party of the past, presented with rare opportunities to assert strong political leadership for the future, has only underlined its fundamental inability to understand or come to terms with the new America. At a time when the Republican party needs to be shaken from its foundations, challenged, renewed and rejuvenated, it has chosen instead the "safe" organizational solution. For this is the era of the caretaker politicians.

While Republicans "organize" to do battle on the old political terrain with increasingly obsolete weapons, events are already overtaking them. In the Congress, the long southern dominance of the Senate is coming to an end. Scores of years of southern Democratic seniority in the House of Representatives have been lost as the one-party South has begun to crack. The Voting Rights Act and Negro registration drive make inevitable a recasting of party competition in the South.

Within the Democratic congressional party, the rise of the Democratic Study Group (a coalition of liberal and moderate House Democrats to which about half of the Democratic representatives belong), after years of careful planning and slow building, is a new and powerful factor in party politics. It is only a matter of time before this "new breed" challenges the Democratic old guard. Generational politics – the division along lines of age and seniority rather than party – has already been felt in some congressional votes. It was a factor in the Republican leadership fights of 1963 and 1965. Reapportionment – its full impact still to be felt in the Congress – will further recast the lines of party competition and draw ever newer and younger faces into contests for public office.

Yet our parties have not really begun to adapt to the new politics that threaten their very obsolescence. We have discussed at some length Republican efforts to "rebuild" after November 1964. Our general conclusion is that the "organizational" strategy avoids the real problems and opportunities for leadership. It is unlikely to redeem the massive Republican defections of 1964. It is even less likely to seize the "issue initiative" that could capture broad new support in the growing sectors of the voting population.

Nor can the Democrats take much comfort from their situation. When a majority party that has had almost unchallenged control of Congress for as far back as most young voters can remember does not speak to the future in a significant presidential campaign, it cannot build confidence in its capacity to lead. The phenomenon of the "teach-in" debates on American foreign policy is only one indication of the inability of a decaying party system to provide a forum for meaningful debate.

Why have our leaders not spoken to the needs of the new America? They have asked for ideas but they do not seem to be really interested in the problems that concern or excite the new generation. They speak another language, content to project their own picture of reality to an audience they do not understand. They speak without communicating. Their political braintrusts and research staffs and policy task forces go through the motions, but their position papers convince few. Little that is exciting or controversial survives committee government under the rule of the lowest common denominator. New ideas fail to break through into the old politics. Too many leaders fear the ideas which will challenge the conventional wisdom and comfortable clichés of the present, and thus their speeches and platforms and slogans and pamphlets do not ring true. Nor do they even begin to realize it.

We believe that a *new* order is coming in American politics. With the end of the Johnson years the last link to the depression and war years will also be cut.

But who then will lead the new order? We would suggest that the future leaders of the Republican party, and perhaps the Democratic party as well, are largely unknown – that the lesson of 1964 was that Republicans must look to the future for their leadership. For those who were found wanting in the past cannot be adequate to the needs of the future.

Many Republicans compare the platform of 1964 with that of 1960 – but not with the demands of a changing world. They still look to the leaders of the pre-Goldwater era – but not to new faces emerging in the states and in Congress. But history will not wait for the Republican party. By the mid-1970s the chances are that none of us will be able to recognize either of our great political organizations.

THE COMING POLITICAL ERA: THE ISSUES FOR A NEW POLITICS

Senator Everett Dirksen of Illinois, Republican Senate Minority Leader, when asked why he supported the 1964 civil rights legislation, replied: "Nothing is more powerful than an idea whose time has come." But even more important than an idea whose time has come is the idea whose time is yet to come. The political party that takes such ideas and makes them its own captures the future.

What are the issues of the future? What revolutionary changes will determine the dialogue of the new politics? Basically they are associated with the coming of age of a new generation that is unlike recent generations. It is a generation born in the depression, and war, and postwar years. It is a generation that does not remember or identify with the great issues that have divided Democrats and Republicans since the time of Franklin D. Roosevelt. The old economic issues are out of date. The new generation assumes and hardly stops to question a growing, abundant economy (though they worry about pockets of poverty), the basic social services of the American version of the welfare state, the right of trade union organization, equal rights for all Americans, and American leadership of the free world. Millions of its younger members, now flooding the universities and graduate schools of the nation, hardly remember Joseph Stalin, Senator McCarthy, Korea, Taft, or Churchill. This is largely a "have" generation, educated, affluent, expecting much from life. It is a generation whose outlook will place new demands on the American party system. Its current and most vivid impression of the Republican party is Barry Goldwater. It remembers John F. Kennedy and cannot quite believe in Lyndon Johnson. It is waiting, searching for something it does not yet see. It is eager, receptive.

When Franklin Roosevelt introduced the New Deal, the population of the United States stood at about 125 million. In 1960 it had grown to 180 million and by 1985 it will reach 275 million. The median age of our population, which has held at 29.5 years since 1940, will drop to 26.5 years in 1970. By the mid-1980s half of our population will be under twenty-five! Before the presidential election of 1972 we shall have become the youngest country in the West. And with this dramatic drop in the age of the population the political center of gravity will shift decisively to the new political generation.

Other trends besides population will shape the new politics. White-collar workers – including managers, sales, professional, and clerical workers – will comprise an increasing share of the working population. They expanded, for example, from 29 percent of the work force in 1930 to 45 percent in 1964. The growing sector of professional and semi-professional employees will mean a steady disengagement from the older economic concerns and from the class polarization of management against labor. Educational opportunity will continue to expand. Since 1900 the number of college graduates in the United States has increased *six times* as fast as our population. Today almost half of those of college age go on for higher education and the proportion may soon increase to at least 70 percent.

Where will the new Americans live? In 1960, the Bureau of the Census located 63 percent of all Americans in 200 metropolitan areas (Standard Metropolitan Statistical Areas). These were not scattered across the country, but were instead largely grouped along three "Main Lines" each close to 500 miles long. One stretched from Boston to Washington, a second from Pittsburgh to Chicago, and a third from San Francisco to San Diego. The nine states that included the largest metropolitan complexes had together 80 million of the 1960 population of 180 million – about 44 percent of the total! During the 1950-1960 decade, population in the metropolitan areas grew by 26.4 percent and the nonmetropolitan population only by 7.1 percent. It is only a matter of time before the separate metropolitan areas begin to blend and merge into each other.

Already the political consequences of population concentration are being felt. The metropolitan complexes (including the suburbs *and* the urban-core cities) are significantly increasing their representation in state and national legislatures, transforming the ground rules of party competition in several states. The nation's Governors, especially in the more populous states, are already assuming a more active role in the national parties, reversing a decline in party influence which culminated in 1960 when it seemed that the Governors had been replaced as "presidential timber" by members of the Senate. Interstate cooperation in the solving of regional problems is growing. Even the South, though it may continue to fall outside the belts of the great supercities, will not escape the forces of urbanization. Over the next decade or two these forces may well succeed in breaking down the regional isolation of the South and reunifying it with the economy and politics of the rest of the nation.

These are the basic dimensions of change. How will they be felt in the issues of the new politics?

CIVIL RIGHTS: THE NEXT PHASE

Civil rights was the first new issue to rise to the surface of domestic politics in the 1960s. The Republican party of 1964 came down squarely on the wrong side of it. Republican members of Congress can take much of the credit for passage of the 1964 Civil Rights Act. They provided political leadership far beyond the promise of their numbers. Republican staff assistance – through groups like the Republican Legislative Research Association – played a key role in a coordinated congressional drive. But the Republican party in writing its platform and in choosing its nominee elected to ignore this congressional record and to fight instead with a disastrous "Southern Strategy."

With the passage of the Voting Rights Bill in 1965, some observers began to speak of the end of the civil rights struggle. The last great legal barriers will have been toppled, they point out, and civil rights will cease to be a major political issue. How short-sighted a view! Can anyone in truth say that the American Negro's fight for equality is finished? The simple facts are that more Negroes are unemployed today than were a decade ago. The Negro unemployment rate is twice that of white workers and the gap is expanding. Among younger Negroes, one of the fastest growing sectors of the American population, unemployment is already an explosive problem, and many Negro jobs – at relatively low levels of skill – are most vulnerable to the real threat of automation.

Negro population continues to concentrate in the central core cities – New York, Philadelphia, Baltimore, Washington, Cleveland, St. Louis, Detroit, Chicago, Los Angeles – as the white flight to the suburbs increases. And with this trend the goals for adequate education and housing become more distant for most Negroes.

The civil rights movement is not just a Negro protest movement. It has drawn much of its support from progressive and responsible members of the white community. The dramatic involvement of the churches should long since have driven this point home to doubtful Republicans. The concern of the movement will turn to the more subtle forms of discrimination – in education, employment, and housing – and to the vicious cycle of poverty in the urban ghettos. As Maine's Governor John H. Reed has said, "Like the metal shackles of slavery, the mental shackles of bigotry must be destroyed."

The Council of Republican Organizations has underscored the great tasks lying ahead. "The removal of legal barriers will not be enough," they said. "The Republican party is committed to equality – in reality – in all aspects of our Society." Then they went on to make a most telling point: "We know that the law is no more effective than the men who enforce it. Administrative performance and social performance must match legislative promise." All the good work Congress has done can be dissipated if the Department of Justice and the federal courts fail to implement the law adequately and fairly, or if personnel shortages cause considerable delays in the administration of justice.

The group – then composed of nine Republican organizations – also urged stepped-up enforcement of the Supreme Court school desegregation decision – and state and local action to correct racial imbalance in public schools. It suggested specific ways in which persistent discrimination in the field of housing, public accommodation, and public facilities and services can be ended. In the area of employment opportunity it stressed how crucial it now is that Negroes be trained for jobs that the law has opened to them. Much work must be done if civil rights is to mean more than the mere absence of legal barriers. Republicans ought to be doing it.

The American Negro still poses the most fundamental challenge to the workability of American democracy. While his fight for equal rights progresses, we will face some of the most critical years in our history. The problems of adjustment and acceptance will be painful and tense. They will call for responsible political leadership of the highest order. In 1964 the Republican party turned its face from this problem. The political temptation to do so again will increase – as white frustration and reaction build. To yield to them will be to fail both party and country.

HUMAN RIGHTS: THE FRINGE OF FREEDOM

But there is much more unfinished business for American democracy than the rights of the American Negro. Even now Republicans must look to the *next* phase in the struggle for human rights and dignity. We must now extend the concept of civil rights to all those who live on the fringe of freedom – to men and women who do not share the legal rights and civil liberties that we assume without question. These include the poor, and especially the poor with handicaps beyond mere poverty, such as the color of their skin, the language they speak, lack of education, or low intelligence.

Those called "mentally ill" comprise one such group of handicapped people. Ten percent of all the citizens in the Republic spend some time in mental institutions. Some 250,000 Americans are declared mentally ill each year. They occupy half of the nation's hospital beds. This is a sector of our population as large as our Negro population. But this problem *can* involve any American. Mental illness can reach into any family. Yet in many of our cities and states, the mentally ill are treated with less sympathy than criminals are – in asylums and in hospitals and in the courts. How is a person judged mentally ill? An incredible diversity of standards exists from state to state, from examiner to examiner. Some psychiatrists even consider political views in deciding whether men are insane – a familiar technique that is as objectionable in America as in countries where it has been employed as the tool of tyrants.

Americans must fight to guarantee the rights of all Americans who are the victims of personal or institutional injustice and discrimination. We must put aside the conventional wisdom about poverty and mental illness. We must champion individual dignity with understanding and compassion. A political party without a genuine social concern for others will not convince the new generation of Americans that it has a conscience. Those who enjoy rights must be convinced that those rights are not secure unless they are extended to everyone.

EDUCATION: FULFILLING THE AMERICAN DREAM

Education will be a central issue in the new politics. Our exploding population will create enormous education problems in the next twenty years. In the twenty-five year period between 1960 and 1985, the population will increase 50 percent! The school age population (5 to 24 years old) will skyrocket from 68 million in 1965, to 77 million in 1970, to 103 million in 1985! No wonder social analysts have started describing America as the Education State rather than the Welfare State.

Education has always been the road to the American dream. Already about half of our young men and women who complete high school go on to college. More and more American parents see a college degree as a passport to economic success or a ticket for social mobility for their children. As a result educators expect at least three million new college places to be added over the next decade! Students prolong their studies for graduate degrees to improve their choice of jobs and increase their options for the future. Graduate school enrollment is increasing 20 percent faster than college enrollment, and an estimated 80 percent of all Ivy League seniors go on to graduate studies. Education will soon surpass defense as America's largest single industry. Teachers are already our largest single occupational group.

Education will be an important political issue for several reasons. Educational spending forms a large and growing sector of all government budgets. State and local outlays for education alone will more than *double* by the early 1970's. But with this massive spending, public attention will shift to the quality and goals of education. For what purpose are we building ever more elaborate schools and great university complexes? Are we entering a new age of Social Darwinism on the American campus where the fittest survive and the losers are forgotten? Student protests on our large university campuses have raised these haunting questions and challenged the familiar answers. Methods of education are coming under increasingly heavy fire. We are now beginning to taste the technological revolution that quantity education will force on us. Teaching techniques must undergo a drastic revolution. New ways of writing textbooks, team teaching, programmed learning, educational television must be evaluated and refined. The number of teachers per student will continue to decline, further upsetting traditional concepts of "the classroom." Three hundred thousand new college professors will be required in the next decade. Yet we graduated only 15,000 Ph.D.'s in 1965 and the rate cannot be expanded to keep pace with the demand.

Americans have too easily assumed that education is an end in itself. From our local school committees and Parent-Teachers Associations to our university boards of trustees and alumni associations, all Americans will have to rethink the purposes of our schools, colleges, and universities. What is taught and how it is taught are questions that the public has not yet begun seriously to debate.

But perhaps the deepest public concern with the educational system will stem from what some social critics have labeled the "diploma elite." There is a clear danger that formal educational qualifications – the mere possession of a college or graduate degree – may introduce new inequalities of opportunity in American society. Paper credentials may bear little relation to native ability or to the skills required for a particular job. Blue-collar and unskilled workers, Negroes and Puerto Ricans, may be denied access to jobs for which they are qualified. The uncritical American esteem for education may lead to new forms of second-class citizenship. Lack of motivation, difficulties of speech and of understanding, poor home environment, are both an effect and a cause of de facto segregation. Diversity of educational standards is another problem. Unless state and local governments in a mobile society begin to coordinate their educational efforts voluntarily, the federal government will have to enforce national education standards as a condition of national survival.

The structure of the old politics is wholly inadequate for solving problems such as these. Forward-looking Republicans must begin to think and talk about the quality of education. We must be sensitive to the human consequences of the massive educational system we have so uncritically constructed.

TECHNOLOGICAL CHANGE: NEW OPTIONS FOR THE PROGRESSIVE SPIRIT IN GOVERNMENT

The new era of politics will be an era of continued technological advance, abundance, and affluence. For most Americans advances in technology will mean increased possibilities to lead a fuller life. Some Americans, however, will not share in this abundance. The problems of poverty, inadequate education, and social and economic discrimination must be recognized as interrelated so that they might yield to a coordinated attack.

The war on poverty and the Great Society are the Democratic party's answer to these problems. Far-reaching legislative and administrative changes are being introduced into the American welfare state by the Johnson Congress. It is safe to predict that these changes will produce a host of new issues. The federal government will be involved in complex decision-making far different from New Deal programs. The financing and coverage of the medicare program is just one example. Medical care, unlike payments of cash out of social security funds, involves services to the recipients and – inevitably – judgments by those who are administering the funds as to the worth and quality of those services. Who will make these decisions? Some doctors prefer one method of treatment, others prefer another for the same illness. There will be differences of cost and, no doubt, statistical variances in effectiveness. Eventually the government is likely to decree that one method rather than others should be used. Will doctors make these decisions or will accountants. Rigidity and timidity are both potential dangers as government expenditure and control extend in the medical care field.

The sheer size of current Johnson Administration efforts is bound to result in some dramatic failures. Major administrative flaws have already been found in the war on poverty. Conflict between local leaders and politically appointed coordinators has threatened to scuttle many programs. Tomorrow's politics must try to institutionalize answers to these problems.

What is the Republican future in the Great Society? There is *no* future in calling for wholesale repeal of major items of Great Society legislation. Certainly there is room for responsible Republican criticism of the administrative failures. But progressive Republicans must themselves join in the search for sensible and efficient answers. The American people sense that the war on poverty, crime, disease, illness, and illiteracy is moving in the right direction. They will respect honest action more than mere negative partisan criticism.

But we can make no more important statement than this: *For Republicans, the real opportunities lie BEYOND the issue of "welfare state."* The technological revolution will afford Republicans new opportunities for humane and efficient reform in governmental bureaucracy and the public services. As the range of possibilities facing government decision makers expands, it will be more important than ever that we continually re-examine the decisions of the past. Are the assumptions upon which they have been based still valid? Can we find new ways to do the same job more quickly and economically?

Where they are appropriate, we should employ the most advanced technical administrative tools – computers, cost-benefit analysis, organization and method studies. Because new electronic computers can store enormous volumes of data in memory banks, they can be used to facilitate the individual treatment of each person on the basis of his special situation. Personalized treatment will become possible in the processing of social security benefits, income tax returns, and student and home-owner loans. The crude operation of today's impersonal bureaucracy can be made sensitive to the personal needs and requirements of every man and woman. The technological breakthrough in computer science means that individual freedom can be increased without contracting the freedom of others. Government can become more responsive.

It also means that tyranny can be tailor-made and extended to cover the minutiae of detail it never could in the past. A central data bank, in the hands of an unscrupulous and unchecked political elite, would be a short distance from the totalitarian controls of George Orwell's chilling *1984.* Already the electronic eavesdropping and recording devices used by American business and government, not to mention the more subtle invasions of privacy represented by much "psychological" testing, threaten to subvert the relationship of individuals and institutions. Can personal freedom be protected in such an age? the new technology will require new techniques of democratic control to insure that governmental power is used responsibly.

The Republican party has often been the party of progressive reform in government, and efficiency in the public services is a basic progressive theme. People want efficient government, efficient in spending their tax money *and* efficient in meeting and anticipating their needs. But new scientific and technical developments have changed the meaning of efficiency. The political party unable to move from the issues of the past runs the risk of becoming irrelevant to the concerns of the present. It most certainly forfeits the options of the future.

METROPOLITAN LIVING: THE QUALITY OF ENVIRONMENT

The growth of the super-city will pose political and economic challenges of a new order for American government. The new metropolitan areas of our country are scarcely governable today. The traditional forms of local, state, and federal government have not been able to keep pace with metropolitan growth. A new generation of Americans will find most of their jobs in the super-cities. The new metropolis offers them the greatest possibilities for career advancement, the range of cultural life they have grown accustomed to and now demand, the educational and health facilities they want for their children. The new Americans are acutely aware of the environment in which they live – of its shortcomings, of the failures and successes of local and state governments in dealing with them. They want clean air and clean water. They want *enough* air and *enough* water. Day after day they experience the inadequacies and frustrations of metropolitan transportation. As a mobile generation, they are sensitive to the need for new air and highway safety programs. They know that a subterranean world of crime and violence may at any moment reach out to them and twist their lives. And in their more hopeful moments, at least, they suspect that it all does not have to be this way. They wait for answers – and they are willing to look to either political party.

The new generation of Americans finds it hard to understand the continued existence of widespread corruption in the governments that supposedly serve them. They fight for school bond issues and constitutional reform in their states. They are increasingly impatient with narrow and exclusive ethnic politics, with the patronage and boondoggling and payoffs of a passing era. They are looking for responsible political leadership. In short, new political demands will emerge at the points of greatest population concentration. The eternal struggle of man to master his environment will find its most difficult challenge in the jungles of tomorrow's super-cities.

THE REVOLUTION IN THE STATES AND LOCAL CITIES: GOVERNMENT FOR TOMORROW

The future of state and local government will be an immediate problem of the new politics. Already state and local governments have expanded at an astonishing rate. For the past twenty years, while critics attacked "centralization of power" and the "enormous expansion of the federal government," the truly dynamic growth has come at the state, county, and municipal level. Since 1946 state and local expenditures have increased sixfold. By the mid-sixties state and local governments were spending *twice* as much as the federal government spent on domestic programs. And the pace will accelerate. Economists estimate state and local spending will double by the mid-seventies.

The Republican party has a unique opportunity to meet the governmental needs of the future, for Republicans have historically been sympathetic to state initiative and responsibility. They have been less inclined than the Democrats to seek the solution of all problems through the federal government. Republicans understand that a "creative federalism" will require the mutual respect and cooperation of governments at all levels.

One problem that responsible Republican leadership will have to meet is the constant danger of "tax revolt." Today state and local budgets, bond issues, tax increases, etc., provide the average American with his only meaningful control on the level of government spending. The federal budget, measured in billions of dollars, has long since passed the comprehension of the American taxpayer. Public discontent with government spending bears most heavily on state and local units. But Republicans must avoid the easy route of encouraging public rebellion and stimulating tax revolt. Republicans have a special challenge in leading the American voter to an understanding of "state responsibilities," particularly in the realm of fiscal policy.

Republicans must face an immediate problem, rapidly approaching crisis proportions – the limited base of tax resources. Property taxes, sales taxes, and state income taxes have already reached or passed the limits of political reassessibility in most of our larger states. Our Governors have, as a direct result, had an unusually high political mortality rate. The ordeal of finding new revenues for existing programs limits their ability to meet new needs.

But our search for a "simpler and better way" is not without hope. For in dramatic contrast to the bleak fiscal picture at the local and state level, the federal government today faces the prospect of increasing revenues. There is expectation that these revenues may soon begin to exceed expenditures. The surplus could act as an automatic "brake" on national growth.

In 1964 Presidential Advisor Walter Heller pointed to a 6 billion dollar annual increase in federal tax revenue and suggested that a part of it be funneled back into the economy through unrestricted grants to the states. The White House supported the plan during the 1964 campaign. So did Senator Goldwater. Both party platforms gave it favorable notice. The Conference of State Governors supported it enthusiastically, as did a special presidential task force. But in December of 1964, President Johnson, angered at news leaks, abruptly shelved the proposal. It has been revived since then, in a joint study issued by the Republican Governors' Association and the Ripon Society in July of 1965* and in legislation filed in Congress by Republican legislators. A similar proposal for bloc grants to the states was also adopted by the Republican Coordinating Committee in December 1965. Such proposals deserve continued Republican attention.

At the same time, reforms are needed in our complicated, contradictory, and chaotic federal tax structure. Republicans can also take the lead in developing a stronger partnership with private enterprise at the state and local level – to tap the creative business process and to build a sound economic base for new industry and jobs.

Most important, sound state government will require constitutional reform. This is a wide open area for meaningful Republican action. Population concentration, reapportionment, out-dated administrative structures, the explosion of needs for services have all compounded the need for structural revisions. But constitutional reform must be more than a re-evaluation of existing governments within state border. It should also look toward techniques

* "Government for Tomorrow. A Proposal for the Unconditional Sharing of Federal Tax Revenues with State and Local Governments." A research paper issued jointly by the Republican Governors' Association and the Ripon Society, July 1965.

of cooperation with neighboring states that share a metropolitan complex or have common regional concerns. Moreover, the cause of constitutional reform offers Republicans a unique means for involving more citizens directly in problems of *their* government. Bold Republican leadership here could be an important step toward rebuilding the Republican party in the states.

Strengthening the state legislatures is a high priority challenge for the new politics. Most state legislatures do not enjoy a fraction of the professional staff available to Governors or administrative departments. The United States Congress has been far in advance of the states in attaining expert staff assistance. But the state legislator is the "forgotten man of American politics" – underpaid, understaffed, underpublicized, he cannot contribute his full weight to the solution of state political problems. His position must be improved. Coordination and exchange of information among state legislators should also be encouraged. The establishment of a Republican State Legislators' Association in August, 1965, under the chairmanship of Monte Montgomery, Speaker of the Oregon House, is an important step in that direction.

State and municipal government will be one of the most challenging frontiers of the new political era. We have not yet begun to assemble the political and administrative talent to meet these challenges. This we must do if we are to build good government for tomorrow.

AN INNOVATIVE FOREIGN POLICY

The contrast between the Kennedy and Johnson administrations is most dramatic in the area of foreign policy. After a relatively short time, the innovating spirit of the Kennedy administration has all but disappeared. The new initiatives of the Peace Corps, the Alliance for Progress, the limited test ban treaty, the AID concept, the new Atlantic Community, whatever their shortcomings, have had no counterparts under Johnson. There have been few "new departures." The Johnson approach has been a very personal, tough, foreign policy. But there is an uneasiness everywhere and the beginnings of criticism from some academicians, writers, and, as this is written in 1965, church leaders. Too often this uneasiness has not been reflected in inter-party debate. Too much of the work of critical opposition has been left to other Democrats. Our parties, as such, have not been responsive to the real foreign policy issues that are exciting public controversy and interest.

As America moved from the Eisenhower to the Kennedy years, it experienced more than a change in ruling parties. It observed a change in political generations and in style of leadership, particularly in foreign affairs. The new style policy was not always accurate, not always consistent, not always effective. But its capacity for historical perspective and its sensitivity to the subtle dynamics of international relations began to accomplish limited but important results. It promised much more.

There is much to say in criticism of the President's foreign policy. Republicans, who have produced some of the nation's most alert and able diplomats, should be saying it. For there is a great need today for that rare mixture of idealism firmly linked with a solid grasp of reality which has characterized the best of this nation's foreign policies. There is a need for a spirit that is patient with small steps because it sees their larger meaning. This was the spirit of the Kennedy Inaugural address, the spirit of "But let us begin." And there are places where this spirit can be put to work. We need, for example, a grand plan for harnessing the atom and restricting the proliferation of nuclear weapons. We must better share our bountiful harvests with those who lack sufficient food. The numbers who must be fed should be limited through an intensive international program of population control. There is a need for cooperation in the exploration of outer space. International student traffic has increasingly contributed to the cross-pollination of cultures, but it should be better systemized. Several years ago President Eisenhower suggested an international United Nations University. One should be created and with it a whole network of international universities using new and existing educational facilities in bold new ways. The new generation will respond to calls in these and other areas. But President Johnson has not sounded the trumpet.

Young America is waiting for a demonstration of leadership in foreign affairs. And it ranks foreign policy high among its potential concerns. Today the new generation of Americans finds little that recommends itself in the foreign policy leadership of *either* of our political parties.

A STRATEGY FOR REPUBLICANS: THE COURAGE TO ENTER THE NEW POLITICS

It is remarkable how slow our political parties have been to grasp some of the issues in the "new politics" – how unwilling to adapt to the new political environment. We believe that this gap provides the best opportunity for a *new* Republican party. But ideas are not patentable, and if the Republican party does not seize them, the Democratic party will. This is the immediate challenge to thoughtful Republicans.

What strategy, then, for Republicans? As Mrs. Clare Boothe Luce has suggested, Republicans must *leap-frog* the Democrats into the issues of the future. They must leave behind the meaningless arguments of conservatism versus liberalism, public versus private, business versus labor, hard line versus soft line, and come to terms with the really new challenges. Republicans, not burdened with administrative responsibility for the present, are in a position more objectively to judge and more freely to reach out to these opportunities. If we truly are to honor our yesterdays then we must grasp our tomorrows.

Republicans, if they are to have a future, must "go hunting where the ducks are" as they look for support. They must go where the new voters *are* and compete for their support. Meaningful competition for these voters in terms of the new issues has hardly begun. How sad, with such an opportunity untapped, that some Republicans should seek and applaud an increase in their numbers from the ranks of discredited southern Democrats. Unable or unwilling to win in the present and the future, Republican leaders have often settled for the trophies of the past, a few discarded "white elephants."

The growth areas that Republicans must tap are not obscure. Geographically they are in the expanding urban centers and suburbs of the North and West and among the Negroes of the deep South. Economically they are America's burgeoning middle class. Occupationally they include the huge new numbers of college graduates, the new business and professional class, the employees of service industries, who already represent the greatest occupational growth area in America. These are the men and women who install and program computers, who service dial telephones, color television sets, and complicated auto transmissions. They are highly trained, continually updating their skills to maintain their jobs. They are can-do people caught up in the present; counterparts of the skilled workers who formed the backbone of the powerful Republican party at the turn of the century, under Mark Hanna, William McKinley, and Theodore Roosevelt.

But modern Republicans have not been good political strategists. They have used little of the creative genius or entrepreneurial skill of the business community and the private sector. They have been more like a stockholder afraid to make investments for the future. Their portfolios have come to include only stocks that are on the wane, past their peak. They have watched a rising market pass them by. They have remained the corner grocery store in the day of the supermarket.

When they have had the daring to invest, they have fallen ready prey to the easy money schemes. They have been bewitched by the flash in the pan, by short run gains and short-sighted strategies – the anti-communism of McCarthy, the anti-labor crusade of "right-to-work," the patent medicines of the radical right, the southern strategy and the backlash.

The lessons are obvious, Republicans must invest in groups with a future, groups on the way up. Republicans must reach out and touch these concerns. We must fight for the interests of Negroes, of the youth, of the middle-class suburbanite, and of the new sophisticated technician, for these are the people who will shape America's political future.

Without *them* the Republican party has *no* future.

THE FINAL PRESCRIPTION: THE INITIATIVE TO LEADERSHIP

The strategy for a new Republican party is clear. All that the Republican party needs now is the leadership to implement it. We need men and women who are not afraid to innovate, to make the bold move, the dramatic appeal. The Republican party needs, in short, the *initiative to leadership.*

The Bible warns men not to put "new wine into old bottles" – "else the bottles break, and the wine runneth out, and the bottles perish." If men put new wine into new bottles both will be preserved. The bottles of the Republican party are growing old. They have been taped and retaped by a caretaker leadership. They bespeak a great weariness. Yet the effort goes on to use them one more time. The caretakers may be fooled but the people will not. The wine is a new vintage and it is only a matter of time before the bottles burst.

Where then will the Republican party find this new leadership? Some of it will come from the younger ranks of Republican Governors and Congressmen. But if these men do not soon develop the boldness to break with the past, history will pass them by as well. At a time when the future is still open, the Republican party needs more men with the courage to win, more men who will stand up and be counted, men who see the future for what it is. The Republicans who will rebuild their party as an instrument of the future may be men and women largely unknown to the politics of today, but men and women who share the purpose, the courage, and the vision of those Republicans who found their noblest hours in pulling against a current that was flowing into the past.

These new leaders of the Republican party will find their greatest opportunity for growth and recognition in the states rather than the Congress. Democratic party inattention to state and local government will afford Republicans a chance for exciting political leadership. Reapportionment will insure new chances to contest state legislative seats and to recruit new candidates for the Republican ticket.

The new political role of the Republican Governors is one of the few bright developments in the Republican party, yet even here the potential has hardly been realized. The Republican Governors and the GOP state chairmen could represent the real hope for a new Republican party for they are on the frontiers of policy, participants in the most dynamic sector of American government, afforded the widest range for political leadership. They are closer to the problems and concerns of a growing population. They have fielded winning teams and winning platforms. They are *the* Republican success story, yet many national leaders have not grasped the significance of this fact. Indeed, Senator Goldwater has attacked the Republican Governors' Association as a divisive moderate "splinter group."

Republican leaders in the states must begin to communicate with each other, to exchange ideas and strategies. The Republican Governors, state Attorneys General, labor commissioners, and other department heads should meet together nationally and regionally as most of these groups already do on a nonpartisan basis. We can no longer afford to compartmentalize some of the greatest resources available to the Republican party.

The new Republicans must organize liaison among young state legislators and among Republican mayors, and the Association of Republican County Chairmen should become more than a polling organization. In sum, the combined levels of Republican organization within and among the states provide Republicans with their greatest hope for rebuilding a new party.

A new generation is coming to power in the Grand Old Party. It is already beginning to reshape and rebuild that party so that it may live a useful and successful political life. It is not easy to trust the young and inexperienced with leadership. Many wondered when they took command whether they would succeed in 1776, in 1860, in 1900, in 1960. Yet the burden of the future will always rest on the shoulders of young men and women. From this generation must now come the leaders of our party and our country. The burden is theirs, and the honor.

CHAPTER 7
THE KEY TO VICTORY

a moderate manifesto

Originally the concluding chapter of FROM DISASTER TO DISTINCTION, "The Key to Victory" sounded many of the same themes and even borrowed some of the language that had first appeared in the "Call to Excellence" several years earlier.

– Editors

Had we world enough, and
time
Your coyness, lady, were no
crime.*

Too often responsible Republicans have resembled the coy lady when talk has turned to action. They ignore the harsh truth that the time to do something about the condition of the party is now! We have not world enough nor time to wait. Republican moderates now bear a heavy and inescapable responsibility to guide their party. To fail at this moment will jeopardize not only the survival of a broadly based Republican party but also the very political health of the American nation. No matter how we may try to escape the unpleasantness of contemporary Republican politics, we cannot escape the judgment of history.

We believe that responsible Republicans must articulate a vital moderate Republican philosophy, they must participate more actively in Republican politics, and they must achieve a long term plan of moderate Republican action. But to succeed, moderates must be "more than moderate" in their commitment. The Republican party needs more activists, more pamphleteers, and more "revolutionaries" of the *center* if it is to keep its mind and soul from falling captive to extremist movements in American politics.

---

*Andrew Marver, "To His Coy Mistress"

Responsible Republicans have been guilty of one *false* assumption that may all too soon become a *fatal* assumption. They have shared a naive optimism, a distant unconcern, an assumption that political parties will take care of themselves. Having won the presidency in 1952 and 1956, moderate Republicans paid little attention to the grass roots of Republicanism, to the need for mature policy discussion, or to the task of building a strong organization. Barry Goldwater and the "conservative" movement were the stepchildren of this inattention. The presidential campaign of 1964 should have taught all thoughtful Americans this – that when one of our political parties forsakes moderate leadership, all Americans must share the cost.

THE COURAGE TO WORK: A CALL TO ACTION

Early in his political career, while he was still a Congressman, Abraham Lincoln wrote William H. Herndon, his Springfield, Illinois, law partner:

> Now as to the young men. You must not wait to be brought forward by the older men. For instance do you suppose that I should ever have got into notice if I had waited to be hunted up and pushed forward by the older men. You young men get together and form a Rough & Ready club, and have regular meetings and speeches. Take in everybody you can get, Harrison Grimsley, Z. A. Enos, Lee Kimball, and C. W. Matheny will do well to begin the thing, but as you go along, gather up all the shrewd wild boys about town, whether just of age or little under age – Chris Logan, Reddick Ridgely, Lewis Zwizler, and hundreds such. Let every one play the part he can play best – some speak, some sing, and all holler. Your meetings will be of evenings; the older men, and the women will go to hear you; so that it will not only contribute to the election of "Old Zach" but will be an interesting pastime, and improving to the intellectual faculties of all engaged. Don't fail to do this.

We believe that Lincoln also wrote that letter to us. We will not wait to be "brought forward by the older men" anymore than he did. We too want to speak and sing and holler. And as we do, we also want to gather up "all the shrewd and wild boys about town" to join us in meeting the great challenges and opportunities which face our generation.

The need for individual participation in politics is just as pressing as it was in Lincoln's time, but much more possible for the average citizen. The leisure age is upon us and sages wring their hands and shake their heads as they wonder what people will do with all their free time. But recent experience suggests that we have not devoted *enough* time to political study and to political action. As ever larger percentages of our population join the leisure class we face a tremendous opportunity and responsibility for achieving a new golden age of democracy.

The coming era can challenge the best in us. Moderates can use their increased time and money as effectively as have the extremists. If they do they will learn that politics can be fun; that their participation can be meaningful. We can all become "happy warriors."

Many moderates throw up their hands, saying that modern politics is a "dirty business" and they want nothing of it. Yet these same people are the first to condemn party leaders for failing to reflect their views. Politics always has been "dirty," and to the extent this is true the blame lies solely with the citizen who would rather complain about the mess than handle the mop. Can we expect men of high caliber to run for office when the public views their participation as inherently corrupt? By the same token, can we expect the Republican party to face national problems realistically, when the vast majority of its members leave the field of policy formation to activists of more extreme views? The active participation of moderates is essential to the growth and responsibility of the Republican party.

Where can a moderate Republican citizen begin? Some answers are fairly obvious.

You can become better acquainted with the local political scene. Attend local Republican meetings and be certain to enroll formally as a member. Watch for indications of what the leadership is thinking. Let them know how you feel; as a member you have at least some bit of leverage. Your leader retains his power by keeping people like you happy. Speak for what you believe in. Make your own proposals and solicit support for them. Bring like-minded friends into the organization.

Make yourself known to fellow moderates – a key point. Often a few extremists are able to take over an organization or dominate a meeting because each moderate thought he stood alone though in reality he was a part of an undiscovered majority. Don't doubt your capacity to make an impact on events. Be proud of your views; pursue your own objectives. Too many moderates keep peace by adjusting to the views of others. Let other people come over to your point of view for a change.

Support good candidates – with both money and manpower. Urge able community leaders to run for office and promote their candidacy in special interest groups of which you are a member. Take on the responsibilities of leadership yourself. Your influence is magnified when you represent others. A precinct captain can speak for a thousand or more voters in his bailiwick. Such positions often go begging for someone to fill them. Able citizens who are willing to put out some energy can quickly earn the right to influence others, the right to speak with authority.

Keep yourself informed on issues. Read carefully; clip and file useful materials. Become an "expert" in something. It takes surprisingly little effort to know more than your colleague about a given issue – and the man who knows a little more is indispensable. Knowledge is power. Form pools of knowledgeable people and make your services available to political figures. Join or support policy and research operations on the local and national level. Communicate your views to editors, commentators, party and government officials. If your opinion is well informed, if your position is well argued, it will be influential.

In all of this, remember that politics is a year 'round business. The elections – primary and general – are high points but their results are the products of the unpublicized ground work which preceded them. Local skirmishes, caucuses, and conventions are where you can best make your influence felt. But first you must dare to become involved. Moderates must make a genuine commitment to political action on the local level for this is the predecessor of effective national party leadership. Here lies the first testing ground for the future of moderate Republicanism.

This, then, is a call to action. Let there be no mistake about that. The responsibilities of leadership have been neglected too often in the unhappy past. All of us must now respond to the challenges of the future. We must change the tone and content of contemporary Republicanism – and with it the nature of political debate in a rapidly changing America.

PART TWO

IDEAS WHOSE TIME IS TO COME

CHAPTER 8
GOVERNMENT FOR TOMORROW

a proposal for the unconditional sharing of federal tax revenues with state and local governments

This research paper was prepared by the Ripon Society and released jointly in July 1965 by Ripon and by the Republican Governors' Association, under the chairmanship of Gov. Robert E. Smylie of Idaho, who gave it their unanimous approval. It was later credited by the New York TIMES with having helped to revive the proposal after President Johnson had rejected it the previous winter. "Here is indeed a field of extraordinary possibilities for Republican initiative and imaginative leadership," the Bakersfield CALIFORNIAN commented. Robert Healy, Political Editor for the Boston GLOBE, wrote: "Politically, the Ripon Society has made an enormous contribution to the Republican Party. For these are things about which the party should start thinking and debating."

The Republican leadership has made the concept a central part of the GOP position. Many Democrats, including Senator Edward Kennedy, has endorsed the idea.

Despite increasing public awareness and despite its own promise to review the matter and report on it, the Johnson Administration did not respond to suggestions that it support the revenue-sharing concept. It can be assumed the principal reason is the unhappy fact that the war in Viet Nam has more than absorbed any projected budgetary surplus out of which no-strings aid would ordinarily come. Some observers suggest that nothing more will be heard of the idea until that conflict is resolved. But the concept has gained some piecemeal success by reducing the number of federal strings through so-called "block grants" to state and local governments.

Meanwhile, the revenue-sharing proposal was given a new shot in the arm by one of its earliest and most important proponents, Professor Walter Heller, former chairman of the President's Council of Economic Advisors. In the Godkin Lectures at Harvard University in the spring of 1966, Heller agreed with those who see Johnsonian apathy and the Vietnamese drain as major obstacles to revenue sharing. But he elaborated on his suggestions nevertheless, and endorsed the concept with new force. If we care about the states, he maintained, then something significant must be done to save them.

The statistical data with which the arguments are supported in the Ripon paper are, of course, representative of the economic situation in 1965. While we have not been able to insert later figures at all points, we have noted that such figures make our points even more dramatically. The trend toward state bankruptcy has not been significantly halted.

The paper was prepared and written by a Ripon task force directed by Lee W. Huebner, in cooperation with the staff of the Republican Governors' Association.

– Editors

For a while it seemed as though everyone was for it. President Johnson and Senator Goldwater endorsed the idea in the closing days of the 1964 campaign. Both the Republican and Democratic platforms gave it favorable notice during the summer. The Conference of State Governors supported it enthusiastically.

Liberal economists and conservative Congressmen joined editorial writers and columnists of all persuasions in backing the proposal. The most popular version of the idea bore the name of the President's chief economic advisor, Dr. Walter Heller. A special Presidential task force, headed by Dr. Joseph Pechman of the Brookings Institution, gave formal approval after a detailed study.

The object of all this affection was the proposal to distribute some Federal income tax revenue to state governments on a "no strings" basis. Economist Robert Heilbroner described the plan as "that rarest of rarities – a really new idea in domestic economic policy." Edwin Dale, economics specialist for the New York TIMES, wrote in the NEW REPUBLIC that it was "one of the most exciting ideas to hit Washington in years." Walter Heller, then Chairman of the President's Council of Economic Advisors, began to publicize the idea in this country early in 1964. Republicans welcomed a plan which expressed the concern for state government which President Eisenhower and other leaders had urged for so many years. Support grew quickly and by December one editorial writer predicted that "it would seem to have at least a decent chance of winning Congressional approval."

But the prediction was never tested. For in mid-December the President did a bristling about-face. He was irritated, he told reporters at a background conference, because the favorable recommendations of the Pechman task force had been leaked to certain newspapers. He was annoyed because the leak had generated criticism. Angrily, and without any reference to its merits, he shelved the proposal – its widespread support notwithstanding.

But it did not stay shelved. Journalists reminded the President of his campaign promises. "It deserved a better fate," the New York TIMES lamented, "at least a thorough airing." Economists continued to plug for it. "(I)t seems a good bet that sooner or later someone will discover its merits," wrote Heilbroner. Later in March of 1965, the nation's governors prodded the President one more time. Republican Governor Robert Smylie of Idaho announced that the governors had asked the President to permit a new study of the Heller plan. They were told that the idea was under review in the Bureau of the Budget. There it languished.

For reasons which are developed in this paper, the Republican Governors' Association and the Ripon Society believe the revenue sharing proposal should be revived. It should be judged on its merits and not removed from the realm of public discussion because of personal peevishness on the part of the President. It is our hope that the resources of the Executive Office, the Pechman task force, in full cooperation with the nation's governors, will soon begin fashioning a workable legislative proposal for revenue distribution to the states.

GOVERNMENT FOR TOMORROW: Opportunity and Crisis

We live in an era when events threaten to outrace our ability to respond to them. Too much of present-day politics is caught up in the rhetoric of the 1930's while the accelerated pulse of life requires that we develop dramatic new solutions to the problems of the 1970's and 1980's. The United States is entering upon a period of political turbulence, in which a new and much younger population will confront issues which are different in kind and in scope from those of the past generation. They are the sort of problems which convince us that the exciting new area of political action, the great new opportunity for boldness and creativity and innovation, will be found more and more at the state and local level.

Consider the most dramatic challenges. "(t)he focus of domestic politics," Peter Drucker has written, "is likely to shift to two new areas: *the metropolis and the school*." The cities, he argues,

> are rapidly becoming unliveable . . . But long before we can hope to come to grips with the city as a human environment we will have to come to grips with the city as a government. And the need is desperate. Within a few years three-quarters of the American people will live in a fairly small number of metropolitan areas, fewer than two hundred.

as for education:

> Five to eight years from now, around 50 percent more students should be in American colleges than there are today . . . Altogether our society will be school centered . . . At least one third of the American people will be in

> school a few years hence . . . Teachers are already the largest single occupational group in the country.

Exploding population, rapid urbanization, higher prices and advanced technology are placing enormous pressures on state and local governments. The country is growing by some 8000 persons every day and the states have had to bear most of the burden. In fact, vast new sums are necessary if even the most ordinary, ongoing functions are to be adequately maintained. Programs such as education, fire and police protection, streets and highways, health and sanitation, recreation, welfare, water, and transportation must not be cut back. Nor can we safely allow control of such concerns to slip further into federal hands.

The states and localities do not want to curtail or surrender these responsibilities. That is why they have increased their budgets to twice the level of federal domestic expenditures. That is why they have doubled their employment over the past thirteen years so that it is now three times that of the federal civilian level. And yet, the states and localities face a crisis. For at a moment when the future is rushing in upon them with such remarkable speed, they are victims of a financial resource base which is decades out-of-date.

All too often headlines announce that the states must "Live on Crumbs": that they are "Frantic for Cash." The pressure of rising costs distorts the whole pattern of state and local performance. Officials are constantly preoccupied with fiscal crises. Mayors and governors are repeatedly evaluated by their ability to wriggle out of one financial squeeze after another. A vicious circle is promoted which produces low esteem for state and local capacities. Ironically, this loss of prestige is occurring during a period when state leaders have shown a remarkable willingness to undertake new responsibilities. Problems result not from lack of will but from lack of money. The effect, as Governor Rockefeller has said, is that, "Our federal system – and the basic concept of responsive government close to the people – is threatened as never before."

THE VIRTUES OF STATE AND LOCAL GOVERNMENT

We dare not let this threat continue, for vigorous government at the state and local levels has several indispensable values.

1. A decision is made more rationally when those who make it must live directly with its consequence. As Professor Otto Eckstein of the Council of Economic Advisors phrases it, there is "a greater coincidence between the distribution of benefits and the costs."

2. A multiplicity of state and local governments creates the possibility of a choice by citizens and forces each government to face the test of comparison with others.

3. Decentralized government permits a variety of values, protecting legitimate minority and regional interests. A widely diversified people need not

submit to a single pattern of public life.

4. Innovation and experimentation are fostered by small scale government. What works well in one setting can spread from state to state as many new ideas did early in the nineteenth century and during the Progressive Era.

5. Healthy state and local government increases citizen participation and reduces the sense of political alienation.

6. State and local governments can provide a source of strength for the party which is out of power at the national level and thus contribute to meaningful two-party politics.

7. Social and economic complexities can often be most easily untangled by state and local units. We repudiate the myth that an increasingly complex society always requires increasingly centralized government. Sometimes new domestic problems call for solutions which can be developed most effectively at the national level. But, the administration of the solutions to these problems can often be managed most efficiently on the local level. We reaffirm our belief that modern society requires flexible, pluralistic government.

Let us admit that we are speaking without apology in defense of a federal system; we are not speaking against the federal government. We believe that we cannot seize the future unless the various orders of government become allies rather than enemies. As former President Eisenhower has said: "The better the states do their job, the better the chance that the Federal government will cooperate properly and effectively with them." To do this "better job" the states need new sources of revenue.

RISING COSTS

Let us consider the way in which the bills have been piling up. Two decades are not a long time, yet state and local expenditures in the mid-1960's were *six times* greater than they were in 1946. State and local outlays for education alone increased from $3 billion at the end of World War II to $22 billion in 1964. State and local governments are spending twice as much as the federal government on domestic programs. Over the past ten years, state and local expenditures have risen at 8 per cent a year – twice as fast as GNP. Let no one say that states have not moved to meet increased demands.

But the dizzying pace is just beginning. Estimates in mid-decade were that total education outlays would more than double by 1972. Health and sanitation costs were expected to increase two and one-half times, housing and community development expenses were envisioned at the present level! Economists estimated that state and local governments, which spent $65 billion in 1964, will be spending $100 to 120 billion by 1970, and as much as $155 billion in 1974. By that time they will have far outstripped federal expenditures for domestic, military, and foreign policy purposes combined.

But the sad fact is that present financial resources are not abundant enough to meet these needs. Nor do they show promise for sufficient expansion in the future. Indeed, almost every imaginable tax resource has already been subject to increasing and often undesirable pressures. State taxes alone have experienced an average increase of over a billion dollars a year since World War II. A sharp jump in 1963 produced a hike in property taxes of 7.3% over the previous year; sales taxes went up 8.7%, corporate and individual income taxes rose 7.5% and 6.3% respectively – all in one year. In 1964, state tax increases siphoned off one-third of the $6.5 billion federal tax cut. Despite warnings from economists, a bewildering variety of consumption, payroll and service taxes have appeared at the local level from Detroit to Oakland, Fairbanks to Mobile, Los Angeles to Baltimore. Over forty cities imposed motel and hotel taxes in an effort to shift their burdens to non-residents. In a frantic search for additional revenues, New Hampshire and New York instituted a sweepstakes.

The end is not in sight. Twenty-six governors asked for tax increases in 1965 and many of those who are relying on larger yields from present taxes have warned their legislatures that tax hikes are a future necessity. Yet there is evidence that traditional taxes have already reached the limits of desirable expansion. Let us examine more closely the current status of the income tax, the property tax and the sales tax.

THE LIMITS OF CURRENT TAX SOURCES

Of all revenues, only the income tax expands quickly with the growing economy. Yet only 12% of state and local monies are drawn from this source. It is clear that state income taxes cannot solve the problem. The distinguished economist John Due explains why in his noted textbook, *Government Finance:*

> The possibility of migration of the tax base is the economic consideration of primary importance. Whenever migration is relatively easy, attempts to tax will yield little revenue and will produce economic effects particularly adverse to the taxing jurisdiction . . . Heavy state taxation of income may induce some persons to leave the state . . . Income taxes can, without question, be administered most effectively and with least migration of economic activity by the federal government.

Professor Due goes on to point out that on the state level *actual* migration is not as great a problem as is the threat of migration on political leaders. Cut throat competition for industry and labor makes it extremely difficult to raise income taxes at the state level. In state after state income tax levies have been rejected by the voters despite support by educational, business, labor and political officials. Several states have constitutional limitations on non-property taxes.

Even if income taxes could be increased, interjurisdictional and other administrative problems make this an inefficient levy. Evasion on the one hand and double taxation on the other create serious problems. State income tax machinery duplicates that of the federal government, needlessly and inefficiently. Moreover, when state increases are added to federal income taxes, the overall tax structure can become illogical and excessive for some taxpayers.

The property tax is more appropriate for state-local use but economists generally agree that it has been over used and cannot be raised much higher. It presently accounts for 45% of state and local income. Property taxes are often inequitable in that they apply to only one kind of wealth. Vast non-property resources can escape taxation while the unfortunate property owner cannot even obtain an adjustment for debt outstanding against his property. An unjust and painful burden falls on homeowners with small current incomes – retired persons and widows are particularly hard hit and often lack cash to pay taxes on homes they bought years before. The property tax can also be highly regressive; it is tied to housing expenditures which are typically regressive relative to income.

Many state and local governmental units are presently looking to the sales tax to get them out of fiscal trouble. Over three-fourths of the states now have sales taxes and several governors are asking their legislatures to add such levies or increase their scope. Selective levies are also popular. For example, twelve states recently considered increases in cigarette taxes – from 3¢ to 8¢ a pack in California, 5¢ to 10¢ in New York, 4¢ to 8¢ in Illinois and so on. Gasoline taxes run very high. Thirteen states allow further city sales taxes and these too have climbed.

Again, consumption taxes in many areas have gone about as high as they can go. Some states have constitutional barriers and in all states 5% is seen as the upper reasonable limit. Moreover, the sales tax is a regressive instrument and tolerable only when it is a relatively small part of an overall progressive structure. It favors those who can save; it places a burden on large families. It can produce pressure for inflationary wage increases, but more often it discourages consumption and investment and thus has a deflationary effect. Selective taxes can change buying patterns when they get too high. Local taxes can drive consumers to the suburbs. Sales taxes are useful within limits but the limits are rapidly being approached.

CONSEQUENCES OF THE SQUEEZE

The sad truth of state and local finance is that costs are rising faster than revenues. The consequences of this squeeze are evident on every hand.

Dramatic evidence of the growing disparity between government responsibilities and government resources is found in the enormous increase in state and local debt. From a $15.9 billion level in 1946, public indebtedness at the state and local level had almost doubled by 1952 when it reached $30 billion. In the next thirteen years state and local debt tripled, an average increase of more than $4.5 billion per year. Approximately $110 billion is outstanding today.

Fiscal problems have also created political blight. Former Republican Governor John Anderson of Kansas described the problem before the Committee for Economic Development:

> the rate of "tax mortality" among state and local political leaders is very high. A governor or mayor must raise taxes in order to meet his increasing responsibilities but he is often voted out of office for doing so. Were he to choose to cut services rather than to raise taxes, he would also be likely to get kicked out.

"Tax mortality" was evident in the off-year elections in 1962 when thirteen incumbent governors were ousted and subsequent elections have shown how taxing policy dominates state politics.

Unfortunately, impoverished state governments have sometimes been forced to abandon or limit needed programs. More often, however, they have managed to raise taxes, increase debt, or – what is perhaps most significant – look to Washington, D.C. for help.

FEDERAL AID FILLS THE GAP

The Federal Government has been ready to fill the gap. From the mid-fifties to the mid-sixties, federal aid to the states has almost quadrupled, from $2.7 billion in 1954 to approximately $11 billion in 1965, about 15% of state and local general revenues. In his text, *American Intergovernmental Relations,* W. Brooke Graves discusses the immense problems he had in trying to just compile a list of all federal grant programs. His roster stretches for twenty-two pages; two-thirds of the entries have been added since 1930. The need for many of these programs has long since disappeared, Professor Graves argues, yet specific grants do not diminish, they multiply.

The 1964 Republican Platform pledged "critical reexamination and major overhaul of all Federal grant-in-aid programs." As early as 1961, the highly respected Advisory Commission on Intergovernmental Relations became so alarmed about entrenched and useless programs that it recommended that each grant program be automatically terminated five years after its establishment unless specifically continued at that time. The Commission, a bipartisan body which includes Cabinet Officers, Congressmen and local officials, has recognized that "there is nothing so permanent as a temporary grant-in-aid." "It becomes a going concern," writes political scientist William G. Carleton. "(v)ested interests are created, the controversial becomes customary, and the opposition vanishes."

Almost all informed observers agree that the thick underbrush of federal grant programs wastes money on outdated operations while real needs are unmet. What is even more reprehensible is that the states are forced to reproduce federal errors and to match federal blunders. Present "conditional" grants-in-aid give Washington important controls over state and local budgeting. Public officials find it difficult to turn down federal money. Yet the requirement that states match federal funds forces them to forego other activities which are often more important. Many governors have spoken ruefully of "those armories we really didn't need," yet built because "we could get them relatively cheaply." The *Reporter* magazine has pointed out that "poorer states in particular feel obliged to put a disproportionate share of their funds into Federally matched programs such as highways and airports rather than into such unaided programs as fire and police protection. The result, writes Professor Due, is that "the overall budget may be substantially different from that which would most satisfactorily meet the desires of the community." He warns of "a precedent for possible drastic interference with the functions of the states."

Furthermore, as the fiscal squeeze tightens, states and localities are tied financially to these outdated programs and they are unable to find matching funds for the more important new federal grants. When the Executive Committee of the Governors Conference endorsed the Heller plan last year, this was one of its most telling arguments.

Conditional grants also involve severe administrative problems. Former President Eisenhower has described "the cloying effects of federal subsidies which invariably are accompanied by an overbearing federal bureaucracy." Facts and testimony support his description. Direct overhead costs alone are pegged at 16%. State officials must frequently wrangle with federal bureaucrats over the substance of essentially local programs, and they almost always lose to the pressure for the purse. No matter how clearly the language of the law appears to support their position, it is virtually impossible for states to obtain judicial review of such administrative actions. Michigan, Oregon and South Dakota have experienced recent frustrations of this sort. Intricate and petty federal rules have come under increasing fire. Pointing to examples of self-defeating regulations and needless red tape, the Advisory Commission in Intergovernmental Relations has recommended that federal controls be "kept to a minimum." Governor Anderson summarizes well our whole discussion of present grants-in-aid when he says, "We are approaching the limits of manageability in the variety and complexity of federal grant programs . . . Many thoughtful people are coming to the conclusion that there must be simpler and better ways of making future federal funds available to the states.

A BETTER ANSWER

What can be done to ease the fiscal crisis in states and localities? Taxes can be reformed and adjusted, credit can be strengthened and extended, federal aids can be reviewed and streamlined. But none of these options can give more than limited relief. Without more dramatic help it is likely that state functions will continue to slip away under the enormous pressures of the next two decades.

But our search for a "simpler and better way" is not without hope. For in dramatic contrast to the bleak fiscal picture at the local and state level, the federal government today faces the prospect of increasing revenues. Because the federal tax structure is highly responsive to economic growth, prosperity generates ever-increasing tax returns. These revenues would soon begin to exceed expenditures were it not for growing expenditures in Vietnam. When defense spending returns to normal an excess of income will result. Unless this margin is returned to the economy, observers fear it will act as an automatic "brake" on national growth. Walter Heller (along with James M. Tobin and Budget Director Kermit Gordon) began to sound an alarm about "fiscal drag" soon after he arrived in Washington in 1961. (He had spoken of it even before the 1960 election.) This concern helped to bring about the 1964 tax cut, but even that did not sufficiently limit "the federal suction machine." In 1964 Heller pointed to a $6 billion annual increase in federal tax revenue and suggested that a part of it be funneled back into the economy through unrestricted grants to the states. This procedure would serve the dual purpose of stimulating the economy across the whole range of fifty states and, consequently, pump funds into the existing sources of state revenues.

The ironic truth of the matter is that where the needs are greatest, current revenue is smallest. The states and localities bear the brunt of the population boom, but the federal government reaps the fruits of the new prosperity. State revenues are embarrassingly small; federal revenues are embarrassingly large. This condition is a direct result of the fact that most revenues can be collected with the highest degree of effectiveness by the federal government. It produces massive federal intrusion into essentially local concerns, the values of local planning and administration notwithstanding.

It is our belief that this logic is not inevitable. We dare to believe that we can have the best of both worlds – the efficiencies of centralized taxation and the advantages of decentralized expenditures. By using existing state facilities for the allocation of these funds to a variety of public services, we would also curtail the monumental growth of the federal bureaucracy with its duplication of services and conflicting jurisdictions. More money would go into services and less into bureaucratic overhead. It is for these reasons that we urge the adoption of a revenue sharing proposal.

THE SHARING OF TAX REVENUES – SOME DETAILS

It was just six days before the Presidential election of 1964 that the White House issued the following description of a revenue sharing program:

> In line with the Democratic platform this administration is moving ahead on development of fiscal policies which would provide revenue sources to hard-pressed state and local government sources to assist them with their responsibilities.
>
> At the state and local level we see responsibilities rising faster than revenues, while at the Federal level an average annual revenue growth of some $6 billion provides a comfortable margin for Federal tax reduction, Federal programs, and more generous help to state and local units.
>
> The national government, as a constructive partner in a creative Federal state, should help restore fiscal balance and strengthen state and local governments by making available for their use some part of our great and growing Federal tax revenues over and above existing aids
>
> Intensive study is now being given to methods of channeling Federal revenue to states and localities which will reinforce their independence while enlarging their capacity to serve their citizens.

The very next day Senator Goldwater urged that the federal Government "give back to the states a share of the taxes collected from them."

This dual endorsement marked the high point of a long search for an effective way to help the states. Republicans like Senator Robert Taft and then Congressman J. Caleb Boggs were leaders in that search in the later 1940's. President Eisenhower sponsored important commissions and investigations during his administration but was able to achieve little substantive reform. The possibilities of budgetary surplus in the 1960's have finally turned an old dream into a very real possibility.

What the Presidential candidates described in general terms, the Pechman task force worked out in detail. It reportedly suggested a 1% return to the states on all income tax revenues, a sum which might total $3.5 billion by 1970. The money would enter a trust fund – so as to keep it out of the federal budget. It would be given in the form of an unconditional grant, subject only to basic prohibitions such as bans on construction of highways or public buildings. Most of the money (⅔) would be distributed according to population, the rest according to state needs.

We would indicate here that many details can be worked out when a more specific plan is presented. For example, a part of the aid could be explicitly earmarked for local governments. Basic prohibitions can guard against flagrant misuse or racial discrimination. Governor Anderson has spoken of requiring a "well developed spending plan," on the state level. Distribution formulas can be negotiated so as to achieve an acceptable and balanced program. Our endorsement is not affected by these specifics. The case we make can be applied to several variations of the plan – including an approach which would give credit against Federal taxes for specified state and local taxes paid. It is enough to note that our states have for years used a variety of methods for sharing tax revenues with local governments, and the experiences of the states should provide useful guidelines for the development of a federal program.

In drawing up a specific proposal, we would do well to examine the experience of countries like Canada and Australia which have made use of the "block" or "unconditional" grant to the provinces for some time. In Australia the process is fairly automatic. In Canada it is subjected to considerable negotiation every renewal period. But even there, says Professor Eckstein, it has "worked fairly well." The last American experience with large unconditional grants came in 1837 when a $37 million surplus from the sale of public lands was distributed to the states. The assumption of state debts in 1790 was another precedent.

Whatever its final form, the revenue sharing concept will help state and local units resolve a dangerous situation. It will enable them to serve the public without future burdening an exhausted tax base. It will not eliminate conditional grants but it will help those who seek to reform them. The grim threat of tax mortality and public penury will be relieved, resulting in governments of higher quality and greater stability. *Commonweal* magazine put it this way: "The Heller plan, properly administered, could improve the states' performance and awaken at least some of the popular interest necessary to make the system work. For arousing the people's attention there is nothing like a gift of $100 million or so."

CAN WE TRUST THE STATES?

We cite this effect on state performance and state morale as part of our answer to critics of the plan. For by and large their objections boil down to a single cry: "We just don't trust the states!" Often the cry comes from well established Washington lobbyists who fear they will lose their influence. It also springs from entrenched administrators who would rather see more money in their own aid programs.

And some "anti-state" opposition comes from those who have lost historical perspective, who forget the states have often led the federal government in their willingness to change, to experiment and to meet new problems. Many people also forget that even today the states and localities spend twice as much domestically and employ three times as many civilians as does the government in Washington. We should not forget that scarcity of funds has not prevented the development of persuasive examples of good state and local government in the fields of education, regional and local planning, and social welfare. Many straws are in the wind; they indicate that the states are in a position to make great advances. Nothing could be more effective than a revenue sharing program in accelerating these programs, and in reestablishing vital state government as a creative partner in a flexible federal system. "If we are serious about the idea of creative federalism," says Dr. Heller, "now is the time to do something constructive about it."

We would emphasize the fact that a revenue-sharing program would not in any way reduce the ability of the federal government to play a creative role in meeting national problems. We are not asking that all our problem-solving eggs be placed in one basket, state or federal. Let us look at one example. In the sense that the War on Povetry is a real "war," it is an all-out "crash" program which attempts to discover and eliminate basic social problems. Everyone hopes that the war will be won; no one plans that it will last forever. The Heller plan will not limit the ability of the federal government to fight that war; it may foster some much needed help on the state and local level. But in the sense that poverty is a persistent and unending threat, we battle against it every day in our schools, our hospitals, our social centers. These institutions will never close, nor will our police and fire stations, our highway and welfare offices, our water filtration plants. Their wars will never be won. The revenue-sharing plan will give the states and localities the wherewithal to more adequately finance these programs – often humdrum and often taken for granted. Those who "just don't trust the states" would do well to reflect on just how much trust all of us must place in state and local government every day.

THE HOUR IS LATE

To those who suggest that federal surpluses would be used to cut taxes, to increase federal spending, or to reduce the national debt, we would point out that all of these ends could be pursued – the margin will probably be large enough to accomodate many desires. But we think the revenue-sharing idea more important than any of them.

Finally we would direct one comment to those who fear that the tax sharing plan would mean further incursions upon state prerogatives, that revenue will mean control no matter how unconditional the original grant. It would be foolish to deny that this possibility exists, but it would be equally foolish to let the matter rest there. The choice we face is not between state dollars and federal dollars, but between federal dollars which bear a vast array of strings and conditions – and revenues which are relatively unburdened. Only the latter alternative can now rescue us from the former. And the hour is late.

Above all we appeal to Americans for a vision which sees beyond the years – beyond the realities of today and into the possibilities of tomorrow. What will our federal system look like then? Critics from the left are convinced of federal virtues and are suspicious of the states; critics from the right defend local government and are suspicious of Washington. But mutual suspicions must not be allowed to produce a deadlock. This country will not be governed well, her problems will not be met, unless government is alive and active and responsible at every level.

No single order of government can be fully effective unless it has the respect and the cooperation of governments at all other levels. The revenue-sharing proposal grows out of an awareness that the federal and state governments need each other. It will depend for its effectiveness upon their capacity to respect each other.

We must act now. For in the last third of the twentieth century, this country will face unparralleled challenges. They can become unparalleled opportunities – but only if we confront them with sensitivity and flexibility, with firmness and with understanding. We must seek these qualities in men and in ideas – and we must embody them in programs and in institutions.

The revenue-sharing proposal can help to prepare our political system to meet the onward rush of events. It can help us to put into practice all that we mean when we speak of "cooperative federalism." It can help us to build government for tomorrow.

CHAPTER 9
URBAN FINANCING
a fair share for the cities

In a special collection of Urban Papers issued in August, 1968, just before the Republican National Convention, the Ripon Society urged the Republican Party to adopt an urban program, to formulate an urban electoral strategy, and to nominate an urban-oriented ticket. It broadened its 1965 paper on Tax-sharing to include payments to beleaguered city governments. The paper on urban finance was largely the work of Robert C. Musser and James Upton of the New York Chapter.

– Editors

I. THE FINANCIAL SQUEEZE

The financial gap in city budgets is growing to enormous proportions. One study of local revenue and expenditure projections concludes that *at the current rate the nation's cities will be faced with a gap of $262 billion during the ten-year period 1967-1977*. The gap continues to widen since (1) cities rely heavily on taxes which are unresponsive to economic growth and (2) the costs of public services are rising rapidly despite decreases in city population.

The demands on cities for services come principally from three communities:

(a) the business and commercial community, which demands transportation, communication and police and fire protection;

(b) the urban middle and upper-class community, which demands these services as well as such family services as schools, playgrounds and entertainment; and

(c) the urban poor, which require the services of the first two communities along with a broad range of special social services.

If cities had only to provide the first two kinds of services, they might well hold their own on the basis of their existing resources. The rate of expansion of social services for the poor, however, has far exceeded the growth capability of present urban revenue sources.

Cities rely most heavily on the real estate tax, which is the least responsive to economic growth. Real property taxes accounted for 60% of the total revenues collected by local governments in 1967. As of that year, however, only ten U.S. cities imposed an income tax. Revenues from the real estate tax increase by only 0.9% for every 1% increase in gross national product, while revenues from income taxes increase by 1.6%.

Cities are reluctant to adopt non-property taxes such as the sales tax or the income tax. The first reason is geographic. The taxable jurisdiction of a city covers a limited area. Corporations and individuals can easily escape taxes levied against them and their property by moving to a lower tax area.

The second obstacle is state control over local finance. Even if cities were willing to levy heavier income and sales taxes, they are prevented from doing so in many cases by state restrictions. In New York State, for example, the power of local governments to incur debt and to levy taxes is limited by the state constitution, which requires that the state legislature must approve any new taxes the cities may levy; approval often becomes very difficult in a legislature which is dominated by non-city interests. The consequence is a yearly trek to Albany by the mayors of major cities in New York State to ask for new powers to tax in order to meet the growing demands on their resources. Adding insult to injury is the fact that in some states city budgets are growing because of programs which have been mandated by state law. New York City expects to spend $1.794 billion in 1968-1969 on welfare and Medicaid programs which arose out of state legislation.

The third obstacle is the bureaucratic machinery and red tape that a community must establish to administer any new taxes, particularly the income tax. Citizens are already faced with a myriad of tax forms to fill out every year and would prefer to deal with a minimum of tax collection authorities.

II. THREE SOLUTIONS

Cities have three major solutions available for their financial problems. First, they can seek increased federal and state assistance for programs whose impact reaches beyond the cities. Second, they can *demand* a larger share of federal and state revenues. Third, they can take greater advantage of existing sources of tax revenues. The Ripon Society proposes that the nation employ a combination of these three solutions.

L. *Increased Federal and State Program Assistance.* Ripon believes that the federal and state governments must increase their assistance for urban programs (a) that help fulfill vital national objectives and (b) that have a regional impact.

The United States has come to recognize that an increasing number of urban programs help fulfill vital national objectives. The high geographic mobility of Americans, rich and poor, has given many local functions a national dimension. The concentration of the poor in the cities is a result of national economic dislocation; and the burden for providing social services to the urban poor thus should fall on the nation as a whole. As indicated in other papers in this issue of the FORUM, the urban social services in most serious need of national assistance are education, welfare and health care.

The cities are becoming increasingly involved with programs in most serious need that have a regional impact, public transportation, air and water pollution controls, water supply, and to some extent, the social services previously named.

Relieving the cities of some of the financial burdens for special social services and regional impact programs should enable them better to fulfill the ordinary responsibilities of government units closest to the people: police and fire protection, sanitation, recreation. The cities cannot surrender all their responsibilities for social services and regional impact programs. Urban influence on national programs turns in large part on the extent of the cities' participation in these programs. Careful balances must be struck between a concentration of federal and state power over city programs and the inability of the cities to finance these programs, without outside help.

2. *Share in Revenue Sources.* The cities must obtain a larger unrestricted share of federal and state revenues to meet their ordinary operating expenses. Communities have a growing need for help in financing even their ordinary local services. It is unwise to finance all of these services through federal and state programs. On the other hand, the federal and state governments remain the only ones that can effectively and efficiently muster the large resources needed to finance the ordinary functions of the big cities.

Federal grants to state and local governments have been rising. In 1950, such grants accounted for only 9% of total local and state spending; by 1965, they accounted for 12%, and further rises may be expected for the 1970's. There has been increasing experimentation with block grants. However, the bulk of federal grants have been restricted and have been limited to specific services that coincide with the national interest, such as highway construction and education.

The Ripon Society joined with the Republican Governors' Association three years ago to propose that the federal government share a portion of its growing tax revenues, chiefly the income tax, with the states. That proposal we believe remains basically sound. The federal government is still in the best position to apportion tax expenditure. However, it is even more clear now than in 1965 that any revenue-sharing plan adopted must specifically provide for redistribution of revenues to the cities.

In view of the financial difficulties facing the cities it is imperative that *any revenue-sharing plan of the federal government include a provision requiring each state to pass a portion of the funds it receives on to the cities.* The federal government should establish certain guidelines and minimums based upon such factors as the percentage of money a state already distributes through local communities; the amounts of money already raised by local communities and spent by them; and the minimum needs of certain low-income communities. The actual formula for accomplishing the pass-through will have to be determined by each state legislature because of the tremendous variety of intergovernmental relationships that exist in each state; but the federal government should set clear standards. Clear federal standards plus increasing reapportionment of state legislatures should help assure that the cities will not be neglected by rural interests in developing pass-through formulas.

It is unlikely that Congress will approve a plan to share revenue with the states as long as defense expenditures continue at their present level. Even now, however, it is essential that the states allocate an increased share of their expanding revenues to the cities. The states increasingly must recognize that the problems of the cities no less than those of rural areas, are responsibilities of the states. Through the federal design of our government the states have the dominant revenue-raising power. State neglect of the cities is an abuse of that power and a threat to the federal system.

3. *Increasing Present Sources of Revenue.* It would be a mistake to think that the cities will be able to get by in the coming years merely by surrendering certain of their functions to state and federal government programs and financing others with revenue-sharing funds. Their needs are too great for such a course.

As noted above, jurisdictional conflict is one of the chief obstacles that cities face in raising sufficient revenues. Overlapping boundaries and tax competition, rightly or wrongly, weigh heavily in the minds of local legislators, whenever taxes are considered. Irrational tax patterns have developed in many states and these in turn generate so much opposition because of their inequities that it becomes very difficult to raise tax rates as high as they should be.

State and local goveenments could do much on their own to correct this situation by entering into tax agreements with each other. They also could give more emphatic support than they have to the Interstate Taxation Act pending in Congress. In a systematic manner, it deals with the thorny issues of corporate net income and capital stock taxes, sales and use taxes and gross receipts taxes. It cuts through conflicting jurisdictional problems by establishing national definations and the administrative machinery to interpret them. It sets out a model sales and use tax and certain incentives to encourage each state to adopt it.

The property tax is another important area where reform is needed in local taxes. One of the great inequities of the property tax today is the unevenness of assessment. Most tax assessment officers cannot develop the economics of scale with which to make rational assessments; they are also open to an exceptional amount of local political pressure. State governments could play a major role in correcting this situation by establishing statewide agencies to handle this work, at least for communities under a certain size. The agencies would determine property values in an efficient and scientific manner and would certify the results to local governments, which would in turn apply their own tax rates.

Reform of real estate taxes should also include the elimination of the obsolete exceptions presently available to charitable organizations. Many such organizations perform laudatory functions in our society; but the public services they receive in the form of police and fire protection, street maintenance and sanitation all have to be paid for. Even properties which are used for direct charitable purposes, such as schools, hospitals and churches, should pay a sum in lieu of taxes to meet these expenses; otherwise they are in effect subsidized by the state. Charitable organizations should pay the full tax rate on properties held for investment; the revenues are needed and private persons otherwise are put at an unfair uncompetitive disadvantage.

* * * *

The Republican Party has taken the lead in recognizing the tremendous responsibilities of state and local government in providing the nation's public services. Similarly, Republicans have been among the first to recognize the financing of state and local government as a national concern. We urge Republican leaders to give high priority to the sharing of federal revenues and to the coordination of state and local tax systems. At the state and local level in particular, we hope Republicans will provide the leadership to accomplish the substantial reforms needed in the nation's property tax system.

CHAPTER 10
BEYOND THE MARLBORO MAN

"Beyond the Marlboro Man" originally took the form of an address to the Boston chapter of the Ripon Society by the Honorable Elliot L. Richardson, Attorney General for the Commonwealth of Massachusetts. Mr. Richardson also served as Lieutenant Governor, U.S. Attorney for Massachusetts, and Assistant Secretary for Legislation for the U.S. Department of Health, Education and Welfare under President Eisenhower. The Richardson talk later took on the form of an editorial in the Ripon FORUM for May, 1967.

– Editors

Too many of the leaders of the Republican party of the 1960's, instead of coming to grips with the problems of contemporary America, still speak the rhetoric of an "Old Frontier individualism" which has long ceased to be relevant to the realities of an increasingly urban and technological society. Theirs is the nostalgic ideal of the "Marlboro Man" whose impact on his environment – and control over it – was his most enviable attribute; they cannot bring themselves to accept an age of big government, giant corporations, and megalopolis in which the fate of every individual is inextricably bound up with the destiny of our whole society.

And so the battered bugles of "Old Frontier individualism" are today summoning the attack on current proposals in the field of general welfare in the same strident tones with which, more than thirty years ago, they sounded the charge against the New Deal. Thus medicare and rent supplements are portrayed as "undermining American values" and "destroying self-reliance"; federal aid to education is seen as synonymous with federal control of education. But the real social needs underlying such programs have gradually produced a broad-based and often bi-partisan acceptance of the practical necessity for such measures. And, although the old rhetoric continues to attack these programs in terms of fundamental policy, most Americans both in and out of government see in them only issues of method and of administration.

The truth is, of course, that there remains little philosophical disagreement between the major parties on the old issue of governmental responsibility for the general welfare. Both parties seem to assume that those significant problems which still persist – problems such as crime, juvenile delinquency, structural unemployment, racial discrimination, and the urban ghetto – will ultimately yield to massive applications of techniques and resources we already know how to use. The blueprints for such programs are indeed at issue, but neither party really questions whether or not such blueprints should be drawn at all.

But at the same time as the rhetoric of the Old Frontier is becoming less relevant, a new and potentially disastrous development threatens us: the growing loss by millions of Americans of their sense of purpose and identity. Living in "little houses made of ticky-tacky" in the densely subdivided tracts of some Marlboro country, overwhelmed by numbers and size, depressed by ugliness, beseiged by advertising, they feel depersonalized and insignificant. While "successful" and "secure" in material terms, they are plagued by a vague anxiety and lack of fulfillment.

Spokesmen for "Old Frontier individualism" do not have the answer, for we cannot go back; nor can we look back to the planners of the welfare state, for the remote bureaucracy which is an inevitable by-product of their plans is in itself a contributor to the crisis. No, the answer must be in a new emphasis on individualism, consciously directed toward so modifying and channeling the irreversible forces of contemporary society as to create new opportunities for individual self-expression and development. Let us call this "creative individualism."

Not all the goals of "creative individualism", of course, can or should be made subjects of governmental policies and programs. Something from within must inspire the awareness that there is no greater satisfaction for any individual than in the development and exercise of a talent or skill. Only individuals can decide that these should be objects of their growing leisure. The demand for beauty and clean air and open space is, in the end, personal, not public. Nor is government action necessary to enable the individual who so desires to play a meaningful role in voluntary, fraternal, and community associations capable of exerting a significant impact on his social environment. And yet it should be our concern to identify and to invent ways in which government can contribute to both the creation and the fulfillment of these aspirations and opportunities.

Within the realm of government itself, one way to begin is by taking positive steps to bring about greater citizen participation in the shaping and administration of governmental programs. We can:

1. Put an end to the practice of assigning operating responsibility for a program to a higher level of government merely because funds are available at that level.
2. Assist lower levels of government to meet their responsibilities through outright revenue sharing, initiation of block grants, simplification of grant-in-aid conditions, and consolidation of project-grant programs.

3. Devise means whereby concerned citizens, as well as the recipients of services, are given a real, rather than a fictitious, role in the formulation of programs aimed at helping them.
4. Involve voluntary agencies – hospitals, day care centers, sheltered workshops – in providing needed services through contractual and fee-for-service arrangements with government.
5. Create roles for individuals, some drawn from the community and some professionally expert in counseling and referral, whose function is to serve as points of contact between the people and their government.
6. Establish at each level of government a joint planning mechanism whose designated function is to plan for decentralization.

But these are only partial answers. Fully to exploit the potential of "creative individualism" will require a degree of sustained and concentrated thought seldom achieved by any active officeholder. And yet the opportunity is one which should particularly appeal to Republicans, since a concern for the individual has traditionally been central to our party philosophy. The Republican party's role should be actively to seek out and to support individuals and groups who are dedicated to exploring new and relevant ideas and who can be stimulated to think with extraordinary intensity about the implications of "creative individualism."

The challenge is present and palpable. We have only to reach out and grasp it. And so urgent is the issue and so paramount is it sure to become that republican political leadership can, in responding to it, deserve and win the broader base of public support our Party so earnestly seeks.

CHAPTER 11
POLITICS AND CONSCRIPTION
a Ripon proposal to replace the draft

Ripon's proposal to replace the draft was first presented in December of 1966 and continually supported by Ripon and by a growing number of adherents to the proposal as the draft debate intensified during the next two years. The paper was prepared in large part by Bruce K. Chapman. It received wide press coverage and was the subject of Richard H. Rovere's column, "Letter from Washington," in the NEW YORKER magazine. "Politics and Conscription," Mr. Rovere wrote, "is not only bold, partisan, and specific in its recommendations but at the same time uncommonly lucid and vigorous . . . an uncompromising document."

– Editors

Americans in the past decade have become increasingly aware of the injustices of life in the nation's poverty pockets and of the blight of racial discrimination. But the fundamental injustice of military conscription, which previous generations of Americans recognized instantly, has unfortunately been blurred.

After fifteen years the draft is again a public question, but the focus upon it is woefully fractured. Many supposed reformers of the draft seek merely to build an even greater civilian conscription on top of the one that served the military. Too many critics accept at face value the Pentagon statistics and bureaucratic judgments used to support a continuation of the draft – something they would never do when investigating the contribution of public housing to the elimination of poverty, or when listening to the apologetics of authorities on the state of the urban Negro.

It is remarkable that the present conscription program has been so little scrutinized. A draft, by definition, is antithetic to a free society. The "nation in arms" has traditionally been a Napoleonic ideal, a Prussian virtue, while in Britain and the United States impressment has always been seen as unjustifiable except when the security of the state requires it. That principle lay behind the drafts of the Civil War, World War I and World War II. It was understood in each instance that when national security could be maintained without conscription, the draft would be terminated.

Today we are arguing in America whether this deferment or that is more "fair;" whether the Selective Service System is consistent from board to board; whether this or that prominent individual deserves his deferment; whether draft-card burners and other protesters should be tried and punished by the courts or tried and drafted by the Selective Service, and so on. Indeed, what should be apparent by now in the debate on the draft is that the only truly fair system of manpower recruitment – in a nation that has reached the point of not needing a draft – is no draft at all. Today, as the result of a burgeoning manpower supply, increased federal revenues, and the rising sophistication of military skill requirements, we have reached that point.

The Ripon Society urges the Federal Government to eliminate the draft, to improve the salary, incentives, fringe benefits, and prestige of the military, and to establish a 2.7 million man volunteer army.

I. THE DRAFT AND POLITICS

The confused focus of the draft issue is largely a product of official indifference and political manipulation. Such diverse leaders as Adlai Stevenson and Barry Goldwater advocated abolition of the draft in their Presidential campaigns, but Congress, with responsibility every four years for extending or ending the draft, gave the matter only the most perfunctory attention between 1951 and 1966. Nor have the tightly controlled hearings of its committees examined the fundamental question, "why the draft?"

Where the Congressional leadership has tended towards indifference, the Administration has tended to pigeonhole the issue into closed studies. In a series of speeches presented on the House floor in early 1964, a group of Republicans were the first to call forcefully and publicly for a draft reform. However, three days before their scheduled presentation, the White House announced a committee on draft reform to be set up within the Pentagon to report within a year, by spring of 1965. This move thwarted the draft reform movement for nearly a year and a half, for it took that long for observers to realize that the Pentagon had no intention of releasing its study.

When criticism escalated a year later, the Administration responded not by releasing the Pentagon report, but by issuing what Congressman Thomas B. Curtis (R-Mo.) appropriately called "a report on a report." The 22 1/2 page, double-spaced, wide-margined release barely got into the draft problem; it raised far more questions than it answered. Rejecting a volunteer military, the Pentagon estimated its cost at from $6 billion to $17 billion with no breakdown of these figures. (Secretary McNamara in 1965 estimated the cost of a volunteer military at $4 billion on one occasion and at $20 billion on another.) Just how such conclusions are reached is a mystery.

For example, to justify its apparent decision that higher pay would not have much effect on enlistments the Pentagon paper described part (and just a part) of a survey of boys 6-19 which asked whether "pay alone" would induce them to join the military if there were no draft. The "surprising" findings were that "equal pay with civilian life was considered the most important inducement by less than 4 percent." But, of course, "pay alone" is not the "most important inducement" to persons planning almost any career, and especially teenagers, who not only are idealistic but have no concept of how really low military wages are now. Good wages unquestionably are *an* important inducement to any career, and previous surveys of public opinion made by the military cited low pay as a major reason for the relative unattractiveness of the military life in the eyes of civilians.

Later attempts by Congressmen and other critics to pry loose the Pentagon calculations were also unsuccessful, though certain tables and charts were later issued. Discrepancies between this data and the Pentagon's oral testimony brought renewed attacks from draft critics. But before they could launch a full attack, the White House once again stymied reformers by announcing a blue-ribbon Presidential "National Advisory Commission on Selective Service." The Presidential Commission is less vulnerable to attack than was the Pentagon study, but considering its origins and the fact that several of the same people who staffed the Pentagon study are working for the Commission, there is reason to believe that at least part of its motivation is similarly political. Nor is there evidence that the Commission's study has gone very deep. Again there has been no opportunity for knowledgeable draft critics – particularly proponents of a volunteer military – to examine the facts, challenge the premises, or debate the theories with which the Commission worked.

We are afraid that all of the confusion over the draft will ignore the fundamental question: should America dispense with the draft? Fifteen years ago – indeed at any previous time in American history – the necessity of *any* draft would have been the first point of contention.

Now, however, the draft critics have scattered their attacks and proposals in so many directions that it will be difficult for any reform to overcome the resistance of the still very strong lobby for the present system. Indeed, most of the proposed reforms would not really provide a system more effective militarily or more equitable than the one we have today.

II. TWO DEFICIENT ALTERNATIVES

Few people truly favor the present practice of conscription. Particularly in the undergraduate community – where the draft is subject to fraternity bull-sessions, student government polls, and "New Left" petitions – resentment is high. Careers must be planned, wives courted, and courses selected, all under the shadow of uncertainty of the draft.

The most commonly mentioned alternatives to the status quo are the lottery and a universal national service.

1. THE LOTTERY

As General Hershey has observed, the lottery would merely substitute impersonal injustices for human injustices. Some people find such a system neater, more abstractly pure, more principled. But to the young married father taken instead of a school dropout, or the future, but-as-yet-untrained, doctor taken instead of the unemployed worker, the system's orderliness would seem small solace. Nor would the country's interest in obtaining skilled technicians and other specialists for the military while insuring the civilian sector a supply of its critical personnel be served by a lottery.

Some lottery proponents protest that certain deferments would be allowed under a lottery. But since the nation has millions more young men of draft age than it needs in the service, those deferments would have to be broad indeed to maintain a semblance of universality. The only difference between that kind of system and selective service would be in the "Russian roulette" arbitrariness of the lottery.

Moreover, the lottery still would not solve the problem of resentment caused by some young men being drafted and others missing service. By what might be called its method of planned capriciousness, the lottery would merely build one more anxiety into lives already troubled by the absurdities and dehumanizing impersonality of modern society.

2. NATIONAL SERVICE

A system by which every young man (and woman?) would perform some kind of service to the country is even more problematical than a lottery. Again it would not even purport to deal with the backward manpower policies that underpin the draft. Indeed, institution of national service would make replacement of those policies even more difficult by building upon them. The illustration, always cited by national service proponents, is the young college graduate who would like to go into the Peace Corps but cannot do so without also (possibly) serving two years in the draft. However, they have yet to consider the men of many skills and patriotic perspectives – including ones with the ability and desire to join, say the Peace Corps, – who still would be drafted under national service to fill up the Armed Forces. While options for service would increase for some, their good fortune would simply mock those unwillingly channeled through an unreformed military draft.

National service springs less from a desire to reform the draft than to reform society. Those men and women who have experienced the fulfillment of volunteer service to mankind would understandably like everyone to enjoy such an experience even though the voluntary element might have to be removed to accomplish it. Moreover, national service proponents are concerned that many young men who might otherwise enjoy such an experience on their own are discouraged by the draft and should be given another option.

It has been charged that if national service is to achieve its objectives, it would require unparalleled state control of human endeavor, far beyond the constitutional provision for conscription to provide for the common defense. Originally, proponents argued in reply that "assignments" to various social projects bearing the government stamp of approval would take into account individual interests and abilities. But the same might be said of the Communist system, the only difference being that national service proposes to conscript persons for only two or three years (though longer periods have also been suggested).

The administrative problems of national service are no less staggering than the philosophical problems. Since many of the projects proposed would be of a social service nature, there would be little fairness in coercing young men into them while letting young women go free. By the mid 70's, two million men will be turning 18 each year – 1.2 million of them unneeded by the military. With another two million women a year (and assuming a three-year term for men and two years for women) a pool of 7.6 million would be potentially available for national service, all drained from an already tight labor market. Obviously, there are not nearly enough jobs to be done through VISTA, the Peace Corps, etc. to occupy any appreciable percentage of such a number – nor money enough to pay them. (Present training costs for one Peace Corps volunteer are $7,800.)

Also, the figures of men to be allocated to various approved national service projects are computed on a yearly basis, as if one year's supply of manpower were all national service was asking, instead of two, three or more. The favorite Peace Crops program is always increased in national service projections to four or five times its present size. Failing even then to note that less than a third of the Peace Corpsmen now serving are draft-age, proponents of national service are completely oblivious of the fact that Peace Corps selectivity is far too tight, even now, to permit wholesale expansion, especially under a system of coercion.

Finally, national service offers no fair outlet for the man whose service to his country simply does not fit some bureaucratic scheme. It is said that the future doctor would be helped in his career if before medical school he worked as a hospital menial through national service. That is certainly questionable, both from the standpoint of the individual and the country's need for practicing physicians. But in any case, what similarly valuable training does the national service offer the future but-as-yet-untrained painter (highway beautification?) or poet (editing the Job Corps yearbook?) or musician? People in our diverse society would be just as misused by national service as by the draft, and maybe more so.

National service would not end the draft's injustices but compound them. There would still be deferments, not only for the physically or mentally unfit, but for young fathers, men with occupations critical to the national security, and probably farmers. Some men would serve and some would not.

One would not want to deprecate the social goals or the contributions, present and potential, of the Peace Corps, VISTA, the Job Corps, the proposed Teachers Corps or Health Corps. But meeting social needs and opportunities by grafting a national service onto the draft would be like taking cough medicine to cure an earache. It would be an inappropriate way of dealing with social problems as well as a counterproductive way of treating draft inequities. Its very proposal is a case of displaced social concern.

Voluntarism is a much more powerful instrument for social advance. It is as hard to imagine Peace Corpsmen who joined only to avoid the draft as it is to imagine "assigning" men to the clergy. If certain social objectives are worthwhile, they are worth pursuing by means of a joint government-private effort. What is needed is a semi-public foundation that would finance on a subsistence basis volunteer work or social worth. Such opportunity for service would be available not only on a yearly basis, but for college and high school students during the summertime.

However, a gargantuan Brook Farm built on compulsion and conscription would, as Harvard President Nathan Pusey has said, be at best "a colossal waste of time." Unhappily, the waste of time occurs in even considering national service, or a lottery, as alternatives to today's draft. Congress for good reason is unlikely to adopt either, beyond perhaps a marginal change or two in the present system. But such changes, whether giving an outright exemption to Peace Corpsmen or drafting from the lower age groups first, would not constitute truly relevant reform.

What the national service and lottery schemes do accomplish is to confuse the issue.

III. WHY VOLUNTARISM

The practical case for a volunteer military rests, in largest part, on the new manpower and financial possibilities for the complete replacement of conscription. Not since the early part of the 19th Century has America had such a high percentage of its population in the draft-age category. As the post-World War II baby-boom comes of age the number of young men is rapidly rising. The American generational revolution reordering political life is relevant to the military institution as well. Where some 1,100,000 men turned draft-age each year in the early '50's, some 1,800,000 turned draft-age in 1966, and in 1975 the figure will be up to 2,100.000. That means an immensely expanded pool of potential volunteers. Whereas 59% of an age group turned 26 in the early 1960's had seen military duty, only 38% of age groups turning 26 in the mid-1970's will have seen military duty.

Secondly, the increasing sophistication of military technology has restructured the nature of manpower needs. A radar technician is several times more expensive to train and several times more expensive to lose. The draft does not attract such people and draftees do not ordinarily become highly skilled technicians. The benefits of the military's famed training schools usually are not lavished on men who will serve only a year and a half after completion of instruction.

It is said that the draft does tend, through its threat, to get men suitable for technical training to enlist on their own. But these men too are largely a manpower waste for the military. While the turnover rate of draftees fluctuates from 90 to 97 percent, the turnover rates for first term enlistees (and officers) is also very high, ordinarily over 75 percent.

Indeed, in a normal year, over 500,000 men – out of a total force of between 2,700,000 to 3,200,000 men leave the military. That is one out of every six men; it is hard to imagine a business operating with such a high annual loss. According to Brigadier General Lynn D. Smith (Army), even before the Vietnam buildup, at any given time some 43 percent of Army men had less than a year's experience.

According to General Smith, "the basic problem of the Army [is] too much personnel turnover." Commanders complain, says Smith, that "As soon as we are able to operate as a unit, the trained men leave and we have to start all over again."

The equivalent of ten divisions are in training at any given time. They tie up the energies not only of themselves, but also of thousands of career men who must do the training. A 1957 military efficiency report by Ralph J. Cordiner, former Chairman of General Electric to President Eisenhower, described the situation at many training camps: "I found antagonism and bitterness over the draft. They were checking off the days until they get out. We must devote 25 percent of our military effort to training men who don't stay. The trainers are discouraged. They resemble the poor teachers whose every class flunks."

Interviews with servicemen, trainers and draftees alike, indicate that the situation has not much improved in the last few years. Cordiner's conclusions seem even more valid now with our increased pool of potential volunteers: "Reduced to its simplest terms, the personnel problem appears to be a matter of quality as opposed to quantity. It is not a matter of the total number of people on hand, but it is a matter of the level of retention of those possessing a high degree of leadership quality and those with technical training and experience the services so urgently need. It is a matter of not being able . . . to keep and challenge and develop the kinds of people for the periods of time necessary for them to make an effective contribution to the operation of the force . . . It is foolish for the armed forces to obtain highly advanced weapons systems and not have men of sufficient competence to understand, operate and maintain such equipment."

The cost of the draft in money and manpower is enormous, and in the last analysis, perhaps incalculable. But it is worth noting that the turnover rate for career men is only 15 percent per year. If that sort of rate, common in Canada's voluntary system, could be maintained throughout our military, we could effect an annual savings of personnel numbering in the hundreds of thousands along with the time and money required to train them.

Low wages lie behind much of the turnover problem. Yet because the draft is costly and provides a certain supply of manpower, pressure to raise the wages of the military (particularly first-termers) has been minimal. Today an entering private in our military makes slightly more than a Rumanian peasant on a collective farm: $90.60 per month. That amount is only 20 percent more than he would have earned per month just after World War II, twenty years ago, despite the 60 percent inflation of the dollar in that period.

The American private also makes substantially less than his counterparts in Canada or Britain – where volunteer systems operate – or his counterpart in Germany, with its selective service system. Indeed, the difference in pay is magnified in each of these cases by the gap in standards and costs of living between other nations and ours. Nor, it must be added, has any of them the great productive margin of the United States to support its military financially.

If a man does make a career of the service he and his wife frequently find themselves living in unattractive military communities. Whether from ignorance of modern planning techniques or from some misguided worship of the spartan mystique, the military has constructed some of the most sterile and unesthetic communal agglomerations in the country. Psychologically, such an environment cannot help but have an influence on a potential careerist's attitude toward the services.

Another negative psychological influence is the draft's own aura of compulsion which carries over to the military as a whole, making it seem less desirable a career to many people than it need be. It is not affirming to an army mechanic, for example, to know that the job he enjoys and to which he has committed himself by choice is done by his fellow worker, a disgruntled draftee, under compulsion. A volunteer system would improve military morale and the popular attitude towards the military career enormously. More enlistments would result, and the entire tone of military life would improve.

Yet another manpower policy change that would abet a volunteer system would be a substantial lowering of unrealistic and irrelevant induction standards, particularly physical requirements.

Rejection rates among our NATO allies are much lower (18 percent in Italy, 18 percent in France, 25 percent in Norway, for example) than the 47-52 percent which is the fluctuating average in the United States. A year or two ago many well-meaning observers saw in the then rising draft rejection rates a sign of increasingly poor physical condition of our nation's young people.

But the truth was that faced with an over-abundance of available manpower and already having loosened requirements for other deferments, the Pentagon and the Selective Service simply were waxing more "selective" by stiffening objective criteria and statistical interpretation. Some months rejections ran as high as 57 percent. However, with the advent of the Vietnam buildup in the middle of 1965, the rejection rate began to drop, until by the summer of 1966 it was down to 39 percent, the Korean War level.

Such manipulation of standards is one of the indefensible inequities of the present draft. Not only do deferment and induction physical test standards vary from board to board, but they vary from time to time. Under a volunteer system the standards would be much lower than the norm of the past few years. Positions and work would be found for men now being judged unfit because they are unusually tall or short, thin or fat, or have some chronic physical problem that would make them unsuitable for combat. Since only one in five military jobs is combatant, there is no good reason to apply standards of combat fitness to every man who volunteers for service. Indeed there obviously are many career men presently in the military who could not meet current standards. But fat or thin they still make adequate supply officers, clerks and – presumably – Pentagon generals.

Similarly, the sophistication of new skills required by the military also makes possible and desirable the greater use of civilians in technical, noncombatant positions. There is nothing radical or untried about such a proposal; the Seabees of World War II are merely one classic example of trained men recruited from civilian life. The principle of hiring people who already are trained is well-established, but it could be much more widely applied – to custodial service, for example.

IV. THE COST

All these proposals would cost money: funds for better recruitment programs, better college scholarship programs for potential officers, more attention to side-benefits and, particularly, higher salaries.

However, the upper estimate of $17 billion dollars given by the Pentagon as the cost of a volunteer military appears inordinately high; it would mean an *average* increase of $6,000 dollars a year for everyone in the services. A much more reasonable estimate is suggested by Dr. Walter Oi, Professor of Economics at the University of Washington and a participant in the original Defense Department study of 1964-5. Oi suggest that the turnover rate for the

Army, for example, should be reduced from 25% per year to 16.9%. This would mean some 144.6 thousand new men per year would be required to maintain an enlisted strength of 857 thousand. Even with no pay boost at all, some 90.3 thousand could be expected to volunteer after the draft's abolition. To obtain the balance of some 55,000 men, according to Oi's detailed analysis, would require a 68% pay boost for all enlisted men in their first tour of duty and smaller pay boost for later tours of enlisted men and for officers. The cost would be an additional 4.05 billion dollars a year for all the services.

Moreover, Oi makes the very important point, neglected by the Pentagon entirely, that society itself bears a considerable cost in order to maintain the draft, a cost that largely would be eliminated under a volunteer system. Included in this cost is the loss to the economy of productive manpower and its foregone goods and services. The draftees and the volunteers who are draft-coerced themselves bear, in effect, a tax which conservatively amounts to 1 billion dollars a year in lost civilian income. If the income lost to all servicemen (and to the economy) is measured, the total is 5 billion dollars a year.

Actually, Oi's draft replacement figure of four billion dollars is upward biased. It does not take into account certain savings that could be obtained through the use of more civilians in servicemen's jobs or for the benefits of improved recruiting methods, such as an enlistment bonus incentive for already skilled individuals. And Oi does not note the possibility of manpower savings through reduced physical standards for acceptable service, nor does he attempt to assess the effect of savings wrought by improved morale and longer manpower experience under the volunteer system. What Oi's figures do indicate is an overall saving to the society as a whole once we achieve a voluntary military.

A full-scale Congressional probe by members of the Labor and Education, Joint Economic and Appropriations Committees as well as the Armed Services Committees is required to explore more fully the economics of a volunteer system. Such a probe should be aimed at setting boundaries of cost rather than establishing a hard figure, because too many intangibles of attitude obtain and cannot be programmed in anyone's computer.

However, at this point it does seem appropriate to note that America's national government treasury is growing by more than six billion dollars *per year.* The United States can well afford an improved military system and the abolition of the draft.

V. OTHER OBJECTIONS

Obviously, many questions remain to be answered. Financial feasibility and freedom from conscription are not sufficient in themselves to justify the draft's abolition.

General Hershey, for instance, has charged that a volunteer, all-professional military would be made up of "mercenaries" and should therefore be prevented. But by this definition "mercenary" would be applied to those men who are "careerists" today. It could be applied to the men who have served in the armed Forces during the overwhelming proportion of our history when we had no draft.

If a "mercenary" is someone who is paid for his living, then we are all mercenaries. If a "mercenary" is someone who is paid an inordinately large sum for his work, then the word still does not apply to the men who would make up a volunteer service; no one has proposed paying military men more than a competitive wage.

Another charge leveled against the volunteer service is that it would soon become disproportionately Negro since it would be relatively attractive financially. However, already there are proportionately more Negroes than whites who re-enlist in the services. While one reason for this is the military's lack of racial discrimination, another is that present low wages are more attractive to Negroes than to whites. Raising wages would tend to attract whites as well as Negroes.

Another dubious assertion is that a volunteer military would be unfair because poor people would be attracted to it and would, as Congressman Charles S. Joelson (D-N.J.) has put it, "be sent off to be killed." This argument ignores the fact that wages would be raised for officers (mostly college educated) and other highly trained men along with everyone else. The services would be as socially representative under a professional system as they are now. It also ignores the facts that four-fifths of the military's jobs are noncombatant and that the actual statistical chance of a man dying while in the service is exactly the same, based on 1965 figures, as in civilian life: 2.5 in 1000. A policeman's job is probably more hazardous than most soldiers', but no one proposes (yet) that we conscript for the police force, or for that matter, the fire department. Indeed, if a man wants a military career and finds he can enter one with hope of reasonable financial compensation, who can be so condescending as to suggest he is being exploited?

A more reasonable argument than any of these against a voluntary service is that such a system would be a less flexible tool for manpower recruitment than would be the draft. It has been suggested that elimination of the draft would result in even fewer enlistments and commissioning ceremonies than occur today; and this at a time when American foreign policy requires mass mobility. In answer, it must be said that to some extent inflexibility of numbers would be compensated by the greater flexibility and reliability of trained, seasoned personnel. The Cordiner report shows that from a military point of view it is quality, not quantity, which matters.

Moreover, the Department of Defense could maintain a slight margin of surplus manpower above that required under normal circumstances. This surplus might be constituted of manpower retrieved from training units as the volunteer system is phased in; it might be made up through over-recruitment, even though that would mean a higher overhead in wages; or, it might result from a truly ready Reserve system, comprised of well-paid veterans whose call-up would be considered routine in times of manpower expansion – not as signifying a "national emergency" as does the call-up of our very unready Ready Reserves today. In any case, the surplus could cushion any minor military manpower reorganization or such a major transition to a massive land-war strategy as would result in temporary restoration of the draft.

The numbers argument also ignores the potential for encouraging enlistment which exists in a volunteer manpower recruitment system. Better pay and housing, better in-service education, and increased prestige through the draftee's absence are four factors which would certainly tend to bolster the young man's enthusiasm for the military. Irrelevant standards can be lowered. Finally, there is some question as to the extent to which the draft influences enlistment. A 1962 survey of first term enlistees in the Army revealed that 63.3 percent counted the draft "very little or no" influence on their decision to enlist, while 17.4 percent said it was only of "some influence." Only 19.3 percent said they were "very much influenced" by the draft.

Some may be troubled by the concept of a professional military establishment untouched by the civilian influence of draftees and six-month reservists. Certainly the quality of their influence and the low level at which it is exerted tends to weaken this objection. Even if the only first enlistment alternative were five or six years and to that extent all service personnel were "career" men, still the objection to "military professionalism" would seem unfounded.

Technological change has rendered the military increasingly dependent on civilian educational resources. Not only are service academies reorienting their curricula, but career officers and enlisted men are returning at regular intervals to civilian universities at government expense. The defense establishment is responding to extra-service influence at every level because its mission is no longer military in the conventional sense of that term – in Vietnam, for example, its job is sociological, economic and political as well. Today's officers are less parochial than yesterday's; the scope of their vocational concern has broadened enormously.

Finally, it seems hardly likely that an institution which for more than one hundred and fifty years has been subject to civilian control will suddenly dominate the secretaries and deputies merely because it no longer drafts 18-year olds. The conclusive fact is that for most of its life the army was a volunteer, hard-core, professional institution, and during those years the principle of civilian control was never subverted.

VI. REACHING THE GOAL

Implementation of a volunteer manpower recruitment system would require a transitional period during which a draft would operate. However, the transitional draft should be quite different from the present system.

It should seek through incentives and lower rejection standards to widen the flow of volunteers as much as possible. The rehabilitation program for men who have failed the military entrance examination for education, instituted under the pressure of the rapid Vietnam manpower buildup, would become (for volunteers only, however) a permanent manifestation of that policy. So too would a completely new project designed to utilize those men who fail the physical tests through special non-combat oriented training programs.

Simultaneously, military pay would be increased, with volunteers paid more than draftees. Congress understandably has opposed such discrimination in the past, but the procedure seems more justifiable when used over a brief period of a year or two as a help in priming the increased flow of volunteers. The present "bonus" program for re-enlistment could be somewhat curtailed as a less effective means of gaining a man's commitment to a military career. A systematic improvement of living conditions for volunteers would be undertaken, as would a special recruitment program for utilizing more civilians in non-combat positions.

Meanwhile, the draft system itself would draft younger men first, and grant customary deferments, though, of course, fewer men at that age would be physically unfit, or fathers, or employed in jobs critical to the national security. Students, however, would be deferred only after they had been notified of their induction; at that time they would be allowed to sign a commitment to serve in a branch of their choice after completion of their college careers and given a deferment on that basis. Of course, they also could opt to serve at once.

Under a transitional draft the Selective Service office would publish and distribute to all registrants a booklet fully explaining the options and broadly describing career opportunities in the various services. Even when the volunteer system was completely implemented the Selective Service would continue to register young men and to classify them, against the day when massive conscription might be essential. The physical examinations given all young men would be designed – as they are only theoretically designed today – to provide all young men, including those from disadvantaged backgrounds, with advice on their state of health, to direct the sick ones to help, to provide the military with an account of their fitness for potential induction.

During the transitional draft, registration and classification of men would remain the responsibility of local boards, though under tighter national guidelines. To end the inequities that result when categories of registrants are inducted in some areas but not in others, actual selection would be made from a national pool.

Even the transitional draft described here would be an improvement over the *permanent draft* that we have today, or, for that matter, over national service or a lottery. But some men would still serve under compulsion while others served by personal choice and others not at all. Such inequity, inevitable under any system of compulsion, and the new reality of manpower surfeit, make the real virtue of the transitional draft just that – it is transitional, planned to smooth the way to an all-volunteer, all-professional military.

VII. THE POLITICAL CHALLENGE

The case for abolishing the draft and replacing it with a volunteer system is not *necessarily* a partisan issue. But then neither are most of the larger national issues, and the draft does unmistakably have partisan implications.

Several outstanding Democrats, particularly from the state of Wisconsin, have contributed much to the cause of draft reform. Libertarians of the left and right alike have sought to restore the priority principle of voluntarism as regards the employment of man's labor – a principle that attracted so many immigrants to our shores in the first place. They have seen clearly that the exercise of control over a man's very physical being, when not absolutely required by national security, is a giant step towards the totalitarian condition, whether or not that condition is ushered in by well-meaning would-be reformers. Indeed, as a great liberal, Justice Louis Brandeis, once wrote, "Experience should teach us to be most on our guard to protect liberty when the government purposes are beneficent . . . The greatest dangers to liberty lurk in the insidious encroachment by men of zealous well-meaning, but without understanding.

But despite the essentially libertarian and non-partisan character of the case for a volunteer military, it unquestionably has been a Democratic Congress that has stymied reform in recent years and a Democratic President who has manipulated the issue in ways apparently calculated to prevent thorough debate. Conversely, Republicans in the Congress have taken up the cause of draft reform, some working individually and with little public notice for years. The Republican Party has a good foundation for reform; it need only build upon it.

Through the Republican program here advocated the contradictions and confusion, the byzantine complexities, discriminations and inefficiencies of one of the nation's most consequential institutions can be terminated. The evasion mentality among the young can be curbed. Lives already anxious in a precarious world can be freed of the draft's additional uncertainty. The insidious, subtle power of a vast bureaucracy to interfere in a citizen's personal plans – to "channel," threaten or punish – can be eliminated.

Should the Republican Party adopt this cause, it can both improve the quality and effectiveness of our military and enhance the freedom of our country. Coupling the replacement of the draft with advocacy of municipal and state government support for a wholly volunteer service in the social fields, the Republican Party can demonstrate a rounded program of reform superior to any other, reform that will rank among the proudest and most significant of our era.

CHAPTER 12
ON THE FRINGE OF FREEDOM
the rights of the mentally ill

This position paper was first published in February of 1967. Its authors were Thomas E. Petri and Norman B. Smith.

– Editors

The history of liberty has largely been the history of observance of procedural safeguards.

– Justice Felix Frankfurter for the U.S. Supreme Court

No one is for mental illness. Everyone opposes it. But too many of us have been indifferent to the problems associated with mental health for too long.

While our indifference has failed to diminish, the impact of mental illness upon American society has mushroomed until today over 300,000 patients are committed to mental institutions each year. This is three times the number of people sentenced to prisons. More than half the hospital beds in America are occupied by mental patients. One out of ten citizens will, at one time or another, suffer from some form of psychological disturbance or mental ill health.

The large number of people committed, the current confinement procedures, and the long terms of detention in public mental institutions make the procedure for commitment and the supervision and treatment of those committed critical subjects of public concern. First, substantive legal safeguards to protect the truly sane from being mistakenly committed as insane are not adequate. Second, the facilities and staff of many mental institutions are presently so inadequate that the regime is custodial rather than curative.

Commitment to a mental institution is for an indeterminate period of time; 40% of those in state mental hospitals have been hospitalized for ten years or more. W. Bloomberg, writing in the American Journal of Psychiatry, maintains: "There is repetitive evidence that once a patient has remained in a large mental hospital for two years or more, he is quite unlikely to leave except by death. He becomes one of the large mass of so-called 'chronic patients.' "

Many patients do not understand why they are confined. They are led to feel that they have committed a horrendous crime, but just what it was is vague and elusive to them. The inmate knows he has lost his freedom. He believes that he has been judged guilty and he learns soon after entering an institution that assertion of innocence is viewed as a symptom of disease.

Furthermore, in many parts of our country, the inmate is subjected involuntarily to various forms of dangerous and mutative treatment such as shock therapy, sterilization, or psychosurgery. He may also be confined by humiliating and painful forms of mechanical restraint, or he may be placed in a "chemical strait jacket" so that his days pass in a stuporous haze. A patient is often deprived not only of his personal liberty, but also of his property, voting rights, contractual capacity, and means of communication by mail and by visitation. In addition, he may be required to labor without compensation.

These abuses must be dealt with now. The time has come for us to look to a new phase in the struggle for human rights and dignity. We must now extend civil rights to those who presently live on the fringes of freedom – to the mentally ill men and women who do not in fact partake of the legal rights most of us assume without question. Legal discrimination against those alleged to be mentally ill is widespread in the United States. Sometimes rooted in ignorance, always based on public indifference, the denial of legal safeguards and adequate treatment to those labelled "mentally ill" can no longer be tolerated.

I. THE NEED FOR LEGAL SAFEGUARDS

How is it decided that a citizen is insane?

Ideally, when an individual is suspected of suffering from mental illness, he is informed of the suspicions concerning his condition. After an appropriate interval during which he and his counsel may prepare his case, the individual is summoned before a judge and, if he wishes, a jury. Only after evidence from both sides has been heard may the subject be confined to an institution.

In practice, this ideal is seldom realized. Many persons are committed to mental institutions for reasons other than insanity. For example, some families are anxious to put elderly relatives into inexpensive State hospitals so that these unpleasant reminders of mortality can be hidden from their view.

Moreover, there are some individuals so mentally disturbed that they cannot evaluate their own condition and seek aid voluntarily. The normal solution in this situation has been to participate in the decision to commit. After all, it is said, he is insane so why should he be consulted? This approach assumes insanity before it is proven. We believe no citizen should be forcibly confined due to insanity, any more than he should be imprisoned for committing a crime, until he has had his day in court.

Some mental health experts oppose formal commitment proceedings because, they assert, notice and hearing produce only anxiety and confusion in a sick mind. It is difficult to believe that the traumatic effect of a hearing is worse than finding oneself in a mental institution without any warning. However, the real vice of denying notice and hearing is that the allegedly ill person is prejudged; the very question that would be settled formally by a hearing is arbitrarily decided in advance by "professionals." Thus, the presumption of innocence is reversed: once a person is suspected of having mental illness, he is considered sick until proven healthy.

The trend today is to further informalize commitment proceedings. It appears that most states now allow officials to serve sole notice of a commitment proceeding on some person other than the individual whose sanity is to be determined. Such substitute notice does not protect the individual's rights; there is no guarantee that he will receive any warning of what may happen to him. Often the members of his family, on whom notice is served, are the very persons trying to get him committed. Before he knows it he is "locked up" – without ever having had a chance to protest.

In about a third of the states even the right to a hearing may be waived. Here the superintendent of a mental institution, or some other person designated by statute, makes the decision to commit. And even when there is a hearing, only about half of the states provide for a jury trial. It has been argued that juries are incompetent to deal with complex medical issues. But this overlooks the fact that the decision to commit a person against his will is, in reality, a social decision of the sort that juries are intended to make. The complaint is also heard that juries tend to err much more than psychiatrists in the direction of committing people who are actually sane. A procedure by which an officer of the court, a lawyer or psychiatrist, makes a preliminary determination of sanity which can then be appealed from by the person alleged to be insane overcomes this charge.

The trend today is toward authorizing commitments without notice and hearing or other formal proceedings. Thus, for example, over 90% of the patients committed under some Maryland statutes never appear in court. In similar Rhode Island cases, the courts have been used only once every four or five years. Even where statutes require notice and hearing in advance of commitment, proceedings often satisfy neither the letter nor the spirit of the law.

For example, the Illinois statutes require that a physician certify a patient is mentally ill and that there be an examination by court appointed psychiatrists and a hearing before the court. But even this elaborate process does not provide justice. A recent study by L. Kutner entitled "The Illusion of Due Process in Commitment Proceedings" revealed the following procedure in Cook County, Illinois: (1) a certificate is signed as a matter of course by one of the staff physicians at the Chicago Mental Health Clinic after the patient is already confined there; (2) the same doctor is the one later appointed by the court (thus circumventing the requirement that one doctor check on another); (3) patients are under such heavy sedation at the court hearing that they cannot intelligently defend themselves. The examinations of patients takes two or three minutes, never more than ten, and over 75% of those examined are committed. Employees of the Chicago Mental Health Clinic who inform patients of their legal rights are reprimanded or dismissed.

Because of such shabby practices, we are skeptical of assertions by institutional psychiatrists that "railroading" never occurs. It does. A dramatic example is the case of a non-English speaking Polish couple in Chicago who returned to their apartment to find their life savings of several hundred dollars missing. They suspected the building janitor. When they informed him of their suspicion, he got in touch with the public health authorities. Soon the Polish couple found themselves committed to a mental institution. They could speak no English, and no effort was made to communicate with them during the examination or hearing. The husband, who spent World War II in a Nazi concentration camp, committed suicide in the institution. The wife eventually obtained her release.

The case of a man called "Louis Perroni" provides another example. Perroni ran a gas station. His lease was canceled so the station could be demolished to make way for a shopping center. But Perroni refused to vacate. When agents of the real estate development attempted to take over the property, Mr. Perroni is alleged to have appeared with a rifle and fired a warning shot into the air. He was arrested for discharging his gun but never indicted or tried. Instead, the judge sent him to New York's Matteawan State Hospital for the Criminally Insane. For six years Perroni languished at Matteawan, trying to obtain a trial. Finally, he secured a court order releasing him from the institution. But he still had to go to court to defend against the original charge of firing his gun. The court sent him to another state hospital. This time Perroni was able to bring his own psychiatrist into the case. This psychiatrist found him competent to stand trial. The state's doctors disagreed. Back Perroni went, without trial, to Matteawan. Mr. Perroni remains at the asylum, even now. He has not yet had a trial.

In the process normally used to determine mental competency, decision making is turned over to experts – to the psychiatrists and psychologists. This has a dangerous consequence: these experts have become an unchecked power group within the legal system. Theories are propounded, procedures which rely on these theories are enacted, practices in accordance with the procedures are individually regulated by the same people who developed the theories in the first place.

What are the theories employed by those charged with passing upon an individual's mental health?

The important fact is that the experts – whose word we take as law and whose conclusions we rarely examine – are terribly uncertain as to what mental illness really is. The reader of mental health literature quickly encounters the most alarming discrepancies. For example, one authority estimates that 2.3% of all criminal offenders are psychopathic while another says that 98% are psychopathic. Such confusion illustrates the dangers inherent in committing an individual on any basis other than that of objective, socially endorsed legal standards.

Unfortunately, the approach of many in the mental health field is characterized by a lack of objective standards. Many psychological experts actually oppose them. They reject limited periods of commitment for the mentally ill, firm procedural rules, and clear standards of misconduct by which to determine eligibility for commitment. To be sure, this opposition is often couched in terms of fear of the cruelty or arbitrariness that might occasionally result from firm procedural safeguards. But always the result of this opposition is to broaden the discretionary power of the experts over the men and women who become objects of their care.

The broad discretion of these experts has often been abused. Consider, for example, the question of whether or not a defendant, in a criminal case is mentally competent to stand trial. Psychiatrists are asked for a subjective opinion – and they sometimes make this critical judgment in a heavy handed manner. As a result, defendants may be committed who are in fact competent. A sample medical report by a psychiatrist reads: "We actually feel the patient could cooperate with counsel but that it would be better if he were to be hospitalized in Ionia." And another goes: "I concluded that we were dealing here with a man who was suffering from an early schizophrenia illness. I realized that it would be difficult to convince a court and jury on this, particularly since all his social and work companions insisted that he was sane. I asked the presiding judge to postpone the trial and the patient was sent for six months observation to a state hospital. This worked out admirably. At the end of three months, I went out to see the patient and he presented the picture of a very seriously disordered, full-blown case of schizophrenia. He was completely out of contact with reality and was actively hallucinating. As a consequence he was never brought to trial and in all probability never will come to trial."

There are already indications in mental health literature that some experts examine a person's *political* views when deciding whether to recommend commitment. To illustrate: 1) One authority in the field of mental health writes: "A man, for example, may be angrily against racial equality, public housing, the TVA, financial and technical aid to backward countries, organized labor, and the preaching of social rather than salvational religion . . . Such people may appear 'normal' in the sense that they are able to hold a job and otherwise maintain their status as a member of society; but they are, we recognize, well along the road toward mental illness."

2) Ezra Pound aided fascism during World War II by participating in propaganda broadcasts directed from Mussolini's Rome to American fighting men in Europe. After the war, Pound was returned to the United States. But the poet was not tried for treason. Instead he was committed to a mental institution. After being confined for over a decade, Pound was granted his freedom. 3) In September 1962, Major General Edwin A. Walker, U.S. Army retired, was arrested at the University of Mississippi for inciting insurrection. Later on the day of his arrest, federal officials hustled him under cover of dark to a U.S. government maintained psychiatric ward in Springfield, Missouri. General Walker was confined for mental observation on the basis of an affidavit signed by Dr. Charles E. Smith, medical director and chief psychiatrist of the Federal Bureau of Prisons. The ex-general's behavior "may be indicative of an underlying mental disturbance," the affidavit said. Dr. Smith reached this conclusion in Washington on the basis of news reports and other secondary sources. Because Walker was in the public eye, he was able to protect himself. He secured release on bail, the first time this has ever been permitted by our government in such a case. He then picked his own psychiatrist (normally a person has to accept the state's doctors), and after another legal battle, Walker was allowed to have a jury hear his plea. The jury cleared him; he is a free man. We report by way of postscript that Dr. Smith was brought before the American Medical Association's Judicial Council. He escaped censure, but the Council expressed concern over "future situations wherein a physician might be subject to political control or be used as a tool for political purposes." 4) After an exhausting legislative session, Louisiana Governor Earl Long boarded a plane in the state capital. He thought he was flying to New Orleans for minor surgery, but soon discovered he was bound for Texas and confinement in a mental institution. After a long struggle, during the course of which he outmaneuvered his wife, the director of State of Louisiana mental institutions, and other mental health experts, Long regained his freedom and returned to the Governor's Mansion.

When it is proposed that authority to commit be given to a small group of experts, to be exercised in their relatively uncontrolled discretion, the dangers are grave. Yet that is what many mental health practitioners seek and it is what they have already, to an alarming degree, achieved. By asking for broad, non-specific criteria on which to base commitment, they require that specifically proscribed acts not be defined in advance. By asking for informal procedures, they require that the most subjective judgment be allowed to stand without challenge or review. By asking for indeterminate commitment, they require that these unreviewed judgments be allowed to detain any person for an unlimited term.

In a constitutional democracy the preservation of personal liberty requires delicate balancing. John Stuart Mill pointed out that the liberty of the individual must be restricted somewhat to increase the liberty of all, but he also cautioned that too much restriction of the individual's liberty will diminish the liberty of all. Somewhere between anarchy and totalitarianism, between absolute permissiveness and absolute conformity, the balance must be struck. We can do this by firmly adhering to the fundamental concept of American democracy – government by law, not by men. Our tradition of due process protections is the greatest protector of individual freedom. It must be applied as fully and scrupulously in the area of mental illness as it is now in the realm of criminal justice.

Too many mental health practitioners invoke health or social goals as ultimate values, thereby implicitly denying consideration of the personal liberty of the individual. If our desire for social welfare is not balanced by a passion for individual freedom, the cure will be more dangerous than the disease.

II. THE NEED FOR ADEQUATE FACILITIES

Once a citizen has been found to be insane, what becomes of him?

The insane are frequently quartered under conditions far worse than those of prisons. The average man can understand the imposition of punishment on criminals; as a result, competent political decisions can be made about it. *Punishment* is a matter susceptible of community judgment. The concept of *treatment* is very different. The usual attitude is that treatment is something for the expert to decide, and that the ordinary person cannot make an intelligent decision about methods of treatment. Because treatment is thus freed from community control, experts have acquired very extensive discretionary powers.

In the past, treatment was often so painful, dangerous, and degrading that when knowledge of it became public, an indignant community insisted upon its abolition. Some of the noblest chapters in the history of American reform have been written by those who fought such cruelties. Any yet, more than a century after Dorothea Dix prodded the conscience of America to rescue the insane from intolerable abuse, a new evil haunts our mental hospitals, uncriticized – often undiscovered. This evil is neglect of inmates.

Albert Deutsch made a two-year investigation of American mental hospitals in 1945-47. He reported that in some wards there were scenes rivaling the horrors of the Nazi concentration camps – hundreds of naked patients herded into huge, barnlike, filth-infested wards, in all degrees of deterioration, untended and untreated, stripped of every vestige of human decency, many in stages of semi-starvation. "The writer heard state hospital doctors frankly admit that the animals of near-by piggeries were better fed, housed, and treated than many of the patients in their wards."

We submit that during the past twenty years, the improvement in conditions in many mental institutions has been agonizingly slow. A 1965 study of every mental institution in New York State, commissioned by the New York

Joint Legislative Committee on Mental Retardation, contained the following language: "What we saw in Building H was shocking. In Ward 23 some youngsters were sitting on benches, others sleeping on the bare floor, clothed in underpants only. This filthy room with defecation on the floor served as the day room and dining room for 130 active children. Their little bodies and faces were dirty and scratched." Of another institution the report states: "There were many emaciated looking, unclothed males lying in bed in their own excrement. The stench was revolting. The patients are spoon fed in their beds, bathed and shaved twice weekly.

"We were ushered to a sub-basement area where about 15 ambulatory patients were eating in a dungeon-like, dirty atmosphere with a commercial dishwasher belching steam at one end of the room." And it was reported that in an institution for children under 12 there is such inadequate staffing that a number of children go unfed at the evening meal because of lack of time.

III. RECOMMENDATIONS FOR ACTION

As a result of these practices, what is ostensibly a regime of treatment for mental illness is frequently a purely custodial system. Because the punitive aspect of such treatment procedures is not publicly acknowledged, political and legal safeguards have not been employed to protect the rights of those allegedly suffering from mental illness or to protect those who have been duly committed and are undergoing treatment.

To end a great tragedy, we make the following recommendations:

1. THERE MUST BE NO DEPRIVATION OF LIBERTY UNLESS PROPER LEGAL PROCEDURES ARE USED.

As we have already seen, it is common for those charged with the care of the mentally ill to inveigh against the formalism of legal procedure. Formalities, it is said, are not only tedious and inefficient, they are harmful to the alleged defective. But the argument can be turned around. An orderly legal procedure, permitting anticipation of a dislocative experience, allows for preparation. Most persons alleged to have a mental illness are quite capable of appreciating and availing themselves of the procedural rights of a formal hearing. They are often hypersensitive to their environment. Participation in a hearing has a satisfying, relieving effect. If commitment is ordered only after the presentation of clear and convincing evidence of mental illness, and only after the defendant through adequate counsel has had every opportunity to present his side of the case, the purpose may be understood by the patient and treatment is less likely to be resisted.

Furthermore, we should abandon the theory that commitment for mental illness is analogous to a civil action, and thus not subject to the rigid due process requirements that accompany a criminal proceeding. *Whenever the state forcibly deprives a citizen of his freedom every procedural safeguard must be em-*

ployed. If it is felt by the court's medical advisors that a full scale trial will adversely affect therapy, this should be explained to the defendant or his court appointed representative by the counsel or the judge, and he should be permitted to waive admission of the public, trial by jury, or other rights. An exception must also be made to allow for a very short detention period without formality in the case of emergency (this, of course, is nothing more than a restatement of the law of arrest). A 1963 Supreme Court decision has encouraging and far-reaching implications. In *Kennedy v. Mendoza-Martinez* the court held that because it is punitive in character, forfeiture of citizenship cannot be administratively ordered, but can only be imposed following a proceeding attended by all of the safeguards of a criminal prosecution. We are hopeful that this doctrine will also be extended to commitment proceedings involving those alleged to be suffering from mental illness. A recent Wyoming Supreme Court decision took this important step.

2. NO PERSON SHOULD BE INVOLUNTARILY CONFINED TO A MENTAL INSTITUTION UNLESS HE ENGAGES IN WRONGFUL CONDUCT AS OBJECTIVELY DEFINED BY STATUTE.

Today's trend is toward commitment of the mentally ill at the first sign of "undesirable behavior." Definite acts of objective misconduct no longer are required. The "propensity" to engage in undesirable behavior is enough. The pattern is: commit today; investigate later, if at all.

This development is unwarranted, because there is no substantial agreement among and within the various behavioral schools as to the criteria for predicting the danger a person poses to society. The decision to confine someone who has not yet engaged in any proscribed anti-social conduct, made on the basis of a psychiatric diagnosis, is based on little more than hunch and intuition.

Today the implementation of the "objective misconduct" standard in the mental health field is more feasible than it once might have been because of the availability of voluntary commitment and the increasing use of outpatient psychiatric centers where help can be obtained without confinement.

We must remember that only the aggressive and violently insane, who comprise a small percentage of those committed as mentally ill, are dangerous to the community. This is the only type who must be committed in order to protect the public.

3. COMMITMENT SHOULD BE FOR A FIXED MAXIMUM TERM: INDETERMINATE COMMITMENT SHOULD BE FORBIDDEN.

Once there has been a finding of insanity, indeterminate confinement is the usual disposition. Those who defend indeterminate commitment argue that a short confinement period may frustrate treatment and that a long fixed term will hang like a dark cloud over a patient. They believe release should be ordered by the institutional authorities when, and if, the inmate is rehabilitated.

Ordinarily, the patient is released when he is pronounced cured and no longer dangerous. But psychiatrists are not agreed as to what constitutes recovery, just as they are not agreed on what constitutes mental illness. Nor are they in agreement as to the degree of recovery that must be achieved before the decision to release can be made.

There is a right in every state for an inmate to apply for release, always by habeas corpus and sometimes by special procedures. But in some states habeas corpus is inadequate because only the initial validity of the confinement, and not its subsequent justification, may be tested. In these states habeas corpus is of little assistance to the patient who wants to secure his release on the ground that he is cured or no longer dangerous. Even where habeas corpus can be used, the person seeking release must discharge a nearly insuperable burden of proof. The inmate may not be able to obtain expert witnesses or counsel, while the state can rely on its power, prestige and own employees as expert witnesses who have observed the defendant continually. The Louis Perroni case, discussed earlier, provides a good example of the patient's predicament.

In addition, there are disparities in the confinement time for different inmates which cause patients to believe they are being treated unjustly. This sense of injustice, along with the feeling of frustration that comes from the uncertainty as to when, if ever, release will occur, causes many patients to lapse into a sense of hopelessness. Further, institutional staffs may manipulate the duration of confinement as a means of discipline and control. There is also a tendency for institutional staffs to postpone treatment procedures, since they are not working under any time pressure.

There is positive evidence that limited terms of confinement are therapeutically valid. Several states permit temporary observational commitment (for a period varying from ten to ninety days) of persons suspected of mental disturbance. The Yale Law Journal comments: "Because the temporary nature of this type of commitment averts the stigma of a final insanity decree and postpones the prospects of a long indefinite confinement, cooperation both by the patient and his family tends to be augmented, thus facilitating early diagnosis and treatment. Consequently, under temporary observational commitment a large percentage of mental patients can be sufficiently improved to justify their release within one to three months."

4. INVOLUNTARILY CONFINED MENTAL PATIENTS SHOULD BE RE-EXAMINED IN FORMAL LEGAL PROCEEDINGS CONDUCTED AT PRE-ORDAINED INTERVALS DURING A FIXED TERM OF COMMITMENT; THEIR TREATMENT SHOULD BE REVIEWED AND THEIR RELEASE ORDERED IF THEY ARE SANE

The absence of legislative and judicial control over the period of confinement of the mentally ill has an unwholesome effect. It undermines what protections now surround pre-commitment procedure. Legislation should spell out in detail exactly what institutional administrators may do. No drastic therapeutic measures (such as personality-changing brain surgery) should be imposed without a prior formal proceeding at which the defendant is given every opportunity to be heard.

These proceedings will not merely provide an inmate with an opportunity to present grievances; they will also review the adequacy of treatment.

The state's attorney or other court appointed inspector should have power to authorize the release of inmates who are cured. The individual should not be required to meet the burden of proving himself sane. At every stage, the state should be forced to demonstrate that a patient is insane if it seeks to continue confinement against his will.

In the light of recent progress in other areas of civil rights, we believe that all of these recommendations would have been accomplished some time ago had the issues we have raised been acknowledged as within the public domain rather than within the exclusive jurisdiction of institutional examiners and administrators.

5. FINALLY, THERE MUST BE APPROPRIATE LEGISLATION FIXING MINIMUM STANDARDS FOR ALL MENTAL INSTITUTIONS, PUBLIC AND PRIVATE, AND PROVIDING FOR FREQUENT, THOROUGH INSPECTION AND FOR STIFF PENALTIES WHEN THE STANDARDS ARE NOT MET.

The passage of the Community Mental Health Centers Act of 1964 represents an acceptance in part by the federal government of its responsibility in the mental health area. The bill recognizes the undesirability of confining many types of mentally ill persons; it is a constructive first step toward eliminating the dilemma of choice between committing an individual or permitting him to remain with his family without adequate care.

But the act is only one step. Other facilities are needed. Most importantly, we need major efforts to secure more qualified people to run these facilities. It is customary to pay the poorly-trained attendant little cash, but to give him room, board and what he can "chisel." The "good" attendant, in his superior's eyes, is the one whose charges give the staff the least trouble. Therefore, the attendant is tacitly encouraged to keep his patients in line by his own methods of discipline.

Poorly-trained personnel are the product of low wages. Where there are competitive salaries, more qualified employees are attracted and fewer personnel are required. Therefore, the net amount spent on wages and salaries may be nearly the same. Also, better personnel means faster cure, a shorter period of confinement and an earlier return to productive employment for the committed. In short, it is clear that higher personnel wages really cost much less than do poor wages.

The history of the treatment of the insane is marked by the gradual abandonment of barbaric practices. Pinel, a figure of the French Revolution, is remembered for striking off the chains of the inmates of the asylums of Paris. The name of Dorothea Dix is associated with the removal of the insane from their wretched quarters in poor houses, jails, cribs, and coops. A drive to reduce mechanical restraint to the minimum in American mental hospitals began a century ago and resulted in widespread acceptance of the system of non-restraint. Many progressive modern mental hospitals are designed so the patients can live comfortably and can move about with considerable freedom. Their patients' time is occupied constructively with psychiatric counseling and occupational therapy.

But this can by no means be said of every mental treatment facility. Legislation is required to foster the necessary improvement.

We call for action now.

CHAPTER 13
ON 'LIBERAL' AND 'CONSERVATIVE' REPUBLICANS

Duncan Foley, an assistant Professor of Economics at the Massachusetts Institute of Technology, began a series of monthly columns in the Ripon FORUM for February, 1967 with this hypothetical dialogue between a Republican and an Economist.

– Editors

REPUBLICAN: I see that Barry Goldwater has a letter in the January Ripon FORUM saying that "there has never been any great division in our Party over basic fundamentals."

ECONOMIST: What do you suppose he means by that?

REPUBLICAN: Most Republicans have a distrust of concentrations of personal power. They are skeptical that any one man can make a good decision on a complex social issue. I suppose I always have a suspicion that personal decisions to interfere with some social process will create as many problems as they solve.

ECONOMIST: That certainly explains Republican reluctance to intervene in economic markets, since they are a perfect example of many small decisions converging to a big social choice without any single person exercising much power. But there are ultimately some social decisions that the government has to make. The most important is the distribution of tax burdens, but there are others. No free market process, for instance, is going to clean up air pollution.

REPUBLICAN: There you have the dilemma of our Party. The "liberal wing" of the party believes that those problems must be attacked in some way by the government. The "conservatives" prefer to live with the problems. As Ronald Reagan said in his inaugural: "There is a simple answer – there just are not easy ones."

ECONOMIST: The simple answer being to do nothing at all, grit your teeth and take the consequences?

REPUBLICAN: I suppose so. The conservatives want to kick the problems down to the smallest, least powerful levels of government and hope they just go away.

ECONOMIST: What about yourself?
REPUBLICAN: I'm in the least comfortable position of all. I don't want to live with problems like poverty, air pollution, inadequate medical care, or poor education. But the only programs I see, Democratic or liberal Republican – just set up another agency, hire more administrators, to tell more people what to do, and pass more laws interfering with the natural course of the economy. It somehow seems barbaric to me just to tell people in trouble to sit tight, or to learn to live with smog or the sonic boom. But there you are. If we didn't have interference in the economy in the first place we wouldn't be building a sonic boom. We also wouldn't be able, as you say, to do anything about air pollution.
ECONOMIST: I only said there was no *free* market process that would get rid of air pollution. There are ways that the government can control the society without administering it. We have talked, for example, about a negative income tax scheme that would accelerate the natural processes which eliminate poverty without agencies or administrators. The philosophy behind that proposal can be extended to most of our economic difficulties.
REPUBLICAN: Just sketch it out quickly for me.
ECONOMIST: Self interest is the strongest force for social change. What Republicans like about the market is that self interest goes unchecked except by competition from other people, and the sum of everybody's selfish actions is often good for everybody. The trouble with agency-administrator approaches is that they ignore self interest. People must conform to the plan whether they want to or not, whether it helps them or hurts them. The result is unhappiness because people are getting pushed around, and new problems when people find the loopholes in the law. Curbing self interest is like squeezing a balloon – if you push it back on one side it bulges out on another.
REPUBLICAN: Which is what I meant when I said the programs create as many problems as they solve. But what's the alternative?
ECONOMIST: The government should control and structure the incentives in the economy, not administer behavior. Instead of setting up agencies and passing laws requiring something like air pollution control, why not just tax every air polluter, factory, dump, or car, according to the volume of pollutants he puts into the atmosphere. Everyone would have the choice of reducing pollution or paying the tax. The people who have to live in the polluted atmosphere would be compensated by paying lower taxes. If we want less pollution, we raise the tax rate.
REPUBLICAN: So no one is compelled to do anything. You just increase the incentives to desirable behavior.
ECONOMIST: Just as the negative income tax changed the incentives to find a job. The point is that by using market behavior instead of overruling it, the government can attack social problems efficiently, without a bureaucratic

agency, and without giving any one man power to decide what other men should do. Would this kind of program be acceptable to both wings of your party?

REPUBLICAN: Thinking that way certainly ought to bring the two wings closer together. But now I must confess to some darker doubts about the conservatives. There are three issues which seem fundamental to me on which conservatives have not clearly joined the rest of the party.

ECONOMIST: Three issues?

REPUBLICAN: First, of course, is civil rights for Negroes. The liberal wing is quite clear about this. There is no question of repealing the law against lynching and replacing it by a tax.

ECONOMIST: Though it just might work better, come to think of it.

REPUBLICAN: No, there is some behavior that laws can and should control. This is not a question of legislating human emotions, as conservatives sometimes say, but of guaranteeing rights. But some conservatives dodge this issue, and sometimes act like a segregationist front.

ECONOMIST: Segregationists haven't won too many national elections lately. What's your second point of doubt?

REPUBLICAN: I have a feeling that some conservative criticisms of Democratic programs hide, not a dissatisfaction with the way the government acts on society, but a desire to obstruct all attempts to change the status quo.

ECONOMIST: If that's true I might as well mail all my stuff to the Democratic committee right now and get it over with. What's your third point?

REPUBLICAN: This is somewhat vague, but I think very important. Suppose we did manage to increase the personal and economic freedom of American society, to open it up as the liberals and conservatives both claim they want to do. People are going to start using that freedom to create whole new patterns of life. Dissent from the old-line puritan, hardworking, churchgoing, family and success-oriented attitudes is going to grow. I suspect that some "conservatives" can't tolerate that. Many of their positive programs seem designed to punish nonconformity and dissent. Is their real emotional goal to return to McKinley, just because they want everybody to think and behave the way people did in 1900? If so, I don't see any hope for including them in any politically effective group.

ECONOMIST: Some of them do seem to insist that only praying in schools, persecuting pornographers, and saluting the flag will build a stronger America.

REPUBLICAN: There you are. Perhaps Mr. Buckley, or Mr. Kirk, or Mr. Goldwater can satisfy these doubts of mine about civil rights, governmental activism, and the right of dissent. If they cannot, there is a deep division in the Party, which will make it desperately difficult for us to win nationally. Yet I do hope Mr. Goldwater is right, and that we can go out together to right the imbalances of power in our government and the injustices of our society. Perhaps liberal impulse and conservative skepticism and individualism can make a program for our Nation.

ECONOMIST: As long as the impulse, the individualism and the skepticism, wherever they come from don't contradict economic reality. And in this case, I don't think they do.

CHAPTER 14
JEFFERSON AND THE GOP

The Society's domestic proposals increasingly involved emphasis on decentralization. They stressed a concept of the role of government as a designer of incentives that would channel the energies of private groups and state and local governments. John McClaughry saw some precedent for the emerging Ripon philosophy in the thoughts of Thomas Jefferson.

– Editor

Admittedly, the Young Republicans of Caledonia County, Vermont, have made no signal contribution to America. Neither have those of Lyndon State College (!), located within that county. But on April 6 these hitherto inconspicuous organizations combined to sponsor an event which might eventually have a far-reaching impact on the Republican Party.

The event was a celebration of the anniversary of Thomas Jefferson's birth (which actually falls on April 13). Its significance – aside from the fact that practically no one observes Jefferson's birthday any more – was that it was sponsored not by Democrats, but by Republicans.

The theme of the occasion was set forth in the initial press release as follows:

"Traditionally the Democratic Party has tried to claim Thomas Jefferson as its philosophical founder. We Republicans are holding this Jefferson Day dinner to emphasize the fact that the Republican Party was formed in the 1850's precisely because the Democrats had lost sight of the principles of Jefferson, particularly his revulsion at human slavery. And today, the Jeffersonian principles of individual liberty, faith in the common man, the unhampered pursuit of happiness and local self-government have been abandoned by the leadership of the Democratic Party."

Not only was this theme unusual for the modern Republican Party, but the format was unusual – intellectually oriented addresses on various topics relating to Jefferson and Republicanism. A Lyndon State history professor, who had studied under Jefferson's great biographer Dumas Malone at the University of Virginia, spoke on "Jefferson's Philosophy of Government," dwelling on the principles of the Declaration of Independence, the Northwest Ordinance, the Statute of Virginia for Religious Freedom and the Kentucky Resolutions. Another professor, also a Republican State legislator and President of the Vermont Historical Society, spoke on "Jefferson and the Founders of the present Republican Party," discussing the influence of Jefferson's thought on the men who founded the GOP in the 1850's.

"Jefferson and Lincoln" was the subject of a third talk, given by a young teacher from East Burke, Vermont. In it he outlined Lincoln's debt to Jefferson, and his use of Jefferson's ideas in making his case against the spread of slavery to the territories. The final talk, by another Lyndon State faculty member, dwelt on "Jefferson and the Republican Party of Today."

This last topic is perhaps of most interest. As the concluding speaker put it, "Can this cultured Virginia aristocrat, this preacher of agrarian virtue, this opponent of bigness and centralized power, this man who, like Washington, eschewed foreign entanglements – can this man teach us – both as Republicans and as Americans – how to chart our course through the troubled waters of the urban crisis, a world in flames, a nation which has grown in magnitude and complexity beyond the musings of his most melancholy moments?" The answer was yes, and the prescription five-fold.

First, Republicans must pledge, in the spirit of Jefferson, to restore the central government to its proper role, redistributing power whenever possible to the local levels of government. Decentralization of governmental activity, in the interest of self-government, of liberty, and even of efficiency, is a platform on which every Republican of 1968 should be proud to stand.

Second, Republicans must pledge to restore decency, integrity and honor to the conduct of national affairs. "Nothing is so mistaken as is the supposition," said Jefferson, "that a person is to extricate himself from a difficulty by intrigue, by chicanery, by dissimulation, by trimming, by an untruth, by an injustice." Republicans must once again elect a President about whom parents can say to their children, "I hope and pray you will grow up to be like the President of the United States."

Third, Republicans must not fear to restore to the nation Jefferson's abiding faith in the common man. Jefferson's dream was of a nation of freeholders, owning a tangible stake in America, their self-government accompanied by the general diffusion of knowledge. The Republican Party of Lincoln carried forth that dream with the Homestead Act, the Morrill Land Grant College Act, and the 13th Amendment. The lessons to today's Republicans, in the fields of education, of expanding the ownership of America's wealth and property, and of assuring equal rights and opportunities to all, are easy to discern.

Fourth, Republicans must recapture the Jeffersonian vision of the American Mission – not to colonize the earth, but to encourage free government by aid and example. He sought a world of justice, law and order and a foreign policy founded on principle, not expediency. These goals, sought diligently by the last Republican Administration, have receded in the past five years. We need to pursue them with renewed vitality.

Fifth, Republicans must become the guardians of individual liberty – not merely the liberty to dispose of one's property as one sees fit, but particularly the liberty of thought, of speech, of press, of assembly, of dissent.

As the history of this nation unfolds, first one Party, then the other, is entrusted with fostering the rebirth of the Jeffersonian vision of America. It is again the Republican Party's turn. This was the principal message of the Caledonia County, Vermont Jefferson Day celebration. Republicans across the country would do well to ponder its implications.

CHAPTER 15

THE NEGATIVE INCOME TAX

a Republican proposal to help the poor

On April 10, 1967, the Ripon Society became the first political group in the country to design and endorse a workable plan for a Negative Income Tax. Its paper, which was written by John R. Topping, Jr. and Duncan K. Foley, received immediate news and editorial coverage in more than fifty major daily newspapers. It was read into the Congressional Record by Ohio Congressman Charles Whalen, Jr., a former professor of economics, it was digested in a special study by the Library of Congress Legislative Reference Service, and it was included as one of the working papers for the national college debate topic for 1968.

– Editors

Poverty means insecurity and dependence. The insecurity of never knowing where the next dollar will come from discourages poor people from seeking new opportunities. The dependence on welfare administrators saps them of the initiative to make their own decisions. The Republican Party believes that the poor man ceases being poor only when he is willing and able to make his own way in the economy, when he takes control of his life. To conquer poverty we must break down the barriers to free participation in the economic life of our Nation. This means providing an adequate education for everyone; it means eliminating discrimination in hiring and housing; it means above all reducing the insecurity and dependence of the poor.

We must find a way to supplement and stabilize low incomes without interfering with the natural freedom and incentives of the market. *The Ripon Society proposes that the United States increase incentives and opportunities for economic advancement through the adoption of a Negative Income Tax system.* Ripon urges the GOP to commit itself to a Negative Income Tax and to make this commitment the cornerstone of an effective alternative to the mismanaged, miscellaneous and ineffectual War on Poverty.

I. WHAT IS NEGATIVE INCOME TAX?

A simple formula (so much per adult, so much per child) determines a "standard" income for every family. The family receives a fixed percentage, called the tax rate, of the difference between its earned income and the standard. These income transfers come in payments, called the Negative Income Tax, which decreases gradually as income increases. All families with incomes below the standard – not just those that are unemployed – receive Negative Income Tax payments.

For example, suppose the standard income for a family of four is $5,500, and the tax rate is 50%. If the family earns nothing, it gets $2,750 (50% of $5,500). If it earns $1,000, it gets $2,250 from the Negative Income Tax, and has a total income of $3,250, $500 more than before. The Negative Income Tax encourages families to move up the income scale until they can begin to pay positive taxes. In 1966 both the national Commission on Technology, Automation and Economic Progress and the Advisory Commission on Public Welfare endorsed similar proposals, as did the National Crime Commission in February, 1967. Yet President Johnson has delayed even a research report on the proposal until 1969.

The Negative Income Tax is not a new concept; already almost 60 countries have a similar program known as the family allowance. The Negative Income Tax has gained the support of many of the nation's most respected economists, both Republican and Democratic. Henry Wallich, a member of President Eisenhower's Council of Economic Advisors, supports the idea. One of its first proponents was University of Chicago economist Milton Friedman, Barry Goldwater's chief economic advisor during the 1964 presidential campaign. Yale economist James Tobin, a recent member of the Council of Economic Advisors, has written extensively advocating the idea. Harvard's Daniel Moniyhan and Dr. Martin Luther King have suggested variations of the plan.

The Negative Income Tax emphasizes individual incentives to find and create jobs, and the natural efficiency of free markets in eliminating poverty. It embodies Republican concern for human dignity, civil rights, and individual free economic enterprise. It is the fairest and most efficient way to accelerate the natural processes through which the American economy eliminates poverty. The United States can institute a Negative Income Tax system providing significant improvement in both incentives and living standards at a cost of ten to twelve billion dollars a year. This represents the natural increase in tax revenues from two years' growth of our economy. This program can be introduced gradually over five years, the cost rising about $2 billion each year, with no increase in positive tax rates.

II. ADVANTAGES OVER PRESENT PROGRAMS

1. INCENTIVES

Current welfare programs actually discourage recipients from seeking employment. A recipient of welfare at the present time cannot increase his total income by increasing his earned income. If a member of a family receiving

$3,000 a year in welfare earns $1,000 the next year, welfare payments drop by exactly $1,000, leaving total income unchanged. For these people the welfare system breaks the link between extra effort and extra income. They have no financial incentive to find or train for a job.

A recent account of the problems of a family on welfare illustrates this. Mrs. Pressley lives in Harlem with six children.

> "That's one reason why I went to work," Mrs. Pressley explained, "so I could have a little more money for my family. It's not much more, though, and it doesn't go very far when you add up the carfare and cleaning bills and such."
>
> Before she went to work in July as a part time neighborhood aide for the Urban League's Open City program that promotes housing desegregation, Mrs. Pressley had received $184 twice a month from the Welfare Department. The Department now deducts her weekly salary ($30) from the welfare allowance but adds employment expenses (carfare, lunch, clothes, cleaning bills, etc.) so that her combined income now comes to $203 twice a month . . .
>
> Mrs. Pressley said that in the past, when she tried to work while on welfare, things did not go smoothly.
>
> "Once, I was working, and I told the investigator not to call the employer and that I would show him my pay receipt as proof. He called my boss to check and I was fired the same day – many people don't want clients working for them."

Mrs. Pressley has the will to work, but it is clear that she is not benefiting from it financially. (When she discovers this, she may stop working.) It is also clear that the whole atmosphere of welfare administration discourages employment. Under the Negative Income Tax, everyone, no matter how small his earned income, can keep something extra if he earns something extra.

2. *FREEDOM*

The Negative Income Tax will also work a radical and constructive revolution in the attitudes of the poor towards their own life.

The philosophy of paternalism pervading our welfare system does little to develop the confidence of the poor in their own ability to direct their lives. The recipient of public assistance suffers a far greater degree of public control over his everyday affairs than the rest of the population. Often, the welfare recipient feels that he is forced to accept the advice of his caseworker. Various detective measures to uncover possible welfare fraud have seriously infringed upon the privacy of welfare recipients. Midnight raids by caseworkers hoping to find female recipients in bed with boyfriends or husbands are not uncommon. The constitutionality of such practices is open to serious doubt, but few welfare recipients are able to mount a legal challenge against these degrading practices.

In fact, the social worker meddles in every aspect of a recipient's life, even to the extent of selecting items in a recipient's budget.

One caseworker complains:

> "Give us some independence in dealing with the clients . . . We come out of college wanting to help people, but we are policemen. We must check how much money they spend. We have to make sure they pay the rent and don't waste any money on cigarettes or a tube of lipstick.
>
> "Every time a welfare client goes to the bathroom we have to make out a form. We can't be their friends. We represent the oppression of the unfeeling state.

A welfare recipient cannot by his own action control either his income or the way that it is spent and becomes accustomed to letting other people make decisions and take initiative. No wonder so many poor people stop caring and develop attitudes of futility and despair. Under a Negative Income Tax everyone will have the freedom to decide his own priorities and desires in spending his income. The experience of buying freely in a money economy is an important factor in developing self-reliance and self-confidence. The Republican Party has long recognized the role the free market can play in enriching people's lives and efficiently satisfying their needs. Must the poor – just because they are poor – be excluded from this part of American life?

3. EQUALITY

The present system puts the heaviest financial burden on those depressed and underdeveloped areas of the country which are least able to afford them. The result is inequitable difference in state programs and standards. For example, even programs financed largely by federal funds such as Aid to the Families of Dependent Children (AFDC) are applied in quite contrasting manners by various state authorities. This variance in standards is an incentive for economically senseless migration to take advantage of more generous programs. Residency requirements instituted to prevent this "welfare shopping" are equally senseless barriers to mobility of the labor force and serve to keep aid away from newly arrived immigrants just when they need it most.

While certain of the wealthier states of the North still possess substantial poverty pockets in their urban ghettos, the greatest concentration of poverty in America is found in the South, the Border States, and the Great Plain States. Economic progress in such regions is virtually impossible today because the inhabitants lack the purchasing power to support an economic expansion. Past poverty and associated low skill levels combine to discourage new industry from locating in these areas. While Negative Income Tax payments will do little immediately to raise skill levels in a poverty area, they will generate considerable purchasing power. In such areas as Harlan County, Kentucky, the added income which will flow from a Negative Income Tax will provide a basis for business vitality and create additional jobs.

4. *WELFARE POLITICS*

In the northern ghetto where welfare has become a way of life, entrenched political machines perpetuate their existence with the implied threat of withholding the essential welfare check. Such political intimidation is a disturbing feature of present public assistance programs. This has happened frequently in Chicago where the Cook County organization of Democratic Mayor Richard Daley holds sway.

The threat of welfare withdrawal was a significant factor in two widely publicized campaigns in 1966 in the over-whelmingly Negro First Congressional District in South Side Chicago. The New Breed Committee, a bipartisan group of young South Side Negro reformers, mounted a serious attempt to defeat veteran Congressman William Dawson, long regarded as the Daley organization's major spokesman in the Negro community. Fred Hubbard, a social worker backed by the New Breed Committee, unsuccessfully challenged Dawson in the Democratic primary. After Hubbard's defeat, David Reed, a New Breed Committee member who had received the Republican Congressional nomination, mounted a campaign with the all-out support of the young insurgents who had backed Hubbard in the Democratic primary.

Several Reed campaign strategists and organizers whom we have interviewed stressed the political potency of the threat of welfare withdrawal. Welfare recipients were exceedingly reluctant to serve as poll-watchers or otherwise publicly identify themselves with anti-organization candidates for fear that they would lose their welfare. The mere fact that a welfare recipient feels vulnerable to such pressure often keeps him politically passive.

Abuses and intimidation are not practiced solely in the ghetto; in many areas of the South, Negroes have been denied benefits for which they are clearly eligible. Often unaware of their rights and lacking access to legal assistance, the unsuccessful applicant can do little to resist this discrimination. The NAACP Legal Defense and Educational Fund has documented some of the glaring injustices:

> In Grady County, Georgia, three Negro mothers, all with young children and no means of support, reported that the Welfare Department had refused in early July of 1966 even to consider their applications for Aid to the

> Families of Dependent Children. All were told that "seasonal employment was available in the fields until October and that no applications would be accepted until the fall."
>
> Another mother who had been receiving assistance since the preceding October had her benefits terminated in May. She was told that "full-time seasonal work" was available. Further, her 12-year-old twins "should work in the fields until October" when benefits might again be granted.
>
> In Grady County, only Negro women and their children are required to work in the fields during the growing season and denied benefits from May to October. Field work is not considered "suitable" for white women and children receiving benefits under Aid to Families of Dependent Children.

Southern poverty, however, is by no means confined to Negroes. Since the Civil War, severe poverty has characterized the large mass of the southern population, Negro and white, and has aggravated racial animosities. Uneducated poor whites have regarded the freed Negro as a threat to their already meager economic circumstances. Yet in every state except Louisiana, Mississippi, and South Carolina, there are more white than Negro families (in absolute numbers, not percentages) with annual income under $2,000.

The Negative Income Tax, nationally and impartially administered, will not be a tool in the hands of machine politicians or white supremacists. It will meet the needs of poor people of all races, in every part of our country.

5. EFFICIENCY

The United States has committed itself to spend substantial sums to raise the living standards of the poor. Agricultural price maintenance, public housing, and the War on Poverty represent only a few of the programs in this area. We can either establish government bureaucracies to spend this money, or give it directly to the poor, letting each family allocate its share to shelter, clothing, food, or education according to its own needs and wants. The Ripon Society believes, in the Republican tradition, that individuals can usually make more efficient economic decisions than any government agency. If a family renovates its home, it will try to get the best work for the lowest price simply as a matter of self-interest. A government agency building a housing project cannot achieve the same standards of personal inspection except at enormous cost.

Our present welfare system is itself riddled with paper work and consumes great amounts of valuable time in making decisions that would be automatic under a Negative Income Tax. Instead of counselling the poor, welfare workers have to police their conduct and scrutinize their assets. Testified a woman case-worker from Harlem: "The woman asked me for three sheets. I had to visit the home and inspect the bed, determine how many used the bed. Were they really torn? If I gave out sheets six months ago, why were they needed today? Go over the records and make sure the sheets didn't exceed the family clothing limit. Wouldn't two sheets be enough? Before I got the sheets I had dealt with the unit supervisor, the case supervisor, and the senior case supervisor."

The Negative Income Tax is a self-liquidating program. As the number of low-income families decrease, the payments automatically diminish, and there is no bureaucracy to look for new excuses to keep up the appropriations. The time of case workers and supervisors represents a valuable social resource which is presently being wasted in policing and paperwork. Freed from the responsibilities of handing out money, social workers could provide counselling services much needed by all parts of the society.

6. *ADEQUACY*

Even if the present welfare system were to correct its deficiencies on the above points, one overriding fault would remain: present programs do not make payments to many of our poorest citizens. The payments we do make are often so inadequate that they create only despair among the recipients. As the Report of the Advisory Council on Public Welfare noted:

> Only a fifth of the poor (7.5 million out of 34.1 million) are now being helped by federally-aided State public assistance programs. Furthermore, they are receiving payment far below the nationally determined poverty figure of $3,000 for a family of four, or $1,500 for an adult living alone.
>
> The national median payment, including vendor payments for medical care for an Old Age Assistance recipient was $77.55 a month, or $930.60 a year; for a needy child, $35.45 a month, or $425.40 a year; or for a family of four, $141.80 or $1,701.60 a year.
>
> The national average provides little more than half the amount admittedly required by a family for subsistence; in some low-income states, it is less than a quarter of that amount. The low public assistance payments contribute to the perpetuation of poverty and deprivation that extends into future generations.

Even a small rise in income from bare subsistence improves the morale of the poor, releases enormous energies toward self-improvement and increases the chances that their children will break out of the poverty cycle. Under the Negative Income Tax every penny spent will go to the poor directly. We expect that this modest increase in standards of living together with the incentives described above will lead to much greater participation of the poor in the economic life of the country.

A large number of people not presently receiving public assistance payments will obtain benefits under the Negative Income Tax plan. Yet, only the most obtuse Social Darwinian could argue that hunger and privation do much to make the indigent a more productive part of society. When people sink into the despair of our poverty pockets, whipped by the lash of hunger, living in rat-infested tenements or tarpaper shanties, and seeing their children without shoes, the erosion of their morale does far more to sap their incentive to work than would the receipt of governmental assistance. Any program to encourage individual initiative must recognize that a certain minimal level of security is necessary for anyone to become a productive part of society – to acquire the skills or take the chances which enable him to become an economic and social asset.

III. ANSWERS FOR THE CRITICS

1. *"Won't a man working full-time for $3,500 a year resent someone else who is getting $2,000 for doing nothing?"*

Since the Negative Income Tax applies to everyone whose income falls below the standard, the $3,500 man will himself be getting some payment. If the hypothetical worker with the $3,500 really covets the status of his neighbor, he has the option of quitting his job; but he must accept a lower income, and consequently a lower standard of living. The incidence of resentment will actually be reduced by a Negative Income Tax. Today, because of administrative, regional, and racial inequalities, identical families receive unequal benefits.

2. *"Won't many people just stop working?"*

The question is suggested by the operation of present welfare programs, which provide no incentive to work. People work for the things they can buy with extra income.

As we have seen, the Negative Income Tax reinforces this positive incentive to work by enabling people to receive the fruits of their labor. We must realistically note that the choice for the poor is not always between honest work and starvation – crime offers an opportunity for an adequate income. The Negative Income Tax will provide many of these people with the margin they need to resist the temptation of a life of crime.

Certainly, a few people will choose not to work even at the very low standards of living provided by the Negative Income Tax ($750 a year for a single person according to the plan suggested below). But many citizens in fact can use this opportunity in ways that will benefit themselves and society: artists, writers and students would be given a chance to have their time to themselves if they were willing to accept very low incomes. In any case, we can always influence the number of people who will choose leisure by altering the tax rate.

3. *"If we pay some people for not working at all, two very different ways of life will grow up in America, leading to class conflict."*

This is a better description of the present situation than of the Negative Income Tax. The poor family in America has no hope of controlling its future. If it is on welfare, its income and expenditures are completely controlled by government administrators. If it is scratching out a living from day to day, it lives in great uncertainty which discourages any plans for the future or for a better life for its children. The result is a growing separation of the affluent middle class from the poor not only in income, but in attitudes toward life. The poor cannot hope for the security and regularity of life which the middle classes cherish. The child who grows up without adequate food, clothing, shelter, or books is already handicapped in his attempt to become a productive member of society.

The Negative Income Tax will alleviate the insecurity of the poor and allow people to plan ahead. It provides a smooth transition from not working to working, from poverty to affluence. The Ripon Society believes that, by extending these features of the middle class environment to the lives of the poor the Negative Income Tax will knit the society closer.

4. *"We already have too many enormous Federal programs interfering in the economy. We need more freedom from Federal control, not an extension of it."*

The Negative Income Tax will shift decisions from the Federal government to individuals. By freeing local resources now devoted to economically burdensome welfare programs, the Negative Income Tax will enable the cities and states to devote their energies to education, the improvement of the environment, and the curtailment of crime, all predominantly local responsibilities which are being poorly met at the moment.

The use of objective criteria that is central to the Negative Income Tax system should insure against an accretion of power in the hands of federal bureaucrats. In fact, local initiative in devising structural approaches to reduce the incidence of poverty may be strengthened by the adoption of a Negative Income Tax system. Under the grant-in-aid approach which dominates much of the public assistance area today, state and local governments often have little room for policy initiative. Instead they find themselves forced to tailor their welfare policies to maximize the matching federal grants. The Negative Income Tax system would not pressure state and local governments to follow any single path in providing for the welfare of their citizens. Assured that their citizens would have at least a subsistence level income, these governments would have more room for initiative and experiment.

The criticism of over-centralization is actually more valid for proposed alternatives to the Negative Income Tax. For instance, the suggestion that the government become the employer of last resort would shift control of enormous resources into the public sector increasing even further the sphere of federal decision making in the economy.

5. *"Won't the money be spent on liquor, drugs and fancy clothes?"*
Most of it will go into housing improvements, into schoolbooks and home study space, into privacy and food and shoes. This is the way most people of all incomes spend their money. As with the earned incomes of the middle class, some of this money will be used for drugs and liquor and will reduce pressures on addicts and alcoholics to support their habits through crime. If making several hundred drug addicts more comfortable is the price or giving shoes to millions of school children, why not pay it?

6. *"Isn't it 'wrong' to pay people for not working?"*

The deepest-felt objection to the adoption of a Negative Income Tax plan or any proposal for insuring a minimum floor under all family income is essentially an emotional one. The idea of "paying someone for doing nothing" runs against the Puritan Ethic. In fact, the notion of "the undeserving poor" leads many Americans to associate poverty with shiftlessness, laziness, and other character debilities. A somewhat more sophisticated version of this attitude recognizes that poor children are not to be blamed for their plight but regards their parents as undeserving of sympathy. Consequently many will advocate large expenditures to educate the children of the poor but will oppose suggestions that these families be given some form of income supplement.

This view ignores the fact that poverty in America is to a large extent an inherited malady. The poor adults of today, more often than not, were the children of the poor of a generation ago. Growing up in an environment which discouraged personal advancement, most of our poor either left school early or merely went through the motions while attending school. Lacking necessary job skills, they have become accustomed to failure.

The effects of this despair upon the family life of our poor have been devastating. Family instability among the urban Negro poor has seriously complicated the task of providing adequate education and citizenship training in the ghetto. Still, the major socializing institution in our society, the family, is the source of most of a child's values. The child who grows up in a broken home in an urban ghetto today is likely to receive little more than a sense of helplessness from his family situation. Though living in a poverty-stricken environment, he is exposed to the blandishments of advertisements urging him to consume. The poor youth in the city, lacking the means to share in the affluent life to which he is exposed, may turn sullen and silent or burst out in anti-social displays of anger and violence.

Society must accept the responsibility of assisting those whose major reason for not finding a job is the accident of their birth and upbringing.

IV. A WORKABLE PLAN

The advantages of the Negative Income Tax are best demonstrated in the context of a concrete plan. The one presented below does not purport to meet all administrative, technical or legal problems, but it does provide a framework for implementing the concept.

1. COST

For purposes of discussion we use the following table for computing the standard income allowance:

TABLE 1

For each adult	$1,500
For the first child	1,500
For the second child	1,000
For the third child	600
For the fourth child	400
For other children	0
Limit for any family	$6,000

These levels represent a reasonable upper limit to the standard income allowance. A family of four, two adults and two children, has a standard income of $5,500.

Our plan includes a "tax rate" of 50%. This means that the family of four would receive $2,750 if it had no outside income. A single adult would receive $750. The incentive to supplement these minimums will be substantial, since a 50% tax rate means a family keeps half of anything it earns. Table 2 indicates the relationship between earnings and total income for a family of four.

TABLE 2

Earned Income	Deficit From "Standard"	Negative Income Tax	Total Income
$ 0	$5,500	$2,750	$2,750
500	5,000	2,500	3,000
1,000	4,500	2,250	3,250
1,500	4,000	2,000	3,500
2,000	3,500	1,750	3.750
2,500	3,000	1,500	4,000
3,000	2,500	1,250	4,250
3,500	2,000	1,000	4,500
4,000	1,500	750	4,750
4,500	1,000	500	5,000
5,000	500	250	5,250
5,500	0	0	5,500

The difference for a family between its present income and the standard is called the "deficit" for that family. In 1965 the sum of these deficits for American families was $20. billion. This figure includes welfare payments as income. Without welfare the deficit is $25 billion. In addition, the Federal Government collected somewhat less than $1 billion in income taxes from families who will be eligible for Negative Income Tax under our plan.

From these figures it is easy to calculate the cost of any proposed tax rate. For example, if welfare payments continue at present levels and a 50% tax rate is in effect, the total cost to the Treasury will be $11 billion ($10 billion representing 50% of the total deficit plus $1 billion representing the loss of tax revenues). Of this $10 billion in direct payments about 80% will go to families with children. If welfare payments are not included as income but are counted as part payment of the Negative Income Tax, the total cost will be $13.5 billion (half of $25 billion plus $1 billion in lost revenue). We expect, of course, that much federally sponsored welfare assistance will be phased out as the Negative Income Tax comes into operation.

[The next section of the paper deals with technical considerations including income definition, deductions, positive tax liability, eligibility, special instances of low annual income among the wealthy, etc. Those who are interested in these topics are referred to the original document, available from the Ripon Society Office. – Editors.]

3. ADMINISTRATION

One of the fundamental simplicities of the Negative Income Tax is the ease with which the program can be administered without establishing an additional welfare bureaucracy. An individual or family which expects its income to fall below the standard in a future period will file for Negative Income Tax payments from the Internal Revenue Service. These payments will be made monthly. At the end of each year, Negative Tax recipients will file returns showing their actual income for the year. Any discrepancy between the actual Negative Tax payments and what a family was entitled to can be made up by a lump sum refund or tax payment or, if the payment is large, by a tax payment spread over several months.

To minimize the variation in tax payments employed, Negative Tax recipients should have tax withheld at the source like other employees. Withholding, together with assistance in filling out forms and modern data-processing, will simply the administrative problems in adjusting tax payments to income.

4. FRAUD

Relatively well-off people who by some legal device can meet the letter of the requirements may abuse the Negative Tax. The incentive for this is small because the payments are small. The chances of its happening can be reduced by making the definition of "income" for Negative Tax purposes as broad as possible.

Another difficulty will be misreporting of income by poor people to avoid the 50 percent marginal reduction in Negative Tax payments for each dollar they earn. The most effective deterrent against this will be the actual requirement of filing a return, since it takes considerable ingenuity to fake a consistent series of fraudulent tax returns. In exchange for the Negative Tax privilege, people may also be required to provide information on returns, such as reports of purchases of durable goods, which will facilitate detection of fraud by computers. The most important point is that the Negative Income Tax criteria are simple and equitable, while present welfare regulations involve a byzantine code of behavior. The combination of deterrence and respect for a good law will help to reduce fraud to a low level.

5. GRADUAL ENACTMENT

The Negative Income Tax represents a substantial though not revolutionary change in our economic environment. For this reason it is desirable to watch the effects of it develop slowly and to gain experience in the problems it raises one by one. The Negative Income Tax should be introduced gradually by starting with a low tax rate, say 10%, and raising it year by year to the target of 50%. The first year this will cost about $3 billion (10% of $20 billion plus $1 billion in lost revenues) which itself is a modest but important contribution to the welfare of the poor. If, as the tax rate rises, significant bad effects become apparent, the program can be halted or reversed smoothly.

The Ripon Society notes that the Negative Income Tax with a 10% tax rate can be instituted immediately with provision for an automatic rise of 10% in the tax rate each succeeding year. If the end of the war in Vietnam provides an opportunity, we can raise the rate by more than 10% in that year. This is a powerful anti-recession weapon, especially since Negative Income Tax payments go to those whose propensity to consume is very high.

Each year until the fifth after the adoption of the program it will cost about $2 billion more. The natural growth of tax revenues is about $5 billion a year, so that the Negative Income Tax can be initiated easily without any increase in positive tax rates. This is true even if the war in Vietnam continues.

V. THE POLITICAL CHALLENGE

We cannot tolerate the low incomes of the poor. Misery affronts our consciences. Ugliness afflicts neighborhoods drained of money and packed with people. Insecurity and discrimination drive their victims to a guerrilla action against the majority who have made it or have it made.

"Massive frontal attacks" on peripheral issues like schooling for four-year-olds do not raise incomes or make anyone more secure. The government's job corps programs, substitutes for on-the-job training, have helped a very few at enormous cost and have not changed the economic environment of the mass.

Direct transfer programs like welfare raise incomes but destroy incentives and erode self-reliance. The poor pay for the security of subsistence incomes by giving up their right to buy what they want or to earn more by their personal effort. Welfare threatens to become a cheap form of institutionalization for people with a problem: like many institutions, it tends to strengthen the problem rather than the person.

If we want to see an improvement in housing and a reduction in crime, we must put more money into poor neighborhoods and regions. If we want to see that money spent efficiently to help people, we can do no better than to let them spend it themselves.

> Eighteen years ago Senator Robert Taft said:
>
> I believe that the American people feel that with the high production of which we are now capable, there is enough left over to prevent extreme hardship, to give to all a minimum standard of decent living and to all children a fair opportunity to get a start in life.
>
> The Ripon Society believes that the adoption of the Negative Income Tax will prove the most viable means of implementing this concept; it will be a great Republican initiative comparable to the Homestead Act and the Thirteenth, Fourteenth and Fifteenth Amendments. No other program to fight poverty can also strengthen free markets and reduce Federal intervention in the economy.
>
> In five years our economy will be producing a thousand billion dollars worth of goods each year. We propose to give one percent to those who so far have been left out. The richest nation in history should do no less.

CHAPTER 16
NEIGHBORHOOD POWER AND THE GOP

Ripon member Howard Reiter contributed this essay to the Ripon FORUM for March of 1968. It was the first of a series of articles which developed a theme of central importance to Republicans.

– Editors

Perhaps no political term since "Communism has aroused as much fear and confusion in this country as "Black Power." Whether it is interpreted as violence, as Negro domination of our politics, or as greater concessions to the civil rights movement (if it can still be called a movement), the phrase has become a rallying cry for black militants and evidence to many whites that "they've gone too far." And what makes the matter worse is the wide variety of leaders who employ the term.

The man who has done the most to advance the slogan is, of course, Stokely Carmichael, former head of the Student Non-violent Coordinating Committee. In an attempt to dispel some of the wild myths surrounding his cause, Carmichael has co-authored with a Negro political scientist, Dr. Charles V. Hamilton, a book entitled *Black Power: The Politics of Liberation in America.* Like Adam Clayton Powell's recording "Keep the Faith, Baby," the book will be a disappointment to those expecting a call to arms or radical proposals. Instead, after being fed on the mass media, which prefer to leave a metaphor dangling innuendoes rather than explain its meaning, the reader may find *Black Power* surprisingly tame. But if it is not revolutionary, its dogma is at least innovative, and indicative of the thinking of black militants and of the entire New Left as well.

The first element of Black Power is pride of the Negro in his race. In effect, it means that a new ethnic minority group is to be created, as close-knit and chauvinistic as the traditional ghetto inhabitants were. Social scientists agree that a critical obstacle to Negro self-improvement has been the lack of a group consciousness and confidence which served Irish, Italian, and Jew so well. Ironically, the blunt treatment of this problem by Daniel P. Moynihan in the report named for him has made him persona non grata in black circles;

yet Carmichael addresses the same issue. After centuries of bowing and scraping and self-effacement, he says, the Negro must act like a man, the equal to the white. If this new-found self-reliance frightens many whites, then so be it.

One of the more intriguing forms that this impulse takes is the search for tradition, a necessity for any ethnic consciousness. The Black Power advocate turns to Africa as the European immigrant identified with "the old country" – names are changed to African equivalents, dress and hair are worn African-style, and parents lobby for the teaching of Swahili in the schools. We might balk at this: only a tenth of Africa speaks Swahili, and it may seem incongruous for American Negroes to turn to an area to which they have no direct cultural ties. Furthermore, while many Americans of European descent can tell you the country, or even the village, of their forebears, African culture was forgotten by slaves centuries ago, and the great amount of mixed blood and ante-bellum miscegenation makes regional identification impossible. What seems even less logical is the feeling of kinship between black militants and Arabs (which explains their feelings about the Middle East war last June). After all, Arabs have traditionally been great enslavers of Negroes. Why all this cultural mythology?

The answer is that there is precious little in American history in which the Negro can take pride. His American existence has been centuries of slavery followed by decades of oppression. While that history is studded with slave revolts, massive labor crucial to American progress, and the achievements of individual Negroes, it is not the kind of history to swell a man's chest with pride. It is a rare man who can take pride in an accomplishment of whose fruits he is unjustly deprived. So the Negro militant goes a step back in history, to the great black civilizations of pre-colonial Africa. (After all, his feeling for Africa is to some extent comparable to that of many American Jews for Israel.) The condescension of American diplomacy toward Africa, the Middle East, and Asia seems remarkably analogous to race relations here at home; so the black militant feels kinship with the have-nots abroad. He sees this analogy in our role in Vietnam, and may even side (as Carmichael does) with the Viet Cong.

This, then, is one facet of Black Power, which involves more vigorous personal and artistic expression by Negroes. It may be repellant to some whites, and may cause others to re-examine their own feelings. But the demand for respect is a natural outgrowth of the demand for Constitutional rights, and it is a healthy development for a people too long submerged in a culture which assumes their inferiority.

Once self-reliant, says Carmichael, the Negro must organize himself into black organizations to demand equal rights. This plank in the program is the result of a profound disillusionment with traditional methods. Specifically, it is alleged that Negro leaders are tinged with compromise and opportunism. Black Congressmen, for example, are thought to be sops to their race; the white Democratic boss carves out a district or two to let the Negroes play with. Even Adam Clayton Powell got his start that way. With this method, the reasoning goes, the Negro will be placated. Yet this token of accommodation is inadequate, for the Negro usually receives fewer districts than he is entitled to.

In general, Black Power advocates contend that the white-dominated groups which bargain in the political arena have not served the real interests of the Negro. Despite Walter Reuther and A. Philip Randolph, the labor movement has too often excluded Negroes from membership and jobs, and the rank and file are the major force in the white backlash. Big business has paid insufficient attention to hiring Negroes or aiding indigenous ghetto enterprises. Worst of all, the political parties have failed the Negro. The Democrats, aside from being represented by Wallace in the South and Johnson abroad, deserted racial equality at a dramatic moment in the history of the civil rights movement: at the 1964 Democratic National convention, when the Mississippi Freedom Democrats (MFDP) were given only "symbolic" representation in the Mississippi delegation.

As an alternative to these traditional forms, Carmichael proposes all-Negro blocs for political and economic measures. One of the most controversial aspects of Black Power is this expulsion of whites, which is often called racism in reverse. Such accusations confirm Carmichael's suspicions that the white liberal is unconsciously racist, like James Baldwin's whiteman who instinctively protects his wallet when passing through a Negro neighborhood. For example, Carmichael asks, did the Sons of Italy recruit non-Italians, or the B'nai B'rith accept Christians? He discerns no logic in requiring that organizations established to fight for Negro rights include whites. White betrayal is too frequent in the history of the Negro for the black militant to trust any outsider.

What forms do these organizations take? Politically, they include third-party movements, partisan factions similar to the MFDP, and groups demanding home rule for the ghetto. The demand for home rule involves neighborhood control of the schools and the exclusion of white policemen from black areas. Objections to these demands are seen as racist paternalism: why must whites think that Negroes are unable to run their own community affairs? Why must they feel that *white* policemen are needed to maintain law and order? Economically, the Black Power program calls for indigenous enterprises, including cooperative businesses and consumer groups, and boycotts of white enterprises which charge exorbitant prices in the ghetto.

It is clear that this program could result in a transformation of the ghetto, one whose ultimate results cannot be foreseen. Yet it may offer an opportunity to the Republican Party, if urban Republicans would take the trouble to study the proposals with understanding and a minimum of emotion. *There is nothing in most Black Power themes that necessarily contradicts orthodox American notions of home rule and free enterprise.*

If, for example, the virtually defunct Republican organization in Harlem were to serve as an instrument for those political objectives, an urban rejuvenation of the party might occur that would help the entire ticket. All talk about a Republican urban resurgence must take into account the fact that by 1970, at least fourteen of our major cities will be at least 40% Negro. If the vanguard of Negro leadership is to be militant, then Republican leaders must strive for a dialogue that has been all too infrequent in the past.

Indeed, if Black Power is appraised dispassionately, there is much in it for all Americans to accept. In fact, it might be seen as the acknowledgment that full-scale integration may not be possible at the present time, and therefore Negroes should at least be masters in their own house. When Black Power is seen not as synonymous with violence, but as an alternative to rioting, perhaps then it will be more widely accepted.

After all, the Black Power program outlined above falls within the bounds of the American ethic. If it remains there, it has a chance of success which depends on how willing white America is to take it seriously. But if Carmichael and his associates develop a new violent black ethic, and reject the program of pride and self-sufficiency within a political framework, they may run up against the wall of hostility and suspicion with which Americans have greeted Marxism and fascism. The great crossroads of Black Power is approaching, and one path leads to possible fulfillment while the other must inevitably encounter frustration and fear.

And so the ultimate course of the civil rights movement lies, as it always has, with the whites. If Black Power is given an opportunity to flourish, it will give white America the opportunity to live in domestic harmony. Republicans, by taking up those themes of Black Power that coincide with their own Party's traditions, can build a new urban coalition and become a force for progress and peace in our nation's cities.

CHAPTER 17
THE CONDITIONS FOR SELF-HELP

The principles of self-help and neighborhood power developed in the March 1968 FORUM were turned into concrete proposals in the August 1968 Urban Papers. In a paper written by Berna Gorenstein, J. Eugene Marans, Stephen M. Minikes and David R. Young, the Society proposed a national system of neighborhood Information Centers to personalize the provision of social services. A position paper on jobs outlined measures to build a viable economic base in poverty-stricken neighborhoods. This paper was written by John R. Price, Jr. and Owen D. Quattlebaum; it was based in part on research conducted by the Ripon Study Group of Williams College. (Williams gave all members of the group full academic credit for their research work). Excerpts from the two papers follow:

– Editors

A. SOCIAL SERVICES

I. THE COMMUNICATION GAP

The social services communication gap is most serious in the cities. The intensity of urban social demands in this decade has caused a proliferation of public and private programs and agencies. At the federal level alone, there are more than 225 major aid programs, involving 400 authorizations, which are administered by 21 federal agencies and 400 regional and sub-regional offices. State and local programs produce additional layers of overlapping services.

The growth of the country's social service agencies in the last decade has been explosive. The trouble is that too few people in the cities know what these agencies do or where they can be found. The failure to communicate the existence of social services to the persons who need them has greatly reduced their value.

The National Advisory Commission on Civil Disorders (the Riot Commission) found that a major cause of the 1967 disturbances in America's cities was a failure of communication between government and the ghetto. This failure extended to the entire range of government services, including law enforcement, and education, as well as social services. The Riot Commission concluded that the failure to communicate the availability of social services heightened the frustration and alienation of the urban residents, particularly in the ghetto neighborhoods.

The Ripon Society believes that establishment of a national network of neighborhood information centers can bring significant progress in closing the social services communication gap. *FUNCTIONS:* The chief function of the NICs would be to serve as an information clearinghouse for virtually all public and private social services. The information at the centers would be extensive. The centers would be equipped with comprehensive manuals on the availability of private and public social services to the individual. Computers would be used in the compilation of the information manuals. Special on-line computer systems, such as those used for airline reservations, could be used to print out up-to-date information on existing services. Inputs of information would come from national, metropolitan, and neighborhood sources. The staff of each NIC would be thoroughly familiar with the services located in their own neighborhood.

The NICs would also have an important referral function. Inquirers could be directed to specific agencies able to provide special assistance or additional information. The NIC would follow up these referrals to assure that they were effective.

In addition, the NICs would perform a limited counseling role. They could, for example, clarify the significance of a statute or regulatory provision; give advice on the procedures to be followed in dealing with public and private agencies; and help individuals and families appraise the range of services available.

At some time in the future, the NICs could also serve as a clearinghouse for job opportunities, as suggested by Richard M. Nixon in a Ripon FORUM guest editorial in May 1968. There are other areas in which the NICs could help provide this kind of locator service, such as finding openings in training programs, housing projects and health care facilities.

The NICs should foster an "open door" atmosphere to help reduce the negative view that many individuals have toward government and its services. Individuals should be able to call or visit the NIC for expert, unbiased and confidential assistance. *STAFF:* The key to the success of the NICs would be the quality of their staff. The staff of an NIC should include professional and nonprofessional personnel, both paid and volunteer. A substantial amount of the staff should be drawn from the neighborhood in which the center is located.

The NICs should have a paid core of full-time professional staff members, who might be recruited in part from public and private agencies which already engage in community counseling activities. These people could be loaned to the NICs, perhaps on a rotation basis. Some of them might prefer to enter NIC career service. The NICs should make efforts to recruit retired business and professional men and women as does the Japanese counterpart of the NICs.

The NICs should have a paid group of full-time non-professional staff members, preferably from the surrounding neighborhood. These indigenous workers would help break down the distrust now existing between the neighborhoods and the social service agencies. The non-professional staff would be trained by the professional staff on the range of services outside the neighborhood. Conversely, the non-professionals would be able to instruct the professionals regarding the people and problems of the neighborhood in which NIC would operate.

The NICs should also attempt to attract volunteer workers, both professional and non-professional. Two thirds of the staff of Great Britain's NIC model, the Citizens' Advice Bureaus, are volunteers, although the volunteer ratio is lower in the cities where the information services are more specialized. Working in the NICs could develop into an exciting new area of volunteer activity for the American people.

The size of an NIC staff would depend upon the needs of the neighborhood. Each NIC should have, as a minimum, a director, at least one supervisor, an appropriate number of experts in the area producing the most questions and the appropriate number of aides and receptionists. A nurse, psychiatrist and other specialists should be available to the staff on a part-time or consulting basis.

LOCATION: At the outset, low income city neighborhoods should have top priority for the location of the NICs. The ultimate goal should be the availability of NICs, or equivalent information services, to every neighborhood in the country. The location of an NIC within a neighborhood would be highly flexible. There would be no need for NIC to be physically independent of other community service offices. It would seem more desirable if NICs could be located within community centers, schools, unemployment offices or other social service facilities. NICs could also be located in public buildings, mobile trailers and transportation terminals.

We recognize that America cannot establish a national network of NICs overnight. However, substantial groundwork has already been laid by the federal, state and local governments in a number of areas. The Office of Economic Opportunity has funded over 800 multi-service centers and 2000 satellite centers in ghetto areas throughout the country since 1964. Within the past year, the Department of Housing and Urban Development has made progress in an experimental program to establish comprehensive neighborhood service centers in 14 pilot cities. These centers would dispense health, education, welfare and recreation services, as well as provide information to ghetto residents. However, the first grants to establish these centers were made only last January by the federal government, and then only for 11 metropolitan areas. The coordination of health and welfare services is being advanced in a number of states by recent authorization of federal grants to locate these services in community centers. Massachusetts Republican Attorney General Elliot Richardson was instrumental in obtaining passage of the bill authorizing these grants.

Neighborhood information or multi-service centers have been operating in California, Michigan and Washington primarily under the auspices of state government. Governor Rockefeller is making efforts to establish a network of such centers in New York State. New York City has oepned four "little city halls," but they have met strenuous local political resistance and have suffered from lack of operating expenses.

The NICs proposed by Ripon would tie in with such comprehensive neighborhood service centers, where they exist. But the NICs would become more widespread in a shorter period, though their services – mainly information and referral – might be more limited than those of comprehensive centers.

II. A NATIONAL NIC COMMITTEE

What is vitally needed now is a national focus for neighborhood information center efforts. We propose that Congress charter a National Neighborhood Information Center Corporation to assure adequate funding and coordination of the NICs throughout the country. Capital subscriptions to the corporation and contributions for its operating expenses would be made by the federal government and state and local governments as well as by private agencies.

The National NIC Corporation would be governed by a National Committee including representatives from the major federal service agencies (Health, Education and Welfare, Housing and Urban Development, Office of Economic Opportunity, etc.), the principal private service agencies (Red Cross, Travelers Aid, Salvation Army, etc.) and the major city governments (New York, Chicago, Los Angeles, etc.). The NIC National Committee would be responsible for the coordination of information of national importance, such as Social Security, Medicare, Red Cross and many similar social services. The National Committee would also help coordinate the funding and planning of NICs in various metropolitan areas.

Each major metropolitan area would have its own NIC Metropolitan Committee to coordinate the establishment and operation of the centers in that area. The Metropolitan Committees would include representatives of the state and city government agencies, the principal private agencies, community organizations (e.g., the Bedford-Stuyvesant Restoration Corporation in Brooklyn, New York), and business, labor and professional groups (Urban Coalition, trade associations, labor councils).

The Metropolitan Committees would in turn help form NIC Neighborhood Committees for the actual establishment and operation of the NICs.

The Neighborhood Committees would consist primarily of local residents but would include members with special expertise from outside the neighborhood.

* * *

Development of neighborhood information centers until recently has progressed much further in other countries than in America. Great Britain established Citizens' Advice Bureaus (CABs) during World War II to help alleviate the dislocation of essential social services caused by war; but the CABs were so successful that they have been given an equivalent peacetime role in British society. The Citizens' Counseling Rooms started in Japan after the War have also been highly successful in providing information and counseling services. Other countries have developed a variety of advice services, ombudsmen, telephone SOS services, administrative appeals machinery and one-stop service centers. The experience of other nations should be of great help in developing NICs in this country, though the United States must fashion its NICs to satisfy its own practical requirements.

The Ripon proposal for a national network of NICs incorporates a number of important tenets of Republican political philosophy. First, it would help separate politics from the dissemination of information to individuals in the cities, thus taking power from urban political machines; second, it would enhance the social services provided by state and city agencies as well as the Federal government; third, it would help coordinate the services of private agencies with those offered by the government; fourth, it would provide a superb new opportunity for volunteer service by the American people; and perhaps most important, it could bring significant progress in the humanization of American government.

Implementation of the NIC proposal presented here would require a strong federal impetus and equally strong state and local support. We urge Republicans at every level of government to lend their leadership to this effort.

B. JOBS

The urban dilemma will continue to resist solution until those Americans who are among the hardcore unemployed are given the chance and believe in the chance to succeed in the market economy. The minority communities where unemployment is the greatest, especially the black community, have discovered that the answer to more jobs lies within their own efforts and their own sphere. Gratuitous paternalism is no longer accepted. The Ripon Society believes that a concerted underwriting of black efforts to run their own businesses and enter into constructive partnerships with white business is the answer of the future. Government must be ready to help with tax incentives and development programs to further this trend.

I. THE TESTING STAGE

The country is still at the testing stage in attempting to solve the problems of urban unemployment. The fundamental defect of many programs from the New Deal to the War on Poverty has been failure to grapple with the unique handicaps of the hardcore unemployed. Fiscal measures to steam up the economy and major public works programs skim off only the readily employable among the nation's jobless. Present recruitment, training and placement programs seem to help primarily those for whom unemployment is a temporary condition. Only a handful of programs, public and private, have reached successfully into the poverty neighborhoods to provide jobs for the hardcore unemployed.

INNOVATION BY BUSINESS: We have seen in the past year a fundamental shift in efforts to reduce hardcore unemployment in our cities. The Government has shifted the primary responsibility for solving the problem to business. The Ripon Society applauds this change. We believe, however, that business must avoid simply producing carbon copies of government programs which have already failed. Business must strike out in new directions to help assure suitable jobs for the hardcore unemployed.

To achieve long term results will require massive efforts on three levels. The first level is to *motivate the individual* by putting responsibilities into the hands of poor Americans rather than relying on middle class leadership. The second effort must involve *a rebuilding of poverty communities* into viable economic units with the greatest measure of self-determination. And to shore up both these efforts must be intelligent local, state and federal *economic programs* and *special incentives* to aid business in poverty neighborhoods.

II. MOTIVATING MEN AND COMMUNITIES

The Ripon Society suggests that it is of prime importance to motivate the hardcore unemployed to become productive members of society. It is a difficult task. They feel alienated from the economy. They are poorly prepared to work and sometimes fearful of working for employers of a different race.

Strong action must be taken to lower these barriers. We urge a system of black representation in the ghetto economy which assures that an employee identifies with his boss and that the neighborhood identifies with the company.

There must be an open-mindedness in industry which exceeds the prevailing attitudes of today. Companies must not only train the poor to hold the basic jobs, but they must continue training through the management level. They must ignore education records and police records in their hiring. They must seek out those people who are leaders in ghettos, who have captured the imagination and won the trust of black Americans. These people must not only be put on the payroll, they must be given responsibility for recruiting, labor relations and other policy decisions – even if they were gang leaders, hustlers or convicts in the past. If black Americans see this happening, their fears of traditional economic exploitation will be allayed.

Ripon believes that improving the economic base of poverty neighborhoods is inseparable from rebuilding the faith of the individual in the possibility of succeeding in our economy. This involves (1) encouraging industry to move or expand in the poverty neighborhoods; (2) assuring thorough community participation in the planning and operation of businesses located in these neighborhoods; and (3) aiding the development of independent, community-owned and operated enterprises in poverty areas.

It has become a source of significant pride for the black American that he now wants to develop his own communities – live there, work there, grow there. As described in the "Neighborhood Power" articles of the March 1968 issue of the Ripon FORUM, this in one sense – perhaps the best sense – is the meaning of "black power." After years of being promised that appropriate improvements in his situation were being made for him, the black man has grown tired of waiting. He now wants to be involved himself.

III. INCENTIVES FOR DEVELOPMENT

The two major federal programs designed to improve the economic base of the poverty communities have been pitifully underfunded. One is the Economic Development Administration (EDA) under the Public Works and Economic Development Act of 1965. The EDA is expected to bring new industry and permanent jobs to areas of substantial and persistent unemployment; yet less than $58 million was appropriated in 1968 to induce industry to locate in poverty areas under this program. Model Cities, a program with even broader objectives, has received far too small appropriations to have a significant impact on improving the economic base of poverty communities in the near future.

Ripon believes that appropriate federal government incentives would provide an important impetus to economic development of poverty neighborhoods. These incentives would help solve some of the critical problems that have hampered development in poverty areas thus far: lack of capital; high initial costs for new businesses; shortage of technical assistance; and unavailability of casualty insurance.

The Ripon Society proposes offering tax credits for businesses locating in poverty areas or hiring the hardcore unemployed. These incentives would be most useful for corporations moving into poverty areas. They would be of only limited value to the development of indigenous enterprises within these areas.

1. *Tax Credit for Investment in Poverty Areas.* We recommend a tax credit for the location and renovation of plants and other business facilities in urban

poverty areas. The existing investment tax credit, first enacted in 1962, applies only to equipment. We recommend that for investment in poverty areas the existing credit be increased substantially and extended to investments in real property and plant.

2. *Tax Credit for Hardcore Employment.* Moreover, we suggest a tax credit, similar to that proposed in the Republican Human Investment Act, for the hiring of hardcore unemployed. The mechanics of identifying and certifying the hardcore unemployed should not be difficult. Business could join with public and private employment agencies to recruit the hardcore unemployed. These agencies could give the job recruits a "green card" or other identifying document for presentation to the employer claiming the credit.

The Riot Commission observed that the existing investment tax credit was taken on 1,239,000 corporate tax returns and 6,904,000 individual tax returns during the period of 1962-1965, representing new investments of about $75 billion and $17.5 billion respectively. The success of the tax credit in its existing application suggests that it may provide a significant impetus to poverty area investment. It is probably the most pluralistic technique available for channeling governmental assistance: the individual decisions of thousands of businesses in making their daily employment and plant location decisions.

We emphasize again, however, the limitations of the tax incentive device for building new businesses within the poverty area. For this purpose, tax incentives alone would not be enough.

3. *Domestic Development Bank.* The Ripon Society endorses the proposal of Senator Jacob K. Javits, co-sponsored by twenty other Republican Senators, for a Domestic Development Bank (DDB). The DDB would aid in overcoming the lack of capital available for investment in poverty areas by providing low-cost loans for the establishment of business and commercial enterprises. Ripon would expand Senator Javits' proposal to include a special "soft loan" program for poverty area businessmen.

The DDB would be funded at the outset by a federal government subscription of $2 billion worth of Bank stock. Of this amount, $400 million would be paid in initially, with the remainder serving as a reserve fund to meet the Bank's liabilities. The $400 million paid in would be raised, not from the general revenues, but from the sale of Treasury bonds. This is the manner in which American contributions to the international development banks have been raised.

The DDB would seek to rectify the fundamental lack of commercial credit for the black business community; it would stimulate black ownership of business in the black community. The DDB would guarantee loans from regular sources to poverty area businesses, as well as providing direct loans to these businesses.

LOAN FORGIVENESS: Ripon believes that the DDB should also have a loan forgiveness program similar to that of the Small Business Administration. A poverty area business would be given a loan, the principal on which would be forgiven in stages depending upon the number of hardcore unemployed persons hired and kept on by the business.

The loan forgiveness program would help meet two principal needs of poverty area businesses: First, it would provide working capital which has been largely unavailable to persons wishing to undertake a business operation in a blighted area. Second, it would provide incentive for the business to reach out and employ and train persons hitherto thought unemployable; the schedule of forgiveness of loans would be designed to offset any net additional cost to the business of hiring untrained rather than trained personnel.

The loan forgiveness program for the DDB differs markedly from legislation to provide tax incentives to established corporations to locate in poverty areas. The tax credit would rarely be helpful to a struggling, undercapitalized, indigenous company; typically such a company has a low cash in-flow and a low tax liability. Far more advantageous for such a company would be a direct loan that may be forgiven in part. The DDB proposal would have the important advantage of encouraging neighborhood capitalism as well as hiring the hardcore unemployed.

4. *Economic Opportunity Corporation.* We also endorse Senator Javits' proposal for an Economic Opportunity Corporation, which could serve essentially as a development service agency. This body would be chartered by a $10 million federal grant; it would be given an additional $10 million to match private contributions. Individuals and corporations could either become members and thus gain access to its services, either by purchasing its bonds or by making a contribution to it.

The corporation itself would be non-profit, but it would have the power to set up profit-making subsidiaries which would act as development and investment companies. Its main function, however, would be to provide research and technical assistance on the problems of investment in poverty areas. In addition, it would serve to encourage private investment in poverty areas by making potential investors aware of the opportunities available in various sections of the country.

5. *Casulty Insurance.* Ripon favors the creation of a national reinsurance facility and of insurance premium subsidies for qualified policyholders in blighted commercial areas.

Premium Subsidies. – We believe that it may be necessary to direct premium subsidies to poverty area businessmen who are otherwise qualified to hold insurance but who cannot obtain coverage at economical rates. Premiums for casualty policies covering commercial establishments in blighted areas have been running greatly in excess of rates for comparable property in other parts of the city. Businessmen should not be penalized for wanting to start a business in a poverty area. Premium subsidies would be a reflection of our public policy to compensate for the additional expenses involved in locating and operating a business in blighted areas.

National Reinsurance Corporation. – The national reinsurance facility was a proposal of the Riot Commission. Congress would charter a National Reinsurance Corporation to reduce the exposure of casualty insurers in poverty areas where the risk of loss is found to be high. Foreign reinsurers, who historically have provided reinsurance for domestic companies, have begun to retrench in the face of the staggering losses suffered in increasingly frequent civil disorders in this country.

6. *Joint Ventures.* The Ripon Society urges that special attention be given to promoting the formation of joint ventures between major corporations and poverty area businessmen. Joint ventures have already been undertaken by Aerojet General in Watts, AVCO in Roxbury, Xerox in Rochester, and Fairchild Hiller Corporation in Washington, D.C. In the latter case, the company will be manned and partially owned by inhabitants of the poverty area. Fairchild Hiller will be only a minority shareholder, though it will provide virtually all the management skills.

Poverty areas have been described as being similar to underdeveloped countries both in their need for capital and the cultural adjustments that must be made to operate effectively within them. American corporations do not hesitate to use the joint venture approach abroad in similar situations. Joint ventures may be an outstanding vehicle for fulfilling the twin objectives of economic development of the community and neighborhood involvement in the enterprise. The Domestic Development Bank and other federal and state agencies should make development of joint ventures a high priority item.

7. *Community Involvement.* It is also crucial that the poverty neighborhoods be given a voice in the activities of the company. Its location, the design of the plant, expansion plans, and other questions are of great interest to the people who live near or work in the plant. A neighborhood board of directors might be established for the company. Its composition should include those militant black leaders who have won the faith of the people.

The need for this was shown recently in Watts, where plans for economic development in that area were strongly opposed by the community because they feared that plants would be built near schools, that residential streets would be congested with commercial traffic, and finally that only whites from outside would be hired. These suspicions are not unjustified. Such things have occurred in the past. Community participation in planning can overcome these fears.

Institutions like community development boards with popularly elected directors can provide regular channels for local participation.

THE LONG VIEW: We recognize the improving the economic base of the community carries the risk of further urban ghettos as one of the involved risks. However, we believe this risk to be minimal. The long range result should be just the opposite. As the resident of the poverty neighborhoods succeeds in performing roles in his community he will become better equipped to seek suitable employment outside the community. Three trends gradually gaining momentum strongly support this view: stepped-up attacks on job discrimination; improved suburban transportation services; and the development of new towns near good jobs. The ghetto traditionally has been a way station for poor Americans. It has also been a training ground for many American minority groups whose members gradually entered the main current of the nation's enterprises. Minority areas still have a role to play as a base for the economic success of the urban poor. There is no longer a reason, however, for minority areas to be depressed areas. The proposals in these Ripon papers would help assure the development of minority areas as decent places to live and work for those who want to remain there and for those who seek the means to leave.

CHAPTER 18
URBAN EDUCATION:
Revolution in Quality

Michael McDonald and J. Eugene Marans wrote the Society's position paper calling for a three-pronged program in urban education. The study was one of the six Urban Papers published in the August 1968 Ripon FORUM.

– Editors

I. THE WIDENING GAP

American education is ready for its third revolution. The revolution of *quantity,* as former Commissioner of Education Francis Keppel tells us, took us to the Second World War. The revolution of *equality* was second, but it is far from complete. Now we find that the revolution of equality cannot be completed without a third revolution in American education – a revolution in *quality*.

America's city schools have become stratified in quality and divided in objectives, and they threaten to produce a society similarly stratified by class and by race. It is incontestable that we have different qualities of education for the black child and the white child, the suburban child, the city child, the inner city child and the rural child. It is usually the inner city black child who receives the worst education.

The bleak record of public education for ghetto children is simply told:

- Black children are already behind white children in achievement by 15-20% by the time they begin school.
- Black students fall farther behind whites with each year completed. By the twelfth grade, they are almost four grades behind white students in the critical skills of verbal and reading ability.
- Once black students feel that they cannot catch up, they are likely to drop out. Six out of ten black students from poverty neighborhoods drop out after the sophomore year of high school. Unemployment and delinquency rates among these dropouts are several times higher than the national average.

- Segregation is growing in Northern urban schools. In the South, the number of black students attending schools with all or nearly all black enrollments continues to rise.
- In virtually every large American city, the inner city schools attended by black students are the most overcrowded. They also tend to be the oldest and most poorly equipped.
- The schools attended by disadvantaged black children commonly are staffed by teachers with *less* experience and *lower* qualifications than those attended by middle class whites.
- Ghetto schools generally are unresponsive to the community that they serve. Parents distrust the officials responsible for educating their children.

The deterioration of inner city education can no longer be allowed. The dangers to American society are too great. States have for too long given inadequate attention to this growing danger, and the problem is now so massive and so complicated that all the local and national resources of America must be brought to bear on its solution.

The Ripon Society believes that basic responsibility for education must remain in the hands of state and local authorities; indeed, responsibility for educational policy should be even further decentralized. Yet every child in this country, as an American citizen, is entitled to the best possible school in order to assume the obligations as well as the rights of American citizenship. The nation can ill afford to allow a large mass of its people to remain uneducated and hence unproductive. The problems which confront education today are thus of grave national concern. Therefore, the federal government must participate with state and local governments in assuring a quality education for every child in the land.

The last five years have seen important new legislation by Congress, breaking ground in almost all areas vital to the improvement of urban and rural education. The Vocational Education Act of 1963, the Higher Education Facilities Act of 1963, the Elementary and Secondary Education Act of 1965, and the Higher Education Act of 1965 have all reflected increasing national concern. Title I of the Elementary and Secondary Education Act in particular is bringing new dollars and new ideas to the children of poverty and neglect, and bringing new awareness among educators that poverty is in part a result of educational failure. Fear of federal interference, which for so long prevented affirmative national action, is yielding to an effective partnership based on increasing state and local capacity for leadership and a respect by the Federal government for local autonomy.

We must build on this base; we must commit ourselves to the expense of achieving quality in education for all our children. The costs of unemployment, welfare and relief, delinquency and crime, high morbidity and mortality – human as well as financial costs – are not the only penalties of failure. Our democratic society has little chance of survival if faced with ever increasing numbers of poorly educated citizens.

II. THE THREE PRONGS

The revolution in quality which we seek has three prongs; (1) *integration;* (2) *compensatory education;* and (3) *community participation.* Each one is critical; but all three together are necessary if we are to succeed in our educational goals.

INTEGRATION: The Ripon Society proposes that the country accelerate its efforts at every level to achieve a significant amount of school integration within the next decade. There are no obvious solutions that will work for every city. The experience of the past decade seems to call for intensive application of a variety of techniques designed to accomplish desegregation. These include school pairing, busing, open enrollment, boundary changes, strategic use of site selection, enlargement of attendance areas and the consolidation of schools.

Racial integration remains one of the most urgently needed changes in American education. The vast majority of urban schools are rigidly segregated, and this segregation is growing. The Riot Commission estimates that by 1975, if current policies and trends continue, 80% of all Negro pupils in the twenty largest cities will be attending 90 to 100% black schools.

Segregated schooling deprives disadvantaged children of one of the most significant ingredients of quality education: exposure to other children with broader educational and cultural backgrounds.

Perhaps most important of all, the sensitive observation that separation is *inherently* unequal has its own effect: segregated city schools are considered by administrators, teachers, parents and the students themselves to be inferior – and the judgment inevitably becomes self-fulfilling.

The Ripon Society considers the educational park to be the most promising innovation yet developed for encouraging integration, because it provides an array of educational facilities in a central area with adequate transportation. Consequently, we propose in another part of this paper the construction of a number of federally financed pilot parks over the next few years and the construction of substantially more such facilities if the pilot educational parks prove successful.

Meanwhile, much can be done in the short run to help reduce segregation in American education. Substantial commitments of federal technical assistance should be made available as soon as possible to state and local agencies planning and executing integration plans. The federal concern with integration to date has been expressed largely in a negative direction. Court orders and Title IV enforcement have been directed primarily against *de jure* segregation in the South.

Use of Title IV funds in a positive manner would require repeal of the present statutory restriction against providing assistance to support and encourage desegration through "assignment of students to public schools in order to overcome racial imbalance." We believe that the time has come for the Congress to proclaim that quality education is inseparable from integration, and that it is national policy to reduce racial concentration in the schools – racial concentration of pupils, teachers and school personnel.

In addition to providing technical assistance for school districts adopting general integregation plans, the Title IV program could encourage development of major educational "magnet" schools to serve all of the students of a small city, different sections of a large city or subdivisions of a metropolitan area. Similarly, supplemental education centers could be established to offer specialized instruction to students from different schools in a city or its suburbs for a portion of the school day. These centers could provide important racially integrated educational experiences.

The states, and in particular, the state educational agencies, have a key role to play in accomplishing school integration. The states are in a unique position to bring about urban-suburban cooperation and metropolitan planning.

COMPENSATORY EDUCATION: The Ripon Society believes that compensatory education is essential in our city schools. If financial and cultural disadvantages are not to be perpetuated, we must drastically improve the quality of our education for children of the poor. If schools wait for teachers and society to reform, a whole generation of children may be lost. We cannot afford to wait.

The Ripon Society adopts the position, stated by the Advisory Council on the Education of Disadvantaged Children (the Advisory Council), that the time has come to provide unequal, exceptional education as a matter of deliberate public policy to every child who needs it. This policy should apply to all the seriously deprived segments of our people – the Puerto Ricans, Mexican-Americans, American Indians, families living in the depressed parts of Appalachia, as well as to black Americans.

Compensatory education may seem to be unequal education, but it is fully consistent with established educational practice in this country. We have been providing compensatory education for our minorities of physically and mentally handicapped children under the name of "special education" for many years. But the largest minorities of our children are not the crippled and the mentally retarded. They are the millions who suffer the handicaps of sustained deprivation and neglect, much of it due to racial discrimination.

Compensatory education became national policy under Title I of the Elementary and Secondary Education Act of 1965. But the billion dollars a year now being spent under Title I is a pittance compared to the need. School districts have tended to spread their funds out too thinly, providing small amounts of compensatory education to reach as many children as possible.

The Advisory Council reports that this tight stretching has caused many Title I efforts to become overextended and ineffective. Ripon agrees with the Advisory Council and other groups of prominent educators that massive actions rather than feeble intentions are required to reach the problems of ghetto children. We recommend that for three to four times more (up from about $165 to $600 per capita) should be allocated to each disadvantaged child to show meaningful results from compensatory techniques.

COMMUNITY PARTICIPATION: The Ripon Society shares the view of most educators that urban parents must be given an important voice in the operation of the schools that their children attend. The school systems of our largest cities have become highly centralized, with decision-making responsibility concentrated in a central board of education. No one seems to heed the parents, whose children after all are the ones at stake.

Moreover, it is time to recognize that the school – at least in some communities – must serve as more than an instrument for educating part of the community part of the time. In fact, the school should be an integral part of the life of the community, on a year-round basis. It should serve all the members of the community, providing basic education and care – including nutritional care – to three year-olds and up, opening new opportunities for education and cultural achievement for adults, and providing recreational and educational opportunities for youth twelve months of the year.

We agree with the Republican Coordinating Committee that federal and state governments should look with favor on recent proposals for school decentralization in larger cities, such as the Bundy Commission Recommendations for the City of New York. These proposals generally provide for centralized control over educational standards and the raising of revenue, and for decentralized control over other aspects of educational policy. The specific design for community participation, or "parent power," will vary, of course, from city to city according to the needs of the local situation. The objective is to restore to the ghetto community the kind of local and neighborhood control and involvement that suburban communities and small cities have traditionally enjoyed. Community participation in education is fully consistent with the Republican Party's concern for participation on the individual citizen in decisions affecting himself and his family.

Community participation should bring benefits in addition to parent involvement in education. The schools can also become a focus for community services. Their facilities can be made available during and after normal school hours for social services by private and public agencies, adult and community training and education programs, community meetings and recreational and cultural activities. Such use is very common in suburban schools with their magnificent physical plants. Community control should also facilitate the employment of local residents – paid and volunteer – as teacher aides and tutors.

We recognize the apparent inconsistency in seeking compensatory education for minority children and community control for their parents, and at the same time stating that integration is essential to achieving equal educational opportunity. However, we believe that these three objectives truly are complementary. Parents want reasonable assurance that the schools their children will attend after integration will be at least equal, and preferably superior, to the ones to which they have been accustomed. Since compensatory education and community participation are expected to be critical in assuring superior inner city schools, it may be essential to the achievement of integration. Within the next five years, measurable increases in quality should be obtainable even without full integration. Within the decade, the mixture of improved inner city schools, new educational parks and accelerated integration plans should bring substantial progress in ending racial isolation in American schools.

We understand that high quality urban education will not alone attract suburbanites back to the city. Equally important are metropolitan commitments to integrated housing and employment, and careful planning of urban renewal and public transportation developments. However, city schools of exceptionally high quality could be the key factors in stemming the flight to the suburbs and in bringing about greater integration in education.

III. SPECIAL PRIORITIES

The quality revolution in American education will require emphasis on special priorities within our educational systems. Three special priorities are: (1) *early childhood education;* (2) *school construction and renovation;* and (3) *teaching quality.*

EARLY CHILDHOOD: The Ripon Society stresses the urgency of developing as soon as possible a comprehensive system of early childhood education. It becomes increasingly clear that children have a better chance to succeed in school if they are introduced to planned learning experiences well before the age of six. Indications are that the basic patterns of learning ability are established even before the child enters his first formal grade of school. We must move ahead immediately to make kindergartens universally accessible to five year-olds and four year-olds, and possibly three year-olds as well. There is substantial evidence that the level of intellectual capability young people will achieve at age 17 is already *half* determined by the age of four, and that another 30% is predictable at seven years. This means that a community that wants to improve its children's opportunities must send them to school at the earliest possible age. The earlier the investment in systematic intellectual development is begun, the greater will be the return.

The early childhood education program must be concerned with the whole child and his environment, medical care and food as well as language training and creative instruction. This must be a joint effort of the teachers, health officers, social welfare workers, and to the maximum extent possible, the parents and others in the community.

SCHOOL FACILITIES: The Ripon Society proposes that the nation embark upon a massive program to reverse the deterioration in city school facilities. This program – including renovation as well as new construction – should within a decade provide new and expanded school facilities in the cities equivalent to, or superior to, the modern and spacious plant typically found in suburban school districts.

The typical school building in central sections of the large cities is overcrowded and dilapidated. These conditions are the result of age, neglect or obsolescence. High population densities often place on the school building a pupil load far beyond its capacity. Double or triple sessions are not uncommon in some cities.

Bad physical surroundings are detrimental to the quality of education and to the quality of life in the neighborhood. They erode the morale of teachers and students. They adversely affect community attitudes toward the school.

We support a massive infusion of federal capital into school construction and renovation. The majority of our inner city schools are as unsuitable for modern education as are country roads for the modern automobile. We propose that:

1) $25 billion of additional federal funds be spent for construction and renovation of inner city schools over the next ten years.
2) $5 billion of federal money be spent for intensive development of pilot educational parks over the next five years, with another $10-15 billion to be spent in the following five years if the pilot parks are successful in reversing the trend toward segregation and unequal educational opportunity.
3) Significant federal bonuses be given to districts with construction projects in progress that recognize the unique need for providing superior education to disadvantaged children in an integrated school.

As with the Interstate Highway System, the construction expenses could be financed in a matching basis with the federal government putting up the major share. The states would likewise provide the supervision of the construction program, subject to certain ground rules agreed upon with the federal government.

This capital improvement program must be accompanied by adequate funding to maintain existing schools at the highest level of quality. It would be folly to spend a decade and billions of dollars rebuilding the nation's educational plant, without adequate provision to maintain that plant at optimum level for the decades ahead.

TEACHING QUALITY: The Ripon Society supports entirely the Riot Commission recommendation that the nation mobilize a national effort to attract to the teaching profession well-qualified and highly motivated young people, and equip them to work effectively with disadvantaged students. The Teaching Corps program, begun as a model program under the Higher Education Act of 1965, may be a sound instrument for such an effort. The Teacher Corps provides training in local colleges or universities for teacher interns – college graduates interested in teaching in poverty areas. Corpsmen are assigned to poverty area schools at the request of local school systems and with the approval of state education agencies. They are employed by the school system and work in teams headed by an experienced teacher.

It is clear that extra incentives must be provided to attract highly qualified teachers to the ghetto and certain deprived rural area schools. The Riot Commission concluded that the most effective means to attract such teachers is to make these schools exciting and attractive places to work. This is an important reason for the substantial construction and renovation program previously proposed in this paper. In addition, we believe that teachers must be accorded the professional status and the pay, equal to the challenge and social benefit of assignment to ghetto schools. This could involve salary increases as high as 50% to properly qualified and motivated teachers willing to work, and in some cases willing to live, in ghetto communities.

Better buildings and higher pay for teachers are not enough to make schools exciting and attractive places to learn and to work. Class size has to go down – probably to a much smaller size than comparable classes in suburban schools. To accomplish this, there must be an expansion of the number of teachers in the urban centers by one-third. A student-teacher ratio of one to twenty-five is considered the maximum for meaningful student-teacher communication. We must develop dynamic teacher recruiting programs and improved certification procedures. There must be a reduction in the time teachers spend on administrative and supervisory chores.

Individualized instruction has to go up – probably through extensive use of nonprofessional workers. There is impressive evidence from experiments such as Homeward Helper programs in New York City that these workers – volunteer and paid – can be exceptionally effective in individualized tutoring and in increasing motivation in ghetto school pupils. Also, adequate supplementary services have to be provided in community schools for severely disadvantaged or disturbed students – of which ghetto schools contain a shockingly high number. The history, culture and contribution of minority groups to American civilization will have to be increasingly recognized in the textbooks and curricula of all schools.

IV. FUNDING THE REVOLUTION

The Federal-State Partnership – The principal burden for funding the revolution in quality of American education must fall upon the federal government. Local tax resources, usually tied to a property base, have reached their limit in most areas. State governments can and should do more than at present, but even the resources available at this level are far from adequate.

The major step toward federal support of elementary and secondary education has already been taken. Primarily as a result of the education laws of the past five years, federal expenditures for education, training and related services have increased from $4.7 billion in fiscal 1964 to $12.3 billion in fiscal 1969. The 1965 laws already provide a comprehensive base for meeting the educational needs of the disadvantaged students.

The experience under the federal education acts has shown that local boards can enjoy the benefit of the federal tax base and technical help without endangering their capacity for initiative and responsibility.

We suggest that Federal government aid to the states be in the form of block grants for broad categories such as building programs rather than monies for specifically outlined projects.

Reallocation of State Aid – The next few years must bring about a critical shift in the allocation of funds between city schools and suburban schools. At present, our big city schools spend one-third as much per pupil as do the schools in adjacent suburbs.

We urge that every state transform its present aid formulas, not merely to provide *equal* per-pupil funds for all school districts, but to assure *more* per-pupil aid to districts having a high proportion of disadvantaged students. The present state aid formulas were designed to give suburban schools exceptional aid to accelerate their development when they were poor. Now the cities are poor, and they need the same kind of exceptional aid to accelerate the development of compensatory education in urban schools.

We urge that the Office of Education, in consultation with the Education Commission of the States, develop prototype formulas for providing this exceptional aid to city school districts. Federal programs aiding states should require, as a basic rule, that funds be allocated within each state in accordance with such formulas.

Republican leadership is desperately needed for the revolution of quality in American urban education. The causes for revolution are grave. They will not go away.

PART THREE
BUILDING A BETTER WORLD
alternatives in Foreign Policy

CHAPTER 19
THE MYTH OF BIPARTISANSHIP
a call for a Republican initiative

Presented in June of 1967, "The Myth of Bipartisanship" gained wide press attention and set the stage for Ripon's Vietnam criticisms and proposals which followed a few months later. The task force which prepared the paper was headed by Robert H. Donaldson.

– Editors

United States foreign policy today is a muddled and meandering mess. A mere glance at the headlines reveals that crisis after crisis has caught the Johnson Administration unaware. American troops continue to flow to Southeast Asia as the President drifts along in a tragic, seemingly aimless policy to fulfill a "commitment" to South Vietnam. Across the world, war breaks out in the Middle East, exploding in the faces of Administration officials frantically searching for a way to avoid fulfilling the U.S. "commitment" to Israel. During the war's early hours, a confused State Department publicly debates whether the U.S. is a "neutral" or a "concerned non-belligerent" in the conflict. In a time of high tension, American policy-makers, unguided by principle, are prisoners of events.

The Republican leadership in Congress, however, offers the public little edification and no alternative. Those GOP leaders, most critical of alleged "mee-tooism" among party progressives, prove to be the worst "me-tooers" on issues of foreign policy. A penetrating and thoughtful study of Vietnam issued by the staff of the Senate Republican Policy Committee is hastily repudiated by an opposition leadership which eagerly proclaims that it stands "four-square" behind the President. American foreign policy, they say, must remain bipartisan; politics must stop at the water's edge.

Two decades ago Republican statesmen, in a time of external threat, formulated the concept of "bipartisanship" in foreign policy. Exhibiting a highly praised sense of responsibility and restraint, they were able to achieve some remarkable successes. Yet, shortly afterward, as the actors on the stage of "bipartisan politics" were replaced and as America suffered diplomatic setbacks, the original techniques of genuine bipartisanship were forgotten. But, the label has remained, sadly distorted, a "sacred cow" which has masked a desire for unity for unity's sake alone.

Today, the opposition party too rarely questions the policies behind which it is asked to unite. Are they really the rational and effective policies required in the nuclear age and on which the original adherents of bipartisanship insisted? As Professor Malcolm Jewell writes:

> "In an age of permanent international crisis, the danger is simply that we may drift to disaster through a chain of uneasy compromises and misguided policies that are protected from effective criticism by the umbrella of bipartisan consultation."

The Ripon Society calls on Republican leaders in Congress and on the Republican Coordinating Committee to take responsibility for American foreign policy, to contribute to the political debate which produces successful international policies.

I. THE DILEMMA OF FOREIGN POLICY

In 1835 Alexis de Tocqueville, the perceptive French observer who offered so many profound insights into American society, wrote:

> "It is especially in the conduct of their foreign relations that democracies appear to me decidely inferior to other governments . . . A democracy can only with great difficulty regulate the details of an important undertaking, persevere in a fixed design, and work out its execution in spite of serious obstacles."

Though well over a century has passed since de Tocqueville confessed his misgivings about the ability of democratic governments to conduct an effective foreign policy, his observations are still relevant. America has emerged from a long tradition of isolation to take her place as the most powerful and active participant in a world charged with danger and difficulty. Never before have the results of foreign policies been so intimately linked with the possibility of instant death and destruction. Consequently, never before have the precious luxuries of democratic control of foreign relations been so seriously challenged.

America's alliances have mushroomed in the past two decades, greatly increasing the need for a dependable and continuous foreign policy; yet in a democracy the opposition can swiftly and legally overturn established policies. Developments in communications and weapons technology make speed and secrecy in the execution of foreign policy even more essential; yet in a democracy both time and knowledge are required for rational deliberation and widespread consent. America's adversaries still seek to blunt effective countermeasures by provoking disunity within the West; yet in a democracy the requirements of unity can seriously hamper the performance of the necessary functions of an opposition party.

Such is the nature of the dilemma facing the Republican Party today. In the nuclear age the requirements of speed and unity in a foreign policy present a strong challenge to the requirements of deliberation and formulation of alternative policies which are the hallmark of the party system of a democracy. The need to engage in criticism and inquiry seem to run counter to the need for national unity in a time of crisis.

II. THE ORIGINS OF BIPARTISANSHIP

The origins of modern bipartisanship can be traced back almost 50 years to a period of acrimonious partisanship in foreign policy which has been unequalled in its fury: the fight over the League of Nations. Following the Second World War, Republicans and Democrats alike – Franklin Roosevelt, Cordell Hull, Arthur Vandenberg and Thomas Dewey – were convinced that the savage controversies in the United States surrounding the Versailles Treaty should not be duplicated. The result was the genuine and harmonious consultation and co-operation which culminated in American acceptance of the United Nations Charter by an unprecedented majority.

That this event was not unique but signalled the beginning of a series of truly bipartisan efforts in foreign policy, most notably the Marshall Plan and the North Atlantic Treaty, was the result of fortuitous circumstances. The widespread recognition of the grave crisis which faced America after the "hot war" had ended, and the determination that this country meet the challenge was not confined to men of one party. Nonpartisan understanding of the need for cooperation was supplemented by constitutional requirements: the elections of 1946 left Republicans in control of both houses of Congress, and cooperation was essential if the nation were to have any foreign policy at all.

Nor should it be forgotten that there existed the indispensable catalyst, the element of personality; men of vision, most notably Senator Arthur Vandenberg, Chairman of the Foreign Affairs Committee, and George Marshall, the Secretary of State, were able to work together in a nonpartisan spirit to achieve policies in the national interest. The goal of this cooperation was expressed by Vandenberg:

> "An unpartisan American foreign policy – not Republican, not Democratic, but American – which substantially unites our people at the water's edge in behalf of peace."
>
> What did the Senator from Michigan understand by an "unpartisan" policy? Was he urging unity as the overarching goal, to the exclusion of debate, a passive acquiescence by the opposition party to the policy of the Administration? Vandenberg's own words are an emphatic "No": "It does not involve the remotest surrender of free debate in determining our position. On the contrary, frank coop-

> eration and free debate are indispensable to ultimate unity. In a word, it simply seeks national security ahead of partisan advantage. Every foreign policy must be *totally* debated . . . and the 'loyal opposition' is under special obligation to see that this occurs."

Bipartisanship, as understood and practiced under Republican foreign policy of the 1940's, was not a label which was applicable to *every* diplomatic strategy nor even to all those to which the opposition had given formal sanction. Certain conditions had to be met for the "bipartisanship" to be *genuine.*

*Vandenberg himself stressed that bipartisanship referred only to those policies on which the Republicans had been thoroughly consulted before decision had been reached and that these had in fact been confined to the United Nations and European treaties.

*Consultation meant more than a mere briefing: Republican views must be accommodated, and the policy should bear opposition "trademarks," with both parties sharing the credit or the blame. Bipartisanship implied a true "meeting of the minds." That this could not be the case with every decision, Republicans fully realized.

*In situations of crisis, such as the Greek-Turkish crisis of 1947, requiring a swift response, there could be little time for consultation and compromise and thus, no bipartisanship.

*With respect to diplomatic maneuvers not requiring legislative authorization, such as the Marshall Mission to China, prior consultation would have only made Republicans responsible for decisions over whose implementations they would have had little effective control. Vandenberg noted that, "it is a fantastic unreality to think that there can be cooperation . . . in any such specific detail."

*Most important, as Vandenberg observed, bipartisanship did not imply "me-tooism" – a shutting off of debate and criticism in the name of "a fake 'unity' devoid of popular consent."

Clearly the Republican architects of genuine bipartisanship recognized that its applicability was limited. The label did not apply to all policies endorsed by both parties, but only to those to which both parties had genuinely contributed.

Many events in American foreign policy over the past two decades have been labeled examples of bipartisanship, instances in which the majorities of both parties have been united behind particular policies. Examples are the Greece-Turkey aid program of 1947, the Formosa Straits resolution of 1955, and the Eisenhower Doctrine in the Middle East in 1957. But more often than not, this unity has been the result of external crisis itself rather than of genuinely bipartisan procedures.

This misuse of labels has led to the Myth of Bipartisanship – a myth which identifies bipartisanship with unity itself, rather than with the procedures used to attain such unity. The semantic difficulty is great; there exists a drastic difference between the bipartisanship as formulated by Arthur Vandenberg and the type that is prevalent today.

The time is past due for Republicans to expose the fallacy of mythical bipartisanship, for it is this – not genuine bipartisanship – which exists today.

III. A BALANCE SHEET

Genuine bipartisanship in the Vandenberg era was and could be applied only to a limited range of issues. Within that range, it resulted in some brilliant successes. Yet some observers have sought to generalize from the peculiar circumstances existing in that day in order to advance the claim that all issues of foreign policy should receive "bipartisan" support. There are four assets which are commonly claimed for the blanket application of such "mythical bipartisanship."

1. Bipartisanship is said to ensure that policies in the national interest, the most effective policies from the standpoint of the nation's values and security, as opposed to policies furthering only partisan interest, are achieved.

2. Proponents cite the necessity of bipartisan consultation during times of divided control of the national government: when one party holds the Presidency and the other controls Congress. Or, they refer to the constitutional requirement that a 2/3 vote of the Senate is necessary in order for a treaty to be ratified, a case which occurs more frequently. The implication is that, because bipartisanship is *essential* in these cases, it is *desirable* that bipartisanship be practiced as a general rule.

3. Bipartisanship, its adherents argue with considerable force, produces unity, stability, dependability and continuity in the face of the totalitarian threat.

4. Finally it is argued that bipartisanship educates the members of the minority party to the realities of world politics and tends to reduce irresponsibility and extremism.

Undoubtedly, something can be said for each of these arguments. If the balance sheet on "mythical bipartisanship" contained only these positive entries, then the case could be decided with relative ease. But, as is usual in the political world, the matter is not so easily resolved. For grave objections exist to "mythical bipartisanship" – objections which are all too frequently overlooked.

1. Adherents of the "national interest" argument usually fail to explain how the national interest is determined, for naturally each party identifies its own policies with those of the national interest. The objection is simple:

without full and searching debate, there is simply no guarantee that the so-called "bipartisan" policy *is* the most effective policy, the policy that is truly in the national interest.

If an entire range of increasingly vital issues is declared to be beyond politics, if politics is said to stop at the water's edge (and there is an increasingly blurred line between domestic and foreign policies), then the party system has lost one of its most crucial functions.

2. Two party cooperation *is* essential in some cases. In those situations when genuine bipartisanship can be effected, it should be. But, as shown above, there are limitations to genuine bipartisanship: there is often no time for genuine consultation in time of crisis. In situations which do not require legislative authorization, there is the danger that the opposition will be sharing in the formal responsibility for policies whose execution it cannot influence.

Furthermore, the insidious notion that debate in the area of foreign affairs can serve no worthwhile function, that it can proceed only from a desire for "mere partisan" advantage, is a notion which counters the very foundation of the party system. This is accompanied by the Administration's assumption that its policies automatically represent a sort of grand consensus. Opposition criticism is said to create disunity – where in fact no unity ever existed in the first place.

Passive bipartisan acquiescence in matters of foreign policy not only shuts off consideration of alternative approaches, but it blurs the lines of responsibility for a decision. The diplomatic failures can be excused as "bipartisan – though rarely are the successes so labeled.

3. The third "asset" of mythical bipartisanship asserts that even though there is no guarantee that the bipartisan policy will be the *best* policy, unity has been achieved and that unity in the face of totalitarian threat is the important goal.

It should first be made clear than the claimed assets – unity, stability, dependability and continuity – result chiefly from the *appearance* of bipartisan unity, rather than from the *procedures* of genuine bipartisan consultation which produce true unity. The uncritical search for the appearance of unity overlooks the fact that unity may or may not be a virtue, depending upon whether in any particular situation the policy behind which it stands actually advances the nation's interest in world affairs.

Bipartisan unity in foreign policy lends an aura of untouchability to the resulting policies; an aura which prevents the search for alternatives, thus leading only to rigidity and to apathy.

4. Does "mythical bipartisanship" produce more *responsible* parties? Unfortunately, such unity as may be achieved behind a "bipartisan" policy may not be lasting. An Administration may temporarily silence opposition criticism

by capturing its leadership, but in the long run such situations lead either to the devitalization of the opposition party or to intensified intra-party divisions. Unrealistic hopes may be aroused behind a policy which seems to be sanctioned by both parties. The failure of such a policy often leads to furious acrimony directed not at the policy itself but to those (perhaps "disloyal") individuals charged with its execution. The Joe McCarthy era, fed by the failures in China and Korea, is unfortunately replete with such instances and it emerged only after genuine bipartisan consultation had ceased to be a reality.

A temporary unity between the two major parties in an area of vital and intense national concern may indeed lead to the demise of the two-party system itself, as third parties arise to exploit the public confusion and concern on the "silenced" issues of foreign affairs. Finally, the silencing of debate through the application of "mythical bipartisanship" permits the Executive to undertake rash, ill-considered adventures which rational and lengthy deliberation could have prevented.

It must be concluded, then, that the assets claimed for mythical bipartisanship are by no means automatically achieved. Unity, stability, dependability and continuity – all these virtues can easily be eroded, or even turned into vices. An educated and responsible minority is produced only through the genuine consultation which has rarely marked recent "bipartisanship."

IV. THE REPUBLICAN RESPONSIBILITY

What then is the Republican alternative to this "mythical bipartisanship?" Is it a return to a purely partisan foreign policy, reminiscent of the furious conflict of the League era?

For a number of reasons, a purely partisan policy is unworkable. First, there is simply no basis in the American political system for a neat cleavage between two disciplined, responsible parties on foreign policy issues on the same lines as domestic issues. Second, American parties are not disciplined parties; there is no way of enforcing unified party support behind a partisan foreign policy (not to speak of the questionable desirability of doing so). Finally, there are still those instances in which it is constitutionally necessary for there to be two-party support on some foreign policies, as in the case of treaties and during those times when control of the national government is divided between the parties. Straight partisanship is clearly not the answer.

If neither irresponsible partisanship nor a continuation of the "mythical bipartisanship" which has simply served as an excuse for the lack of thought is the solution, then the solution must lie somewhere between. *The Republican approach to foreign policy must be one of responsible and principled partisanship. Such a Republican position assigns to the party a few basic roles.*

1. When opportunities for genuine bipartisan cooperation are available, they should be pursued diligently. Collaboration between the Administration

and the opposition should not be ruled out, but it must be limited to those areas in which such cooperation is meaningful.

2. The opposition party must demand to be kept informed. They must not acquiesce in the application of the mythical label of bipartisanship to mere briefings. In seeking explanations and clarifications of the Administration's policies, the opposition forces the Administration to examine its own positions and to articulate publicly their rationale.

3. The opposition party must offer constructive criticism of the Administration's policies. In a day when the Democratic President is obsessed with secrecy, when management of the news is blatant and misleading, it is the duty of the opposition to keep the nation informed. The American public must be kept aware of the facts, alternatives and issues involved as the administration makes decisions behind doors which mock the true meaning of bipartisanship. As President Dwight D. Eisenhower remarked during the Cuban Crisis of 1962:

> "A foreign crisis must not become an excuse for silence or submission by us Republicans."

4. Finally, the Republican party must debate and resolve its own foreign policy views, that policy the GOP would employ were it in control of the White House. It is naive for any party to hope that voters will return to power a party which remains silent while the great international issues of the day are being debated by the party in power. Only when the GOP has established its own principles and policies does it have a scale against which to measure the performance of the Democrats.

Responsible and principled partisanship does not entail an extreme ideological alternative to the Administration's policies. It must be based on the broad foreign policy consensus in this nation regarding both goals and means. At the same time, it must base disagreement on a confident commitment to *principles* – without which the United States will find itself constantly acquiescing in the status quo or extemporizing when it changes.

> As Senator Jacob Javits has written: "We would deny ourselves the vitality of debate that gives strength to our democracy if we claimed that because a President of one party and his Secretary of State have made a policy proposal, the members of the opposition party must say nothing but Amen."

Policies that extend "beyond the water's edge" are too crucial in the twentieth century to be declared off-limits for responsible debate. Without rational deliberation, vital problems which have been neglected by the Administration will continue so until they explode in the faces of policymakers; courses of national policy which have been poorly charted by Administration planners will lead, if not criticized and corrected, to sure disaster. *Bipartisanship in its mythical form is a luxury which this nation can ill afford. It is not merely the right but the clear duty of the Republican Party to employ all its available resources in the responsible study and debate of the pressing issues of foreign policy.*

CHAPTER 20
CHINA TODAY – CONTAINMENT AND CONTACT

The Ripon position paper on China summarized the group's conclusions after several months of research on Asian affairs. First released in May of 1966, it continues to reflect an important dimension of Ripon's approach to Far Eastern Policy. A New York Times editorial described the paper as "a breath of fresh air for many Americans."

– Editors

The problem of China is an immense and significant as any which presently confronts the American people. The Ripon Society believes that the present generation of political leadership in both major American parties has failed to confront this problem with the creativity, subtlety and flexibility which it demands. On the one hand are the advocates of a rigid policy which would deny the Communist Government of Mainland China any role whatever in the diplomatic area. Describing China as a great power bent on military conquest, they would force the United States to frame its response in solely military terms. With some logic they insist that the only way to keep China from military conquests is to make the costs of such conquests prohibitive. They ignore or write off the possibility that China's will to make war could be reduced by building understanding and contact between China and the rest of the world.

On the other hand are those whose passion for a policy of understanding and contact is so great that they overestimate its potential for short run success. They would have our government forsake its policy of military containment and allow China certain prerogatives within its historic sphere of influence. They would wisely encourage China to travel a diplomatic road by making that road more attractive. But at the same time they would further increase the attractiveness of the quicker military route by making it less costly to the Chinese people.

It is our belief that both of these approaches are unrealistic and ineffective. The rigidity with which they are frequently proposed results from the context of the bitter foreign policy debates of the late 1940's and early 1950's in which they first arose. Each side has allowed the acrimony of those years to blind it to the insights of its opponent. Extreme advocates of containment are unwilling to see any value in accommodation; extreme proponents of bold initiatives for further contact view all military confrontation as frustrating their aims.

We speak today as members of a generation which did not participate in the debate which followed World War II. We grant that we have experienced certain aspects of the China question less directly than some. But we also believe that this fact may free us to see the tangled matter with less emotion and greater perspective than some of those who have been strongly committed to a single position for so long. It is our conviction that the China problem cannot be adequately understood unless the collective wisdom of both military containment and diplomatic accommodation is appreciated.

CHINA AND CHANGE

It is clear that China will have a major impact on this history of our planet in the decades immediately ahead. Her ancient culture and proud traditions remind us that this is the oldest continuing society in human history. Her large land area, huge population masses, and recently acquired nuclear weapons potential guarantees her future importance.

China's role as an independent and powerful force has grown since the Communists came to power in 1949. For a century before that, Chinese history had been marked by internal disunity and humiliation at the hands of foreign powers. For a decade afterward, China's destiny seemed closely bound to that of the Soviet Union. This powerful alliance threw the West on a defensive alert. The Korean War confirmed western suspicions about the expansionist tendencies of Asian Communism. Support for the Koomintang government which had fled to Taiwan became a symbol of American resistance to this force and of our official desire to displace the Communist government on the mainland.

In the last seventeen years the People's Republic has consolidated its power to the point where very few expect the Nationalists to ever retake the mainland. Yet official American policy seems to have held to this vain hope and to the consequent refusal to deal diplomatically with the Communist Chinese. At the same time China has become increasingly independent of the Soviet Union and that independence has recently erupted into open hostility and a threat to break off diplomatic relations. Yet too many Americans (including some Administration officials) still speak of a monolithic "Sino-Soviet bloc." We believe that both of these new facts, Chinese power and Chinese independence, must be better reflected in American policy. Pretending that the Communist government of mainland China does not exist will do no good. Neither will a merely sentimental call for understanding and sympathy. Our very best scholarship, information, intelligence and judgment must be marshalled to meet this difficult challenge. The recommendations which follow are our immediate contributions to the searching reexamination of American policy which must come about.

I. MILITARY CONTAINMENT

We believe that any Chinese attempt to absorb an independent nation or reduce it to a state of vassalage militarily or through internal subversion must be stopped. If force is required, then force must be applied, but carefully and in appropriate quantities. We must not allow the stated Chinese policy of expansion through "Wars of National Liberation" to succeed. This policy argues that violence and terror are legitimate means of promoting the Communist goal. The United States and her allies must maintain the patience and the will to prevent this policy from being successful. An orderly and peaceful world will be impossible unless such doctrines are resolutely opposed and finally abandoned.

It should be noted however that effective resistance to Chinese threats against Korea, Formosa, in Thailand or India require that we not become preoccupied by the less significant Chinese role in Vietnam. That conflict began, after all, as a civil war. While it is true that China would like Hanoi to succeed, it is misleading to view the conflict as a test of Chinese will and power. To be bogged down endlessly in Vietnamese jungles will not necessarily strengthen our capacity to contain Communism in Asia.

II. FIRST STEPS TOWARD CONTACT

If blocking the military road is the first step to peace, then opening wide an alternative realm of contact is also essential. For unless China can turn elsewhere, she will probably not give up her military methods. Then the result of our containment may only be a mutual escalation of violence which could produce nuclear war. It is true of course that American initiatives cannot guarantee Chinese response. There are limits on American policy and it may be that there is nothing the United States can do to modify the stand of Peking. But let us at least reduce the possibility that China will walk the road to war. Let it be a mark of our maturity that we are willing to take the bold first steps toward peace.

It is perhaps unfortunate that the search for contact has focused almost exclusively on only two American actions: diplomatic recognition and support of China's entry into the United Nations. Both steps would represent abrupt changes in American policy, so abrupt that they may be politically impossible. Moreover, both moves might well be viewed as hypocritical maneuvers and would probably produce no more than bombastic rejections from a still suspicious Peking. A full normalization of relations, including an exchange of ambassadors and admission to the United Nations, are desirable goals. They should probably be looked upon, however, as the result, not the cause, of an improved diplomatic atmosphere.

We believe that the quest for such an atmosphere can immediately be furthered by the following recommendations:

1. Our government pronouncements must reflect a less hostile attitude. Our tendence to picture China as a villain and outlaw makes it more likely that she will behave that way. We must criticize Chinese policies without insulting Chinese leaders. (The Secretary of State might begin by discontinuing his insistence on calling the Chinese capital by its Nationalist name, Peiping.) Our rhetoric concerning the Soviet Union is much more mature than it once was. Certainly a similar adjustment concerning China would entail no retreat, no loss of face, and it might remind American citizens as well as world opinion of our sense of responsibility and our desire for peace.

2. We must more insistently and more dramatically pursue the goal of increased contact between American and Chinese citizens. Through diplomatic channels in Warsaw and elsewhere, we must continue our attempts to work out an exchange of newsmen, scholars, doctors and cultural groups. The current library exchange program offers a small base upon which to build. The United States might draw world attention to such programs by formally appropriating the funds with which they could be implemented. And if such overtures are again refused, then we must offer the hand of friendship again and again. Chinese leaders and Chinese positions will almost certainly fluctuate from time to time. We must do all we can to encourage a change in the right direction.

3. It is almost certain that the People's Republic of China will be voted admission to the United Nations within a few years, no matter what the United States does, and, for that matter, whether or not Peking requests admission. Accordingly, we believe, it is unwise for the United States to continue to commit her prestige to denying that result. Rather let us maximize our chances to influence conditions under which such an invitation is extended. This does not mean that we have to sponsor or even support Chinese admission. It does mean that we should let it be known that we will not continue in active opposition. The United States would thus demonstrate its desire to see that every opportunity for better understanding is explored.

There need be no loss of prestige in such an action, but rather an indication that a great and secure power does not fear the participation of its detractors in this international organization. Such an action would be much like last year's decision to drop our insistence that peace-keeping dues be paid to the United Nations by all member nations. In that instance the United States showed its magnanimity by rising above a relatively minor consideration so that the United Nations might continue to function.

It is frequently argued that Chinese violations of the United Nations Charter should preclude her acceptance in the organization. Our response is that if the United Nations is to be a meaningful force for peace, then it cannot be viewed as an exclusive club of moral nations. The Charter is not so much a standard against which outsiders are judged as it is a goal to which members aspire. Membership in the United Nations should be an encouragement to more responsible international behavior rather than a reward for such behavior.

4. Because the problem of Taiwan and its continued claims to the Chinese Mainland is so much a part of all of these matters, the United States must once again review our commitment to that aspiration. What is the extent of the commitment? Are we merely bound to defend Taiwan against aggression or are we committed to support all her ambitions? Is our commitment to support Chaing Kai Shek personally, to guarantee his return to the Mainland, or to preserve the integrity of his government? How does this commitment square with our current involvement in Southeast Asia? A further complication is the fact that the Taiwanese may some day elect to rejoin the Mainland of their volition. The answer to these questions should not call for the abandonment of Taiwan to the overwhelming power of the Mainland; but it might well involve rethinking a position which considers Taiwan the only "legitimate" government of all China.

5. We must prepare the American people for a more flexible trade policy toward China. Certainly an embargo on strategic goods should be continued. But greater trade can build effective contacts and a community of interest which is to the advantage of both nations.

6. The thorny problems of arms control and prevention of nuclear proliferation can never be solved without the meaningful participation of modern China. Again, it may be some time before Peking will agree to such participation, but the United States, together with other nuclear powers, should continually encourage Chinese representation at all international conferences dealing with this matter.

Certainly it would be foolish to expect an overnight change in Chinese opinion once these initiatives are taken. But these overtures must be made nevertheless. As China grows in power and in security, as her economic and social problems ease, she may develop leadership and attitudes which will bring her into a responsible role in the community of nations. There is little for the United States to lose in attempting to encourage such a development. But it is painfully clear that everyone will lose if the Chinese people develop their awesome potential without a corresponding sense of moderation and maturity.

THE REPUBLICAN ROLE

While many Americans still oppose any change in this nation's attitude toward mainland China, recent opinion polls indicate definite and growing support for greater flexibility. We believe that it is the responsibility of our political leaders to mobilize and encourage this element of public opinion. Unfortunately some of the recent rhetoric of President Johnson, Vice President Humphrey and Secretary of State Rusk have – if anything – discouraged it. It may be that the current conflict in Vietnam has led them to believe that this is not the time to redirect this nation's opinion concerning the Far East. But it is the essence of the Ripon Society's position that the United States can and must bear the shield of containment in one hand at the same time that we proffer the olive branch of peace with the other. With the shield we discourage the aggressive force which is China today. With the olive branch we seek to encourage the responsible power which might be – and must be – the China of tomorrow.

If the Administration fails to encourage the second half of this dual response, then the responsibility to do so falls upon the Republican Party. Republican history reveals a rich strain of realistic and responsible leadership in foreign policy. This strain has not always been the dominant one within our party, and in the last few years it has often been eclipsed, particularly in matters concerning the Far East. But we believe that our party has the resources from which to create principled policies which are imaginative, flexible, and progressive. Republicans can and must fill a leadership vacuum which has developed in the formulation of American policy toward China.

As members of a new generation of Americans and of Republicans we can no longer be silent while vital issues are discussed in a manner which is narrow-minded and unimaginative. We can no longer be content with cliches and sterotypes, from either the rigid "right" or the sentimental "left." This most challenging of all current problems can become only more critical if we are bound by the thinking of the past. Even as we hope for a new and more flexible generation of Chinese leadership, so we also suggest that the perspectives of younger Americans should be broadened beyond the rigid points of view which have led to the current impasse.

We know that there are many Republican leaders today who share our quest for an intelligent, forthright, common-sense foreign policy. We believe that the American people are ready to join and support such a quest. The hour is late and the stakes are high. The quest will demand the very best that is in us. Surely it deserves no less.

CHAPTER 21
THE REALITIES OF VIETNAM
an alternative for Republicans

Christopher W. Beal researched and Josiah Lee Auspitz wrote the Ripon position paper on Vietnam during the summer of 1967 and their final draft was edited and approved by the Society's twenty member National Governing Board in September. It was released to the public on October 2nd through a nationwide mailing and a press conference in Washington.

The immediate response to the proposed Confederal Strategy indicated that Ripon had said something new and worthwhile. Granted, as Chalmers Roberts wrote in the Washington Post, *this was a "political document." It argued the Republican responsibility to provide an alternative to the President's policy; it claimed that a meaningful alternative would require the election of a Republican administration. But, as Mr. Roberts also wrote, President Johnson's "persistent question of 'what would you do?' has finally produced . . . thoughtful answers." The* Boston Globe *called the report "one of the most thorough and scholarly proposals yet injected into the Vietnam debate." The* Providence Journal *suggested it was "like a fresh wind blowing through a smoke filled room."*

General James Gavin indicated that he would discuss the proposal in detail with General Westmoreland when he visited Vietnam. It was, he wrote, "a brilliant analysis . . . one of the best things I have read on Vietnam." Eric Sevareid discussed the paper on the CBS Evening News and called it "A bold blueprint, almost the total opposite to the one we are now trying to follow in Vietnam." Senator Clifford Case, a member of the Foreign Relations Committee, told the Senate: "I hope to make that G*Ripon's proposals*H *the basis of a good many discussions about what goes on in Vietnam."*

The paper was later made the title essay of The Realities of Vietnam: A Ripon Society Appraisal, *a book published in April 1968 by Public Affairs Press, Washington, D.C., with introductory essays by Senator Mark O. Hatfield (Oregon) and Congressman Paul Findley (Illinois) and discussion by a number of leading academic experts. Some of the Ripon proposals had already made their way into government policy. Hence Elizabeth Pond of the* Christian Science Monitor, *pointing out that the paper had first appeared "in the pre-McCarthy period when serious debate on Viet-*

nam policy had not yet entered the internal political process in the United States," called it "one of the best pieces of Vietnam analysis available M *and also a model exercise in political responsibility."*

– Editors

Better is a poor and wise youth than' an old and foolish king
who will no longer take advice . . .
(Ecclesiastes 4:13)

With one eye fixed on remote posterity and the other on the Gallup polls, President Johnson has had little vision to spare for the real constituency of his Vietnam policy: the generation of men who are expected to fight the war and live with the results.

As members of that generation, we have sought the advice of experienced men; we are conscious of the informed and responsible counsel that is available to the makers of American foreign policy. But even seasoned observers agree that on the subject of Vietnam *rigor mortis* has set in. A bureaucratic coalition within the administration has reached a rigid consensus that repels knowledgeable advice. It has set its own terms of discussion, enshrined its own version of the facts and has for the most part succeeded in imposing its internal verities on public debate as a whole.

Thus, the American people have been asking whether more bombing, more troops, more diplomacy, more refugee relief, better elections, or more economic aid hold the key to our difficulties in Vietnam. And the administration has graciously suffered "dissent" on these questions. Small wonder, when dissent on tactical issues is easily preempted by bureaucrats who have the power to act: when "hawks" have the public ear, the administration can intensify military activity; when "doves" seem ascendant, it can treat them to a flurry of diplomacy. But the basic structure of administration policy remains untouched by these fluctuations. The larger questions of our involvement in Vietnam remain to be asked.

Why has a conflict which has been repeatedly defined as "political" and "essentially Vietnamese" become a largely military, largely American undertaking? Why, after six years of "limited" war, punctuated by glowing predictions of success, has no upper limit yet been reached on American troops or expenditure? Why, despite American talk about bringing peace and democracy to South Vietnam, has American policy led to the further entrenchment of a regime of generals, who are dependent for their power on the continuation of the war?

Answers exist to these questions, answers that demand an unflinching reappraisal both of the structure of our Vietnam policy and of the conduct of our foreign affairs as a whole. The Johnson administration is incapable of carrying out this reappraisal. It is motivated, as the President and his advisors assure us, by a sense of commitment. A commitment to a brave little nation? To the cause of freedom and democracy? To the containment of aggressive Communism? No, these broader goals have been obscured behind commitments of a different sort: a prideful commitment to continuing a misconceived policy, an ignoble commitment to covering over mistakes, an imprudent commitment to the unlimited use of American resources and moral energy in a dubious cause.

The time has come for simple commitments to reality and the national interest. Vietnam is the place to begin. The course of this war may well shape American thinking on foreign policy for a generation to come, just as the bitter neutrality controversy of the 'Thirties dominates the thinking of many officials reponsible for our present position. It is important, therefore, that the proper lessons be drawn early. And it is appropriate that they be drawn by young men who will have to build from the pieces that the Johnson administration leaves behind.

The Ripon Society proposes a thorough reorientation of American foreign policy in Vietnam and new departures in our conduct of foreign policy as a whole. It calls for frank discussion of American goals in Vietnam, the costs of fulfilling them, and their place in a larger context of priorities for global foreign policy and domestic spending. It proposes the following agenda for debate and action.

1. There must be an examination of present policies in the light of the facts of Vietnamese political life. It is the conclusion of the Ripon Society that the present structure of policy is built on an expensive fiction about what South Vietnam is and what it can become. The American people should know how much it will cost to make this fiction into a reality.

2. New concepts are needed for Vietnam. Instead of our present military, centralized, "nation-building" approach, the Ripon Society calls for a flexible, political approach to the problem that will reduce American troop commitments in the long run and take cognizance of the strong ethnic and religious rivalries that divide many non-Communist South Vietnamese from the Saigon government.

3. The conflict in Vietnam has increased certain imbalances in American political instutitions: the imbalance between our ability to wage war and our administrative capacity to seek peace; the imbalance between Congress and the Executive in the formulation of foreign policy. These imbalances as well as the present administration's failures in foreign policy, provide both an opportunity and a duty for the Republican Party. The Ripon Society calls on the Republican Party to bring the issues of foreign policy to the people in the 1968 elections.

I. THE COSTS OF IMPLEMENTING A FICTION

Visiting Congressmen and journalists who ask to see the success of pacification programs in South Vietnam are often taken to An Gaing providence. There they are treated to the spectacle of orderly village life directed by respected local leaders who have a long history of resistance to Communist control. These villages, stable and secure from attack, have been electrified; aerial land surveys have been carried out; American-sponsored improvements in sanitary, educational, and medical facilities have been made. To extend similar benefits to all the villages in all the provinces of South Vietnam is the American goal, and it is a noble goal.

But there is another remarkable feature about the model villages of An Giang province. They are under the sway of the Hoa Hao sect, which as recently as 1963 was declared by the Saigon government to be part of the Viet Cong. American officials in nearby provinces and in Saigon fully accepted this interpretation, and U.S. equipment and support enabled Premier Diem to carry out a program aimed at the destruction of Hoa Hao power. Had Diem succeeded, there would be no model villages in An Giang province today. There would be refugee camps, large numbers of U.S. troops, and fragmented settlements that would be easy prey for the Viet Cong.

Happily, the Hoa Hao were able to hold out.against their enemies both in Saigon and in the Viet Cong until Ngo Dinh Diem was overthrown. In 1964 they negotiated an agreement with the new central government: Hoa Hao areas, considerably reduced by Diem's attacks, were grouped within the newly drawn boundaries of An Giang province; the autonomy of local leaders was assured; and, in return for allegiance to the Saigon government, the new province was guaranteed immunity from harassment by the Army of South Vietnam. Almost overnight, An Giang became a "pacified" area, and U.S. teams were able to enter to improve the lives of the villagers and to help them in their long-standing effort to defend themselves against Viet Cong infiltration. Thus, the most successful example of "pacification" is an area that has never had the advantage of occupation by American or Army of the Republic of Viet Nam (ARVN) troops. It is a region in which a local group has been "redefined" from pro-Communist to anti-Communist status and which has been allowed a measure of autonomy in return for allegiance to Saigon.

Other local leaders have not been so lucky as the Hoa Hao. They have been defeated by the combined efforts of the Viet Cong, the Saigon government, and American policy. But since particularism runs deep in Vietnam, local leadership may reemerge, just as the Hoa Hao resurfaced after American officials proclaimed them to have been "for all purposes eliminated as a powerful political and military force."

The tenacity of local loyalities is a product of the ethnic and religious diversity of South Vietnam. South Vietnam is a fragmented country; it is the product of several waves of conquest and a long history of ethnic, religious and geographical rivalries that have left divisive hatreds. Even before the arrival of nearly a million refugees from the North, it was rent by localism in the rural areas and factionalism in the cities. A realistic approach to the country must build from this legacy. It must recognize that there are many non-Communists who, like the Hoa Hao, hate the mandarins and the army of Saigon just as much as they hate the Communists.

As a first simplification, the real South Vietnam may be divided into three regions, each of which has a distinctive political culture: first, the northern Coastal Strip, an area which is characterized by an imperial tradition and deep-seated contempt for the government of Saigon and where the militant Buddhists are the most important non-Communist faction; second, the Central Highlands, populated by mountain tribesmen who are not ethnically Vietnamese and who are willing to ally themselves with any force that will protect them from Vietnamese cultural domination; third, the southern part of the country (old Cochin China), which is divided among important religious groups (Catholic, Buddhist, Cao Dai, Hoa Hao), each of which has strong political interests. The presence of ethnic Cambodians adds an element of racial diversity to the southern part of the country.

Finally, in all these areas are the Viet Cong, whose cadres control fully one-fourth of the rural population. They have developed an intricate network of front organizations that include youth groups, women's clubs, and civic action groups in villages which, taken together, contain three-fourths of the rural population. For many villages the cadre's authority is inseparable from village life, and indeed, the cadres have become a new social class in rural Vietnam.

To build a stable coalition from the non-Communist fragments is an ambitious undertaking that might be accomplished by skillful bargaining. But the American aim in Vietnam has been more than ambitious. Under the Kennedy and Johnson administrations the United States has been the partisan of a policy of centralized government in South Vietnam. Instead of seeking to foster a political system built upon grass-roots support, American policy has been preoccupied with a dream of centralized democracy radiating out from Saigon, much as communism is thought to radiate from Hanoi. (In actuality, the North allows some local autonomy to ethnic minorities, a fact which the Viet Cong use to good effect in their propaganda campaign among the mountain tribesmen of the Central Highlands.) The American mission in Saigon has accordingly been engaged in a search for a "national leader" capable of carrying out a program of "nation building," a sort of man on a white horse who will be the South Vietnamese counterpart of Ho Chi Minh.

In the beginning this national leader was Premier Diem, and we acquiesced while he persecuted the Hoa Hao and made political prisioners of more than

40,000 of his non-Communist enemies. Later he was Premier Ky, and we supported him in smashing the Buddhists in the northern provinces and in sending lowland Vietnamese with American troops to organize the mountain tribesmen of the Central Highlands. Now our candidate for national leadership is General Thieu, who has been chosen president in an election from which all "neutralists" (including a former Cabinet minister) were excluded.

But whoever the man, there must also be a white horse, and unfortunately only one group in South Vietnam has even a remote possibility of being ridden to power over the factions and fragments of political life. This is the army, most of whose top officers were born in the North or fought for the French. The American dream of making South Vietnam into a centralized, unified state thus inevitably means military government. From the experience of other underdeveloped countries, no reason exists to hope that a military regime will turn itself quickly into a constitutional democracy or that it will be responsive to the interests of the rural population. "Nation-building" as it is now conceived in U.S. policy means nothing if not military rule in South Vietnam, and indeed within the State Department the military regime of South Korea is given as a model for South Vietnam. It would be enough if we could hope for a military ruler who was capable simply of administering the countryside.

But even here there are enormous difficulties. The army does not have sufficient contact with the rural areas to understand peasant problems or to administer them effectively. The army of South Vietnam has had only one top-ranking general of peasant origin, General Thi, and Premier Ky relieved him of his command of the I corps area soon after the Honolulu Conference. The social distance between officers and enlisted men is great. Officers despise their troops with the traditional contempt of the high-born for the manual laborer. Enlisted men are rarely promoted into the office corps; in the last three years only one field grade officer in the army of South Vietnam has been wounded leading his men into battle. The pruning out of ethnic Southerners and former members of the Viet Minh in favor of Northerners has further divorced the officer corps from the country.

The army of South Vietnam is thus not to be compared with the popularly-based armies of some other underdeveloped countries. It lacks their social base and political skills. What is more, the generals cannot even command the respect of the mandarin class, the traditional rulers of the country, who have always asserted the superiority of civilian to military authority.

On its own merits, the Army of the Republic of South Vietnam is not, then, a good bet for unifying the country on a centralized model. But with the thrust of American policy behind it, it is an even worse bet. Just as U.S. military support relieves the ARVN from going into the swamps, so U.S. political support relieves the Saigon generals from the need to bargain with civilian factions. Indeed, the one ruling general whom the United States Mission publicly criticized, General Khanh (now stripped of power), was also the only one, tragically, to bring the militant Buddhists into a ruling coalition. American policy has become fixed around the idea that a nation-building war must be carried out on all political and military fronts at once, against Communist, neutralist, and anti-Communist rivals alike.

Can such a war, carried on without regard to the political terrain, aimed at imposing central government in a country with decentralized bases of power, dependent on the administrative capabilities of a narrowly based and politically unskilled military elite, can such a war be successful? Probably it can. Implementing a fiction is not impossible, merely expensive. It is now costing the United States, according to reputable estimates, upward of 24 billion dollars a year and casualties of 7000 a month. The budgetary figure represents three times the total of American overseas investment for the current fiscal year and about seven times the total foreign aid budget. The monthly casualty figure equals the total number of Peace Corps volunteers who went abroad last year. The troop commitments to Vietnam represent an almost total investment of our available troops for flexible response to unanticipated crises in other parts of the world. If unexpected trouble should occur abroad or in American cities, the U.S. strategic reserve would be inadequate to respond. To ask whether this represents a prudent investment of American resources, manpower, and moral energy is now academic. The question is whether we can hope for any substantial reduction of cost if present policies continue.

The costs of Vietnam have been built up on an installment plan. First a little more bombing, then a few more troops for conventional operations, then a few more for counter-insurgency warfare, then more investments in the "other war." With these four major elements – and with well-advertised elections and peace offensives to legitimize its operations – the Administration has attempted to implement the fiction of unified central government in Vietnam and to protect this government against external aggression. The Administration clearly believes that more installment plan increases hold the best prospect for a long-run reduction in the costs of the war. But what are the likely results of intensification of the four major elements of present policy? What are the prospects for success of the two legitimizing devices?

EDITORIAL COMMENT

[*There followed a detailed discussion of tactics showing that a continuation of present policies could only raise the costs of the war without appreciably hastening its end. The paper did not seek to predict the precise mix of tactics that the Administration might use, but it did chart the "upper and lower limits" of likely costs to the United States within the existing structure of policy.*

The "lower limit" of cost to the United States would be a "refugee camp" solution, in which upwards of four million Vietnamese would be homeless, the rural social order would be destroyed, the rice supply would be reduced and the country would be turned into "a nation of beggers and thieves." Such a country might be administered by a centralized military government in Saigon, but it could count only on the "temporary allegiance" of its refugee constituents and its existence would represent an intolerable moral cost to the United States.]

As for the upper limit to the American commitment, there is none. A different mix of elements – more emphasis on bombing or conventional warfare – could lead to an invasion of North Vietnam, an extension of the war into Laos and China, a confrontation with the Russians. So long as it is conducted in accordance with the aims of the Johnson Administration, the war will, in sum, get worse before it gets better.

What should the upper and lower limits to the American commitment be? The Ripon Society believes that the proper upper limit of the American commitment has already been exceeded. A prudent policy would demand that the level of present involvement be taken as a ceiling and that steps be taken to reduce the drain on American resources. To do otherwise is to further distort our sense of priorities away from other, strategically more important parts of the world and away from necessary expenditures of money and idealism at home.

But President Johnson's policy, however unrealistic and costly, has also created obligations that put a lower limit on the American involvement. The United States has a moral commitment to the one million refugees from the North who have been resettled in South Vietnam with our aid. It has an obligation to the 1.8 million refugees generated in the South during the past two years of heavy fighting. It cannot lightly abandon these people and the others of South Vietnam who are not Communists to the vengeance of the Viet Cong and their Northern supporters. Nor can we accept a solution that would pose a military threat to Thailand, which, unlike South Vietnam, is a signatory member of SEATO.

The Ripon Society believes that an honorable approach to Vietnam can be found that will work within these new upper and lower limits. i.e., an approach that will reduce American troop commitments in the long run and minimize the destruction of Vietnamese society. It is an approach that does not demand precipitant withdrawal or imprudent escalation; its effectiveness does not depend on the panacea of immediate negotiation. It does demand something perhaps more difficult at this late date: a patient, realistic, flexible, and humane vision of what can reasonably be achieved in South Vietnam.

II. THE NEED FOR A CONFEDERAL STRATEGY

At selected moments in the unfolding of its Vietnam policies, the Johnson Administration has challenged its critics to provide alternatives. After Hanoi failed to respond to the bombing pause, for instance, the Administration asked whether there was any choice but to resume bombing. When intelligence reports showed increases in Viet Cong troop strength, the Administration paused to ask whether it could do anything but increase American troop commitments. And so it has gone. By posing stacked questions sequentially, the administration has proven to its own satisfaction that its critics are naive and incapable of posing feasible proposals for a change in policy.

Now the real basis for a responsible alternative in Vietnam is not to be found by manipulating elements within the present structure of policy. The alternative to policy based on a fiction is policy based on reality. In reassessing the American undertaking in Vietnam, two central realities must be confronted.

The first reality is the fragmentation of the traditionally anti-Communist forces in South Vietnamese political life. In addition to the regional, religious, and ethnic rivalries traced in the Appendix to this paper, there is a wide gulf between the French-educated urban middle classes and the rural population. The former have a typically French faith in centralized government, to which the United States Mission has somehow been converted under the conviction that it represents "nation-building." Non-Communist peasants, on the other hand, have fought to resist centralized control, whether from Hanoi or Saigon. If both urban and rural sources of support are to be drawn into a stable non-Communist government, it will have to be on the basis of decentralized rule. Regardless of the protests of the French-educated centralists, local leaders will have to have a greater degree of autonomy than they have yet been granted. If they are not, if local leadership, however ignorant and unsavory it may appear to city folk, is further undermined and destroyed, the result will not be a democratic government from Saigon. The result will be no government from Saigon, save for refugee camps and American troops to carry out the policing functions normally performed by local leadership. American troops would then be the objects not merely of Communist hostility but of opposition from all traditional groups seeking to protect their social order from alien interference.

The second reality is the political and social innovation that is the basis of Viet Cong strength throughout South Vietnam: the local cadre. Viet Cong cadres are the only effective link between many Vietnamese villages and centralized commands, and they are the strongest such link in Vietnamese history. The cadre member is trained to live with the people of his village, to seek out those with grievances against Saigon-appointed officials and local notables, and to provoke incidents which mobilze the peasantry against the government. He is instructed in the techniques of organizing front groups, engaging in the selective use of terror to intimidate his opponents, accumulating intelligence from children and village spies, and co-existing with potentially hostile groups until he is ready to overthrow them. Very often "coexistence villages" that are well-infiltrated by cadres admit U.S. medical teams, vote in elections, and listen to Saigon-trained propagandists by day, while the Viet Cong maintains control by night. Cadres are an important new part of the village social structure in three-fourths of the rural population of South Vietnam, although only one-fourth of the rural population is under their total control. Careful analyses of their training and internal messages indicates that they have taken on a new social rule that is more important to most of them than adherence to Communist ideology. Hence, recent American usage of the term "cadre" does not recognize the Communists' claim to mechanical control. In our usage, "cadre" is not a collective noun denoting a well-disciplined group of men; it denotes an individual, professional agitator.

If the cadres are to be dealt with realistically, both the Saigon government and the American mission will have to abandon the goal of extripating them from village life. And the United States will have to recognize the futility of a Chieu Hoy program designed to encourage individual defections from cadres without guaranteeing a continuation of their social role. Viet Cong cadres are presently tying down nearly all the ARVN troops and more than half the American troops in the country. To destroy them means either the destruction of a large part of rural South Vietnam or an enormous drain on American manpower. A means must be found to allow them to hold their social function, while neutralizing their military threat.

A *confederal stategy* would deal with these two realities in a way that both Americans and Vietnamese would understand.

In its first phase, a confederal strategy would aim at developing an effective and stable non-Communist coalition between the cities and the twenty-seven per cent of the rural population that is subject to government control. In cases of conflict among factions, American support would go to those which have effective control of rural areas, since their loyalty and local policing efforts are alone able to free American troops for their proper function of checking infiltration from the North.

The concept of a coalition based on a confederal approach requires the concession to local leaders of formal guarantees of autonomy in the following ways:

*Control over local police and militia.

*Election of provincial and district officials who are now centrally appointed. (Provincial and district chiefs, most of them military men, now approve candidates for hamlet and village elections and make the major civilian decisions affecting their areas.)

*Government officials of local origin. (This is crucial in Vietnam where administrative rules are traditionally loose, allowing for wide discretion.)

*Local rule in formulation of land tenure regulations and reforms.
*Redrawing of provincial boundaries to correspond to the realities of political control.
*Cultural guarantees to ethnic minorities (*e.g.*, preservation of customary law, use of ethnic languages for primary school instruction).
*Right to collect local taxes, supplemented where necessary by direct access to U.S. aid. (A recent amendment to Title IX of the Foreign Assistance Act of 1967 permits the United States to find local channels for the distribution of aid.)

In other countries similar measures for decentralization might be accomplished by informal understandings, without written guarantees. But the time for that has passed in Vietnam. Too many promises have been made and broken for regional groups to trust any authority in Saigon. Nor can the United States serve as guarantor of informal bargains, for our Mission, too, has found it convenient to forget pledges made to minority groups in South Vietnam. National elections may give the regional minorities temporary leverage because of their ability to deliver bloc votes, but in a national legislature overwhelmingly dominated by urban Vietnamese the ethnic minorities have no continuing means of enforcing their interests. They will be restive whenever they are not actively courted by the ruling faction in Saigon.

In the September, 1967 presidential elections, for example, the Thieu-Ky ticket actively sought the support of the Hoa Hao in An Giang province, of the Cambodian minority in Ba Xuyen province, and of the Highland tribesmen. If Thieu is able to deliver on his promises of financial aid and autonomy, these ethnic minorities will no doubt continue to hold anti-government feelings in abeyance. But their loyalty is not to the constitution of South Vietnam, which provides no guarantee of their rights, but to the military faction. Should it break its word or be replaced by a rival coalition (*e.g.*, one composed of Coastal Buddhists, Southern army officers, and Mekong Delta Vietnamese), the ethnic minorities would again feel isolated. Thus, before any form of parliamentary coalition politics can be stable, prior confederal steps must be taken to give all important non-Communist groups a stake in the idea of national government.

A first, obvious step is to make formal and public the arrangements already in force with the Hoa Hao in An Giang province and to ratify similar arrangements for the enclaves of Cham peoples in Binh Thuan province.

Second, the government of South Vietnam should fulfill promises already made to the mountain tribesmen to draft guarantees of cultural autonomy.

Third, confederal decentralization and redrawing of boundaries should be carried out to give other strong local groups authority over their own regional affairs; the Buddhists in the northern coastal provinces; the Cao Dai and the settlements of Catholics and Northern refugees in the lowlands; and, the ethnic Cambodians in Kieng Giang. Ba Xuyen, and Vinh Binh provinces. Measures of this sort, which could be adopted almost immediately, would give non-Communist groups a state in the South Vietnamese government and constitution regardless of which faction happened to hold the reins in Saigon. There is no other way to deal with the problem of fragmentation of the non-Communist groups.

Once the rock-bottom non-Communist groups are consolidated the same confederal framework can be offered to "co-existence" villages, which comprise much of the contested half of rural South Vietnam. Local Viet Cong cadres and ARVN troops who have developed a relationship of tacit collaboration would be encouraged to formalize their relationships in exchange for regional autonomy from Saigon. Provincial boundaries can be redrawn for such areas, just as they were redrawn for An Giang province in October 1966.

These agreements might require the marketing of all surplus rice through Saigon, the payment of nominal taxes, and other signs of allegiance in exchange for separate access to U.S. aid to repair the devastation of war. The second phase would provide an alternative to the ravages of war that does not now exist for these villages. There is at present no way in which a Viet Cong cadre operating in contested villages can submit to popular war-weariness without losing his social function. And villagers have no incentive to denounce cadres so long as the alternative is not local control but administration by a Saigon-appointed military governor.

It is, of course, likely that the Viet Cong cadres would receive orders from above not to participate in confederal bargains, in which case a clear conflict of interest would be established within the Viet Cong ranks. Cadres who are not ideological Communists or not dependent on the North for supplies would perceive differing interests from those trapped in the Communist hierarchy. This would put pressure on the Viet Cong where it is economically most vulnerable, for those cadres who are independent of Northern supplies currently provide surplus rice for the Viet Cong efforts in weaker areas. Bidding away independent villages would begin the process of crippling the Communist movement by alienating cadres whose local social role is more important to them than the ultimate Viet Cong aim of winning the cities.

In its third phase, a confederal strategy would be offered to villages under the full control of the Viet Cong, which now hold approximately one-fourth of the total rural population. Such hard-core villages would face increasing isolation as the earlier phases of the confederal approach progressed. At this point the Viet Cong hierarchy would face three alternatives: 1) remaining in the South while their villages are losing food and manpower; 2) fleeing to the North; or, 3) retaining much of their local power in Communist enclaves and participating in the confederal framework. Once their prospects for taking over the entire country are cut off by a consolidation of non-Communist groups, it is likely that the Viet Cong high command would negotiate for the third alternative.

A confederal strategy provides a vision of a feasible outcome that South Vietnamese and Americans both lack. Urban Vietnamese can now envisage only a French-style solution, with the urban classes playing the role of colonial administrators and the army securing the countryside. The American Mission, on the other hand, seems infatuated with the model of South Korea, where a military junta has taken steps toward democratization. Both of these models fail to cope with the fragmentation of South Vietnamese political life and the new social role of village cadres. A decentralizated solution, by contrast, would permit both local leaders and rural cadres to keep a stable base of power now denied to them under the slogan of nation-building.

The minimal result of a confederal approach would be a consolidation of non-Communist groups, whose territory the United States could then defend with conventional forces until they were given legal guarantees. The maximal application of the confederal framework to the rest of the countryside would make possible a political system that accommodates sharp political differences (as does Italy) and deep cultural diversity (as does Switzerland).

A confederal strategy is designed to reduce the American commitment in installments much as the present policy seems destined to escalate it by installments. Barring massive invasion by North Vietnam, a confederal strategy would operate well within the present troop commitment.

It would save manpower almost immediately by winning the cooperation of the local population in the northern provinces of the Coastal Strip and Central Highlands. It would prevent vast numbers of American troops from being sent for new counter-insurgency operations south of the Mekong River. Saigon can no more surely lose its influence in this area than by permitting the entry of U.S. forces, which Communist propaganda convincingly identifies with the French, to enter.

Finally, by lowering the level of violence in selected "coexistence villages," it would put steady political pressure on the Communists, who would be faced with possible defections by their non-ideological cadres. The present policy of Saigon to root out all cadres gives them no choice but to continue obeying orders from the Communist hierarchy. A confederal strategy would promote factionalism in the Viet Cong and unity among non-Communists; the present policy does the reverse.

It should be emphasized that the confederal concept is a *strategy, not a rigid blueprint.* It is designed to keep the costs of the war below the upper limit recommended in the previous section. It permits a rethinking of Vietnam policy that provides not merely an alternative vision to that of the Administration but alternative emphases at every step of the way. This can be best illustrated by showing how the major elements of present policy will fit into a new pattern under a confederal strategy, how such an orientation cuts across some of the well-known "hawk-dove" distinctions.

1. Bombing North Vietnam

Even if bombing some day leads Hanoi to nominal capitulation and negotiation, the Viet Cong can still conduct intensive guerilla activities, and they will do so unless they have an alternative that permits popular southern Viet Cong leaders to retain political power. A confederal strategy encourages the formulation of such alternatives. It can be adopted regardless of one's attitude to the effectiveness of bombing in inhibiting infiltration.

But we would claim as an advantage for confederalism the fact that it will allow for a de-emphasis on bombing. The effect of bombing in fulfilling its two major purposes has been very much overrated by the administration.

Punitive bombing north of the 18.5 parallel simply does not save American lives. It risks conditions under which more lives, American and civilian Vietnamese, will be lost. And it is irrelevant to the insurgency in the South, which is the major drain on American fighting forces. *For these reasons, a confederal strategy would heavily de-emphasize bombing the North. Interdictory bombing south of the 18.5 parallel would continue as long as it was necessary to cut infiltration and troop buildups.*

2. Conventional Ground Forces

Invasion and insurgency are the two major military problems the United States faces. A confederal approach would employ conventional ground forces to defend areas where the Saigon government had won the loyalty of the people. It would also use them along the demilitarized zone and at crucial mountain passes to prevent an invasion of the northern I corps area.

While military leaders have been debating over bombing, barriers, and infiltration, they have failed to remind the American public that the North Vietnamese seem to be preparing an invasion of the I corps area, where American troops are already stretched dangerously thin. A confederal strategy would release troops from policing and counter-insurgency operations to counter a conventional thrust by the North Vietnamese. South Vietnam is not worth the millions of troops needed to counter both invasion *and* insurgency. Hence a confederal strategy provides a political framework in which present troops could be deployed against the invasion of areas in which the local population ceases anti-government activity.

3. Counter-insurgency

The United States can win the counter-insurgency war, but at the standard ten-to-one ratio of conventional to guerilla forces it is not worth the price. Under a confederal strategy counter-insurgency operations would not be extended to new areas of the country. Plans for an offensive south of the Mekong River and based in the town of Can Tho would be permanently abandoned. In areas where counter-insurgency operations are now underway, the promise of selective withdrawal of American forces would be used to increase the attractiveness of piecemeal negotiations under a confederal framework. With counter-insurgency as with bombing and conventional warfare, military action is used in a confederal strategy to advance feasible political goals.

4. The "Other War"

Under present policy the "other war" is too often the camp follower of military initiatives. After bombing, search and destroy operations, and refugee generation have taken their toll, American teams offer food, medical aid, and réfugee relief. The confederal strategy would use the economic, psychological, and social programs of the "other war" independently to fulfill political objectives.

A. Chieu Hoy

The Chieu Hoy program, which encourages individual defections of Viet Cong cadres, would operate in a wider context. Defections would still be welcomed, but primary emphasis would be placed on negotiation that permits cadres to retain their social role.

B. Land Reform

A centralized program of land reform is unrealistic. In many areas where land records have been destroyed, the attempt to resolve tenure disputes from Saigon can only be capricious and corrupt. Local administration of reforms is needed, not more centralization.

A confederal approach would use land reform to further the political goal of developing local leadership. Saigon might limit the size of family plots; it might provide surveying teams and keep a central record of land transactions. But the administration of reforms and the settling of disputes – a powerful source of patronage – would be left to local leaders. The power to implement land reforms would provide an added incentive for local leadership in coexistence villages to participate in a confederal framework.

C. Economic Aid

To make a confederal strategy credible the United States will have to demonstrate its willingness to aid areas that are not under direct American military control. In principle, President Johnson has committed himself to such a course, and indeed An Giang province provides an isolated example of the purity of American intentions. The most dramatic symbol of American aims, however, was the proposed project for a Mekong Dam to aid people of Laos, Cambodia, and South Vietnam who are not under American military occupation. After publicizing the project and engaging in preliminary studies, the Johnson Administration dropped it without explanation. There is perhaps no single act that would better symbolize the American commitment to the long-term interests of Southeast Asians than the revival of this project. Because it would take years to complete, it would make Communists and non-Communists alike believe that the United States has a permanent concern for the welfare of Southeast Asia and that, unlike the French, Americans will not leave when they grow tired of the war.

A confederal strategy will also implement the Foreign Assistance Act of 1967, which stipulates that "emphasis shall be placed on assuring maximum participation in the task of economic development on the part of people of the developing countries through the encouragement of democratic private and local government institutions." (Title IX, Sec. 281) This would depart from present policies which emphasize channeling aid through the Saigon regime, which regularly tries to deny American funds to its non-Communist opponents.

5. Negotiations

A confederal strategy will steadily improve the negotiating position of the South Vietnamese government by consolidating its support and enabling it to bid away Communist cadres. It will create a basis for national negotiations that cannot exist so long as the Communists perceive that the government of Saigon is inherently unstable. Should Hanoi and the Viet Cong hierarchy become reconciled to the impossibility of a conventional military victory, they will still have the choice of reverting to guerilla warfare or of trying to bargain for partial control of their enclaves in the countryside in general negotiations. A confederal approach will then make possible a stable solution. It should be emphasized that as long as all efforts for limiting American costs are directed at securing general negotiations, military escalation will go unchecked. A confederal approach, by coordinating military and political initiatives, will assure a lessening of the conflict until such time as peace talks become feasible.

6. Elections

A confederal strategy would attack the endemic cause of instability in an overly centralized system by conceding a measure of power to local leaders. Instead of placing preponderant emphasis on village and national elections, it would promise elections on the district and provincial level. Under present policies almost all provincial and district chiefs are military officers and all middle-level officials are appointed and promoted from Saigon; under a confederal strategy many of these administrators will be elected.

Vietman's local leaders need something to fight for. An increase in their own authority is a more plausible incentive than the imposition of corrupt officials from Saigon. A confederal strategy would accordingly urge that provincial and district elections be offered to all areas that are able to maintain internal security.

Elements of the French-educated middle class of Saigon and perhaps all the refugees from the North may greet a confederal strategy without enthusiasm, and even with outright hostility. Thirteen years of American support have accustomed many Saigon residents to the illusion that they themselves have ruled the provincial towns and the countryside. French intellectual habits have made them see Saigon as the Paris of South Vietnam, as an administrative capital of a thoroughly centralized regime. Northern refugees, for their part, are likely to oppose bitterly any scheme emphasizing regional bases of power and implicitly denying their right to return.

But Vietnamese political and military leaders, however adamantly they may oppose a change in their comfortable assumptions, have also shown a remarkable ability to adapt to political realities when they are not protected from them by American troops and economic aid. The confederal strategy will remind recalcitrant Vietnamese leaders that the illusion of centralized rule was possible in the past only because of massive American support and that such support will henceforth go to a vision of government that is more consistent with democratic ideals and more appropriate to Vietnamese political realities. The United States can begin distributing its aid in a decentralized fashion even during the period of readjustment to the new idea.

A second possible objection is that thanks to thirteen years of suppression of local leadership, there may be no popular regional and ethnic leaders with which to bargain on a confederal basis. The Appendix to this paper should satisfy doubts on this matter. It demonstrates the tenacity of particularistic loyalties in South Vietnam. American officials and Vietnamese politicians who deny these loyalities should spend more time outside Saigon.

[*The Appendix traced the history of local leadership in the three principal regions of South Vietnam.* – Eds.]

Finally, must not areas be pacified militarily before they can participate in a confederal framework? An Giang province suggests not, as do the repeated demands by northern Buddhists and mountain tribesmen for a measure of self-rule. In a counter-insurgency war the loyalty of the population is invaluable for reporting and resisting Viet Cong infiltrators. Wherever such loyalty can be won by the mere extension of local democracy, massive military pacification is neither necessary nor right.

One cannot, of course, reduce the costs of the Vietnamese undertaking without eliminating certain options now open to American policy-makers; and it is only fair to list two options that a confederal strategy forecloses. The first is the possibility of ridding the countryside of all Communist influence. This has been the expressed aim of a few Saigon army officers, but no reputable American official has ever publicly favored sending the millions of counter-insurgency troops required.

The second option is that of destroying North Vietnam and thereby provoking the Chinese into a war in which their nuclear capacity would be destroyed. This would presumedly be done by creating a situation in Vietnam analogous to that in Korea. If the Chinese were convinced that the United States had extended its original war aims to include heavy punishment and possible invasion of the North, they might intervene and provide an excuse for pre-emptive war.

A confederal strategy assumes that the United States can contain the Chinese without destroying neighboring states, much as it contained the Russians in Europe. Those who disagree with this assumption will of course find the cost of this strategy too high. They will find it intolerable that the United States adhere to its declared war aims, which include a perservation of the South but not the destruction of the North.

A confederal strategy is designed to:

I. *Reduce American costs without sacrificing America's moral obligations to its Southeast Asian allies.* In contrast to present policies which increase the level of United States military involvement installments, a confederal strategy aims at a decrease from the present troop levels. It accepts as a lower limit any troops necessary to defend from conventional attack those areas in which the local population is loyal to the government and constitution of South Vietnam and able to maintain internal stability.

II. *To confront the significant a) political, b) military, and c) diplomatic realities of the Vietnamese situation.* These are: a) the fragmentation of non-Communist political groups and the social role of the cadre; b) the primacy of insurgency and the possibility of large-scale invasion; and, c) the unlikelihood of any diplomatic resolution of the conflict until there is a stable government in Saigon with a framework that will permit the Viet Cong to retain power in the countryside.

III. *Provide a direction for change and a vision of a feasible outcome.* Depending on the fortunes of war, such an approach would result in anything from non-Communist enclaves to a stable non-Communist government with Communist enclaves in the countryside.

IV. *Coordinate military and political initiatives so that they are mutually reinforcing.*

A confederal strategy offers a coherent overview of the Vietnamese conflict that specifies *operational* political goals for every province and district of South Vietnam. The present goal of centralized government is unprecedented in Vietnamese history and is accordingly incapable of inspiring any real comprehension or loyalty in the countryside. A confederal strategy reasserts the primacy of the political element in limited warfare and does so on a level where political guidelines can save American lives.

For these reasons the Ripon Society endorses a confederal strategy. If great obstacles to its implementation exist, they are not to be found on the terrain of South Vietnam. They are to be found in Washington.

III. THE REPUBLICAN RESPONSIBILITY

It is not necessary to blame the entire structure of present policy on any one man or party, or any small group of officials. For although President Johnson and his advisers seem stubbornly committed to an imprudent and costly course of action, and although they will continue to use every available form of political leverage to avoid being confronted with their mistakes, the fault is not entirely theirs. Their misconceived policies could not have developed unchecked were it not for deeper malfunctions in our political institutions.

There has been, to begin with, an administration imbalance between our ability to take military risks and our ability to take political risks. The Department of Defense, reformed under unified civilian control, has been able to offer flexible responses to world problems. It has adopted a method of planning and budgeting that enables it to see clearly the costs, interrelations, and long-range military implications of its programs. And it engages in planning for contingencies so that it will be prepared for crises.

No comparable comprehensive effort in cost analysis, coordination, and contingency planning has been undertaken among the cluster of civilian agencies charged with economic and political elements of foreign policy. As a result, the relations between military and non-military instruments of foreign policy have often been determined by blind bureaucratic momentum, which naturally favors the better-prepared agencies. Because the Department of Defense is unified, massive and engaged in stand-by operations, while civilian agencies are fragmented and devoted to day-to-day details, American policy has a built-in tendency to drift toward military measures in times of stress.

South Vietnam provides a tragic example. America's power to wage war in that country is enormous. But we have been unable to wage peace, to formulate a political strategy that would limit the loss of life and build a basis for a negotiated settlement. American forces destroy entire villages on less hard intelligence than the Viet Cong use in assassinating a single village chief. Military contingency plans exist for invasion of North Vietnam, for bombing of Haiphong, for bombing of dikes, for counter-insurgency operations south of the Mekong River and doubtless even for use of nuclear weapons. But do similar plans exist for a confederal initiative or for any realistic settlement? Perhaps in a sub-basement of the State Department. But so long as there is no public indication of them American talk of negotiation lacks credibility. Political preparedness, like military preparedness, has to be publicized to be believed. It is meaningless for officials to talk of America's desire for peace and for a "political solution" so long as the administrative means to implement these hopes are not known to exist.

A second imbalance, between Congress and the Executive branch, has permitted bureaucratic mistakes to go unchecked. The Legislative branch faces long-term problems in adapting its procedures to the growth of executive power. In recent years it has begun laying plans for such adaptation: plans for Congressional reorganization, for improved staffing, for proper access to information and expert advice. But the Vietnamese conflict came before any innovations could be made and although it has forced many responsible legislators to revise their own roles in the making of foreign policy, it has caught Congress as a whole off guard.

Congress has neither the staffing nor the machinery to assert its prerogatives in the making of Vietnam policy. Its right to be consulted has been compromised into a right to ratify. Bureaucrats come before its inquiries in a contrived atmosphere of crisis with answers which are predetermined by carefully controlled information. Congress' right to know has been reduced to the right to be briefed. Legislators have been informed promptly of the *results* of policy in Vietnam, but no body of Congress has had continuing access to the political intelligence and strategic plans from which decisions are really made. Even Congress' right to set broad aims has been undermined by executive decisions which, although apparently "tactical," have altered the character of the war. Congress, in sum, has been unable to check the bureaucracy from without. Since significant checks are also absent from within, the pattern of Vietnam can easily be repeated: American policy can drift toward military solutions where political ones will suffice; American youth can die because its elders lack decisive civilian leadership.

President Johnson did not create the imbalances in our political institutions, but neither has he tried to correct them. If anything, his personal style of administration has accentuated the difficulties. His is a style of secrecy and silence. He has been willing to consider only proposals that filter noislessly through bureaucratic channels. He is famous for rejecting out of hand programs that originate outside his administration and for cancelling plans that are leaked prematurely to the press. He has been criticized for this, and he has also been praised for relying more than any recent president on career civil servants.

But the Johnson style has more important consequences than its occasional outbursts of pique or its encouragement of career service. Its charm for the President lies in its ability to stifle effective criticism. By keeping programs secret until the moment of their release, the President given opponents no time to prepare alternatives. He subjects legislators to a blitz of proposals that overwhelms their meager staffs. The President's practice of withdrawing nominations and programs that receive advance publicity also keeps dissidents within the administration from taking their case to the public. Since a public row means the sure rejection of a proposal, civil servants seldom dare to express their preferences outside official channels. The President's style thus excludes the public (and Congress) from bureaucratic debate and in so doing leaves the natural momentum of the bureaucracy uncorrected by external pressures. In foreign affairs this means that however many skirmishes may be won by proponents of political initiatives, the main thrust of American policy remains in the hands of the strongest agency, the Pentagon. Even if the President should reorient his Vietnam policy, his administration is unlikely to overcome its dependence on military plans and its habituation to military risks. It presents a classic example of self-entrenching bureaucracy that cannot be reformed from within.

If foreign policy is to change, if the serious imbalances in our institutions are to be corrected, if the lessons of Vietnam are to teach anything, a new administration must be elected. An alternative in foreign policy will have to be Republican.

Not any Republican alternative will do. A Republican administration must be committed to reducing the costs of the American undertaking in Vietnam. We have described a general approach to Vietnam that exchews escalation, that can succeed without the good will of the North Vietnamese, that keeps the cost below an acceptable upper limit, and that can lead to an honorable outcome. It remains for a new administration, undeluded and free to act, to adopt a confederal strategy.

A Republican president must also commit himself to long-range reforms in the administration of foreign policy. Future involvements should be shaped by realities abroad rather than bureaucratic inertia in Washington. Numerous analyses and proposals for administrative reform already exist. It is time to review these materials and to lay plans for a change. Here is one area in which the appointment of a Presidential Commission could be more than a publicity stunt.

A Republican Congress (or at least a Republican House) must adapt Congressional machinery to the demands of global foreign policy. Congress should consider establishing a joint committee on intelligence and strategic planning which would require the Executive Branch to report periodically on America's international position, much as the Joint Economic Committee requires it to report on budgetary policies. Such a new Committee should have access to the on-going information from which decisions are made in the manner of the Joint Committee on Atomic Energy.

The need for changes in foreign policy imposes a responsibility on the Republican Party. On all fronts the Johnson Administration has failed to provide prudent, realistic leadership. Its political policies, which remain open-ended, will require many more American troops unless a hard decision is made between countering invasion and countering insurgency. Its failure to take steps for long-term administrative reform assures that these deficiencies will persist, that American policies will drift by installments toward an ever wider, ever more senseless war. The Republican Party can provide a way out of this fiasco. It can grasp the realities of local politics in Vietnam; it can reassert the limited nature of American aims; it can reduce the costs in human life; it can bring into Government men from our universities, our professions, our business community who are better qualified to run this country's foreign policy than the self-deluded men who try to make reality out of fiction from their desks in Washington. The best men, the best minds in this country are not making American foreign policy.

The Ripon Society calls on Republicans to undertake new departures in foreign affairs. Though the issues are complex, their essentials can be brought to the people. In 1952 the Republican Party demonstrated that it could extricate America from a war on the Asian mainland. The issue now is whether the American people think our present course in Vietnam is worth more deception, more resources, more lives.

If they do not, there *is* an alternative.

* * * * *

This argument is, on the surface, more reasonable. Multilateral aid, for reasons of maximum efficiency and value of aid, is not *tied* to purchases in the subscribing countries, and might threaten to increase the net drain on a donor's currency. But, as argued above, the tying of foreign aid has not actually reduced U.S. trade imbalances significantly, and is certainly no permanent answer to the problems of exporters who cannot compete competitively.

It is important to note, moreover, that many of the purchases made with these funds will still be going to U.S. exporters. David Bell has estimated that about 75% of the money currently given to the World Bank was returning to the United States in the form of purchases by World Bank loan recipients. The U.S. contributed 44% of the foreign exchange used by the Indus Basin Fund, and received 54% of the contracts let by this agency. Of total contributions we have made to eight U.N. aid agencies, we have received back in U.S. procurement approximately 70%.

At current levels of assistance, the difference between this proportion of return and the 80% currently returning to us as a result of our tied, bilateral programs would amount to about $200 million extra drain on the balance of payments. We conclude that the international political and economic benefits to be derived from untied multilateral aid are worth far more than the tiny differential that such expenditures would entail in the U.S. balance of payments.

* * * * *

The Ripon Society is not the first to be impressed with the great benefits of an expanded multilateral aid program. Republicans such as Henry Cabot Lodge and Senator Howard Baker and Democrats such as William Fulbright have argued that it is the only effective method of implementing long-term economic development.

The benefits of an internationally supported multilateral aid program can be realized without the labor pains which accompany the birth of any international political institution. The agencies necessary to implement the multilateral approach are established and respected. All that is required is for the United States to resolve to bury its misconceived and unrealizable goals. Foreign aid should – and need – no longer be either a subsidy to inefficient American exporters or a crude instrument for bribery and pressure of foreign governments. Multilateral aid can provide an exciting departure from the stagnant foreign policies of the Democratic administration. It should be a central element in the Republican approach to international affairs.

CHAPTER 22
MULTILATERAL FOREIGN AID
a better way to foster development

Ripon's foreign aid proposals were first presented in January of 1968. The paper was written by Robert H. Donaldson and based on a draft presented by Michael W. Christian at "Commemoration Marshall" in Brussels, Belgium in June of 1967.
– Editors

America's involvement in Vietnam is costly and tragic – a reminder that it is unquestionably in the national interest to use our resources in an attempt to guide the "revolution of rising expectations" in the developing world along a peaceful path to prosperity, stability and freedom. Former Vice-President Richard M. Nixon put it succinctly in the October 1967 issue of *Foreign Affairs*: "There can be no security, whatever our nuclear stockpiles, in a world of boiling resentment and magnified envy." A central instrument for the task of eliminating this resentment and envy is the foreign assistance program.

Two decades of experience in foreign aid now lie behind us. The results have been disappointment, matching neither the needs nor the expectations. The Congressional appropriation for economic aid in fiscal year 1968 was the lowest in twenty years – approximately $1.9 billion. But the problems of our current aid effort are not limited to an inadequate level of expenditure; this is merely symptomatic of an underlying confusion as to both the dimension of the task and the goals of our policies.

If foreign aid is to become a truly positive force in the developing world, we must radically realign both our concept of the program and the methods of implementing our policies. *The Ripon Society proposes that direct or bilateral assistance for economic development be phased out and that future funds for the development of the Third World be channeled through international, multilateral agencies.* The United States must exercise its leadership in the developed world by revitalizing and expanding the existing multilateral aid network. Only then can foreign aid become an effective tool for the task of development, rather than a useless device which embroils the United States in unwanted controversy and commitments to stagnant societies.

1. OUR CURRENT AID EFFORT

A. CONFUSION OF GOALS

Any discussion of our present foreign aid program must recognize the absence of a consistent underlying strategy. From an initial concern with the reconstruction of war-shattered Europe, our focus has shifted first to a reliance upon military assistance and "defense support" in areas bordering the Communist bloc, and then to the present effort which promotes the simultaneous military and economic build-up of "friendly" nations throughout the "free" world. The goals of foreign aid are described variously as the desire to block Communist expansion, win new friends for America, spread the democratic system, enlarge world markets, or relieve the world's misery. Frequently contradictory, these aims are also unsupported by a clear understanding of the possibilities for success or the ordering of priorities.

Even more dangerous for the long-term future of the assistance effort is the fact that both officials and public have failed to recognize that foreign aid *alone* could never achieve this panoply of purposes. Economic assistance programs have been oversold: too many results have been promised within too short a time-span. As misery and backwardness, hostility and suspicion, Communist subversion and totalitarian rule continue to flourish in the less developed countries, the resulting disillusionment focuses on foreign aid, and leads to cries for abandonment. As Egon Neuberger of the RAND corporation has noted:

> The fault is not fundamentally one of poor administration of the program, but rather the imposition of goals that are beyond the possibility of achievement with the instrumentalities of aid . . . These excessive expectations explain in large part the disillusionment with foreign aid.

To a significant degree these excessive expectations were a result of the brilliant Successes of the Marshall Plan. These were interpreted as evidence of an optimistic future for the field of economic development. Yet the job of helping the less developed nations to achieve self-sustaining growth has been different, both in degree and kind, from the tasks of the Marshall Plan.

The less-developed countries, usually new nation-states, are more accurately described as "pre-developed." The task is not one of reconstruction; in many, the whole fabric of education, commerce, and industry, and political life is in its earliest stages. Modern social institutions, management, and a supply of skipped labor are almost nonexistent. Even as assistance continues, the less developed countries are wracked by chaos more pathetic and complex than the turmoil in Europe in 1947. Former World Bank President C. E. Black has estimated that it is "likely that there will be ten to fifteen revolutions a year for the foreseeable future in the less developed societies." Political unrest, which unfortunately postpones or cancels economic development, now seems an unavoidable part of the development process. The enormity of the task is clear.

Still, given a realistic set of goals and purposes, and an awareness that foreign aid exists as only one instrument for achieving them, policy-makers and the public alike can divest themselves of pie-in-the-sky expectations and appreciate the *real* possibilities of foreign assistance.

Fourteen Western European nations, in addition to Japan, Lebanon, and Iran, no longer require American aid. Greece, Israel, Taiwan, Mexico, and the Philippines will be added to the list in the near future. But even nations such as India which still cope with gigantic economic and social problems, have achieved much during the last two decades. Since the early 1950's, India's steel production has increased sevenfold, her electrical power capacity in 1972 will be ten times the level of 1953, four times as many of her children are attending school, and malaria has been reduced from 100 million cases annually to less than 50,000 in 1966. Foreign assistance, together with able administration, has indeed achieved an exemplary record.

B. THE GROWING GAP

Despite such successes, prospects for future achievement are very much in doubt. George Woods, another former President of the World Bank, has offered the following gloomy assessment:

> The available amount of international development financing is falling further and further behind the economic capacity of higher income nations to provide it, and further and further behind the capacity of developing countries to use it productively.

How much growth is required if the gap between rich and poor nations is to be narrowed? In 1966 the per capita gross national product of the U.S. was $3648; in India it was $104, in Indonesia, $70, in Nigeria, $117, in Bolivia, $149. The average gap between these four and the U.S. was $3538; in 1960 this figure was $2896 – a six-year increase of 22%. To fill this gap halfway by raising per capita incomes to $1000 per year would require 200 times the current aid flow; to achieve the equality of the poor with the rich in 50 years would take $65 billion annually! Yet, the present rate of aid flow has leveled off, and grants to multilateral agencies have in fact decreased.

..How does the present effort of the developed countries compare? The average total economic aid from *all* sources to the less developed countries from 1961-65 was $6.7 billion annually, one-tenth the "equality" requirement. What proportion of even *this* burden does the U.S. bear? In 1962, U.S. bilateral assistance accounted for 56% of the non-communist aid; in 1965, less than 50%. But, while our total share is still impressive, our commitments seem less so in terms of our relative ability to pay. In 1946-48, our total aid budget represented 2.1% of the GNP; in 1949-52, 1.8%; in 1965, 0.9%. When *economic* aid alone is considered, the 1965 figure falls to 0.6%, and the 1968 figure to *one-quarter* of 1%. The relatively modest goal urged on the developed countries by the 1964 United Nations Conference on Trade and Development (UNCTAD) is a level of aid amounting to 1% of the GNP. This, we too believe, is a *minimal* commitment in light of the enormity of the task.

C. DEFICIENT TECHNIQUES

A discussion of confused goals and inadequate levels by no means exhausts the catalogue of ills in our current foreign aid effort; very serious problems exist in the techniques through which current United States assistance is administered.

1. Loans vs. Grants

It is essential to note that the recent shift in emphasis in aid distribution from grants to loans does not represent to the United States a significant reduction in monetary expenditure. From the developing nations' view, it does, however, almost negate the possible accomplishments of the program.

In the early years of the U.S. foreign aid program, assistance was given primarily in the form of grants of U.S. dollars to foreign governments. From 1948-52, 90% of our aid took this form. By 1965, however, only one-third of our bilateral economic assistance was disbursed as grants. This shift was political: Congress' concern with saving the taxpayers' money, plus the insistence that the exercise of the discipline to repay loan strengthens the moral fiber of the borrower and demands that he use his resources more economically.

But is a grant really a "giveaway", and does it constitute "unbusinesslike relations?" To the businessman supplying the equipment purchased by the recipient through his foreign assistance there is no difference between a loan and a grant. The profit realized by the exporter is the same. To the importer in the recipient country, the end-user of the equipment, there is also no difference: he pays his government in local currency and, if the transaction results from a grant, the money is deposited in a "counterpart fund" in the United States. For both supplier and user the transaction is businesslike. As for the stimulus to more efficient allocation of resources which is alleged to flow from loans, John Lewis has aptly remarked that, if the immediacy and urgency of the domestic needs are not sufficient stimuli to efficiency, "it may be doubted that much marginal stimulation will be afforded by deferred repayment obligations."

And Robert Asher concluded:

> In the foreign aid business, the character-building virtues of loans versus grants are for the most part figments of the imagination.

On the contrary, it can be argued that loans of the current type, repayable in dollars at 2.5% interest, actually *retard* the economic development of the recipient. The ability of the recipient to service the loan depends not, as is usually argued, on the profitability of the project for which the loan is made, but on whether all its industries and services together earn enough foreign exchange to pay for essential imports *and* provide a surplus to be applied to debt servicing. Given present skyrocketing public debts in the less developed countries, the existence of this ability to repay is highly doubtful.

In the past decade the public debt of these nations has risen from $10 billion to $45 billion. A World Bank survey revealed that in 1963, 73 aid-recipient nations were forced to spend $2.9 billion of their foreign exchange in repayment of past loans. Debt service in Latin America now amounts to 47% of all aid expenditures that region receives from the U.S. It has been estimated that, if the present volume and terms of lending remain unchanged, the net benefit to the poorer countries – the incoming aid minus the outgoing payments – will drop to *near zero* by 1975. In the next twelve years, India alone will need $18 billion in foreign assistance, of which $14 billion is required for debt servicing. It is evident that foreign assistance loans, on their present terms, are mortgaging away the futures of the less developed countries.

2. "Tying" and the Balance of Payments

Prior to 1958 the United States required competitive global bidding for the bulk of its aid procurements. But understandable concern for increasing gold losses led the government that year to begin to tie American aid very tightly to purchases from American producers. By 1965, 80% of American economic assistance was tied.

Critics of U.S. foreign economic policy have claimed that tying was merely a device for "dumping" surplus or over-priced U.S. goods. In addition, they contended that this process was creating a dangerous degree of aid-recipient dependence on American industry and commerce – in clear contrast to our stated aims of promoting economic *independence* abroad.

Charges of economic colonialism appeared strengthened when President Kennedy and AID chief David Bell, in attempting to develop increased public and congressional support for foreign aid, stated that foreign aid would reshape trade patterns in areas which had formerly traded almost exclusively with Europe. And in the mid-1960's, legislation was passed which prohibited the use of aid to support projects which could result in export goods competitive with U.S. products. As a result, Professor John Montgomery has noted, "the nation seems to be becoming mercantilist in spite of itself."

Besides creating resentment, tying substantially reduces the efficiency of foreign aid. It harms both donors and recipients. So long as aid-giving nations adhere to this practice, each is deprived of the opportunity of earning funds from the expenditure of others, to the detriment of its most efficient producers. In addition, tying prevents the less developed countries from expanding their purchases from each other. In general, Asher notes:

> the tying process tends either to raise the total cost of aid programs over what they would be if purchases were made in the cheapest market, or to procure less aid for the same amount of money.

AID itself estimates that the average aid dollar's value to the recipient decreases at least 15-20% as a result of tying. In a sample of twenty development projects financed by six different countries, an item-by-item comparison of the lowest quotations from the tied source with the lowest quotation in international competitive bidding showed the weighted average to be 51% higher from the tied source.

What effect has tying had on the U.S. balance of payments deficit? Commerce Department figures show the direct balance-of-payments drain resulting from the heavily-tied 1966 foreign aid program to be $750 million. But a recent study demonstrated that whereas the 1958 (pre-tying) U.S. trade imbalances with 25 recipients of non-military assistance was $1.8 billion, in 1965 – *with* tying of aid – the imbalance had shrunk by only $200 million. John Lewis has concluded that:

> the balance of payments improvement that can be accomplished by tying American aid to dollar purchases is comparatively slight since, even without country-of-origin tying, a substantial portion of American loans would be spent in the United States anyway and since . . . some of the loans spent elsewhere would indirectly facilitate additional dollar exports.

At any rate, aid tying is no *solution* to the basic problem, the relatively poorer competitive position of American exporters. Tying in effect subsidizes these exporters, removing them from the necessity of re-sharpening their competitive talents and conditioning themselves for the long pull.

In conclusion, not only does tying distort and reduce the true economic value of the aid funds to the less developed countries, but it also, as George Woods argues, makes "aid become a hypocritical misnomer, a disguised subsidy to domestic manufacturers in the export business."

3. the Counter-productivity of Bilateralism

The proportion of U.S. economic aid channeled through multilateral agencies from 1956-65 averaged 6.5%. Clearly our aid program, like those of most developed countries, is conducted overwhelmingly on a bilateral basis.

Yet bilateralism has distorted the goals of foreign aid. Programs which were conceived and justified in long-term perspectives have been too readily convertible to the use of short-range interests. In the early days of assistance, the foreign offices of the developed countries quickly learned that aid provided a convenient and expedient political lever. Gifts in money and kind, an old and embarrassing tool of foreign affairs but now re-labeled as assistance, became an open and respectable means of bribery. Donors came to use assistance in a number of ways: to preserve power in a former colony; to sweeten negotiations for a military base; to obtain a manifestation of resistance to Communism; or to gain or close access to markets. During the 1950's when rice was listed as a U.S. surplus item, aid was denied to Vietnam's most important domestic crop. Irrigation, pest control, and extension services went unaided; all would have had the forbidden effect of increasing rice production.

By the time foreign aid reached its present level, it was inextricably bound up with the short-term external political and economic ambitions of the donors. Yet it continued to be justified with promises of long-range mutual benefits. Tailored to fit these political policies of the donors, bilateral assistance has become counter-productive, working against the interests of both donor and recipients.

When financial and technical assistance are undertaken on a bilateral basis, a complicated relationship is born binding the donor to the recipient. Rigidities arise which, in effect, pre-commit the donor to a future course of action, a course that the donor may find undesirable in the future.

To the extent that the donor's diplomats, parliamentarians, and public are conditioned to supporting foreign assistance for reasons of national self-interest, this assistance is increasingly seen as an "investment" in the recipient. The more aid is "invested" in a less developed nation, the more the donor is forced by public and parliamentary opinion to defend its own investment in the recipient country. *The United States' increased sensitivity to the internal affairs of the recipients of our aid results in artificial extension of our vital interests.*

The result is the increased possibility that the donor will respond in a manner far out of proportion to its actual interests when an unfriendly act occurs in a recipient nation. The response is often in the form of a termination of all assistance; e.g., the abrupt withdrawal of German aid from Tanzania.

The more serious possibility of military response from the donor is also implicit in the aid relationship. Bilateral assistance tends to relate the great powers more closely to the unpredictable events in the Third World and increases the possibilities that accidental or planned chaos in some remote nation will involve them intimately.

Assistance locks the donor and the recipient into a downward spiral; incidents within the recipient nation result in the donor's retaliation, which further accents the recipient's bitterness. Aid-giving nations, hoping to bank a fund of goodwill, often find themselves staring only at red ink. The experience of the U.S. foreign aid program in Burma is a classical example of bilateral assistance creating resentment. As John Montgomery notes:

> So long as a sense of obligation remained . . . the Burmese were not able to free themselves of fear that their neutrality was somehow being weakened by the mere acceptance of U.S. aid.

While donor nations have shown exaggerated reaction to events in the countries linked to them by aid, this reaction is usually minimized by the stability of their own governments. The less developed nations, however, enjoy little stability, and aid is often the most important national issue. Thus any adverse effects of aid tend to be greatly magnified in their impact on both a recipient's economic and political development.

The flow of bilateral assistance often begins with a stream of predevelopment study teams which flock to the new country, monopolize the few efficient ministers' and economists' time, and often merely duplicate the efforts of previous survey groups. Once projects are chosen, the U.S. often has to "sell" the local government on the project that corresponds to our particular interests. The recipient government, unable to match the competence of the American technicians, accepts a project it half wants and half understands. Backed by the donor for its visibility and the recipient for its political value, a particular assistance program can leave the recipient committed to the local costs and the long-range servicing of the loan, often with sizeable interest rates. Thus saddled with the recurring costs of a number of such projects, a recipient can no longer afford to borrow on any terms. Moreover, when these nations defy a tenet of American foreign policy, they can usually measure our displeasure by the size of the cut in the next year's funds. The see-sawing aid levels to Egypt and Yugoslavia are two of the sharpest examples of the influence of Congressional pique.

The seeds of difficulty are sown as the recipient government begins to serve two masters, its own constituents with their mounting desires for land and the products of technology and its donors with its relatively inflexible view of stability and desire for protection of private investment. When the local government is drawn from the privileged class, we and that class are together on one side of a widening gulf between their government and their people.

The recipient, then, is expected to dance to the foreign policy tune played by the donor and maintain a stable and westernizing society in the face of the tremendous internal pressures inevitable in newly independent states. Because of the nature of bilateral assistance, the donor, even when its aid springs from a well of good intentions, denies the recipient government both a freedom of choice in foreign policy and tools of government which would broaden its support and increase its long-term stability.

Assistance to less developed nations is necessarily difficult and frustrating. Even at best, however, bilateral assistance is an inefficient means for the development task.

The greatest inefficiency is also the most obvious: each donor must maintain an entire backup administration for its assistance programs, necessitating an enormous number of government personnel both in the capital and in the field. When administrative overhead is multiplied by the dozen major donors, the waste involved is enormous. Ironically, the legislative suspicion that aid is wasteful has resulted in a very costly supervision of each project at every stage by an unwieldy number of bureaucrats and their attendant red tape.

In addition, the bilateral system cannot take a global or even a regional view of assistance and determine priorities. Sometime multiple goals conflict. In the 1950's the World Bank's insistence on private ownership of a steel mill it was financing in the Philippines was undermined when the U.S. Export-Import Bank provided a loan for a publicly-owned mill.

The waste and destructive components of bilateral assistance are inherent in the very nature of the donor-recipient relationship. The many renovations and re-organizations of the bilateral programs have done little or nothing to lessen the naturally corrosive effect of these bilateral aid relationships. These arguments have been summarized by Senator Howard H. Baker, Jr., who recently observed that bilateral aid

> certainly does not seem to be winning us many friends, even in the recipient countries, and there is some question about how much true help is being given to the economic development of these countries . . . It leads to all sorts of ill feeling in the recipient countries when we try to impose a minimum of control over how our money is being spent . . . One way to avoid such pitfalls is by channeling our aid dollars through multinational lending institutions . . .

II. A MULTILATERAL AID PROGRAM

The Ripon Society proposes that the United States discontinue the extension of bilateral foreign economic assistance through the mechanism of tied loans and that it move toward a multilateral aid program. The emphasis should be on aid funds which are untied and are disbursed by Congress as grants to the multilateral agencies. Respected institutions through which a large part of an expanded multilateral aid program could be channeled are already in existence.

The International Bank for Reconstruction and Development (World Bank) and its associated institutions, the International Finance Corporation (IFC) and the International Development Association (IDA), are institutions of proven ability. The World Bank is financed through subscriptions by member government, a fixed percentage of which is lent to applicant governments, and the remainder of which exists as a guaranty fund for private investors. Only 40% of its loans are made from its own capital; the rest is financed through the sale of bonds on the public market. The voting power of the member-nation directors is weighted according to the size of subscriptions, with the U.S. currently holding 30% of the vote.

Loans have concentrated primarily on the development of "infrastructure" – power, communications, transportation, and the modernization of agriculture. Loans are extended only after a thorough investigation by the Bank's staff into the applicant's economic situation; they act as a "guarantee of a nation's probity," and are usually followed by an increased flow of private investment.

Free from the taint of power politics and backed by its ability to raise money from the most skeptical donors, the bank's professionalism stands in sharp contrast to the political maneuvering which usually characterizes the bilateral approach. IBRD loans have been used to dredge the port of Bangkok, to free Baghdad from floods, to electrify the Cauca Valley in Colombia, and to reorganize the Ethiopian telephone system, among other projects. Its good offices have been made available to relieve international tensions which impede development: it mediated the issue of compensation for the Suez Canal; provided advisers to represent the Congo and Belgium in their disputes; and conducted a nine-year mediation between India and Pakistan which culminated in the Indus Basin Development Fund Agreement.

The World Bank, however, disburses "hard" loans and, while its accomplishments are legion, it has almost been priced out of its market due to the shortage of countries that can afford to get further into debt. Thus, it is the Bank's "soft loan" affiliate, the IDA, which can serve a more crucial function in the current aid crisis. Extended on a long-term basis – a ten-year grace period followed by 40 years repayment – IDA loans require no interest payment and only a small service charge (3/4%). Thus IDA is more able to invest in enterprises which are not immediately commercially profitable, but, for the same reason, is forced to rely on its members' munificence for funds rather than the private market. The IDA is currently out of funds, and has met with only limited success in attempting to increase government subscriptions. The U.S. government should drop its attempts to achieve a tying arrangement within IDA and should substantially increase its grants to this, "the agency best equipped to cope with . . . the growing debt burden of the poor."

The World Bank should also be given authority and funds to institute a supplementary financing program as proposed by UNCTAD. Less developed nations which submit country development plans and policies for scrutiny by the Bank and which agree to adhere to certain financial standards should be eligible for compensation in the event of a loss in export earnings due to events beyond their control. While costing donor nations only $300-400 million per year, such a program would substantially lessen the severe foreign exchange fluctuations of poorer nations and enable them to plan development more confidently. The appointment of Robert S. McNamara as World Bank president provides a new opportunity to strengthen this international institution.

The United States and other developed nations should make more funds and personnel available to the United Nations Development Program (UNDP), an excellent conduit for the massive technical assistance and pre-investment work required by less developed nations. Laying the groundwork for institution-building and human resource development programs, and emphasizing pilot plant projects and pre-investment surveys, this agency's work aids nations by increasing their ability to absorb investment funds. Twenty-five of its projects costing a total of $19.2 million have called forth $751 million in additional foreign investment.

In addition, a multilateral approach to foreign aid would allow a consortium of donor nations to channel funds through a multilateral body. In particular, the funding of costlier projects would be resolved at the consortium level, thus preventing an excessive drain of funds from the IBRD family and regional banks, while still retaining for the donors a considerable degree of flexibility.

IBRD-led consortia now exist for India, Pakistan, Nigeria, Sudan, Tunisia, East Africa, Colombia, Thailand, and Malaysia. An Inter-American Bank-led consortium exists for Equador, and a Dutch-led group, for Indonesia. Greatly expanded use of this multilateral device would lessen the strains and stresses of bilateral giving and promote a sounder division of labor among developed countries.

The Inter-American Development Bank, the Asian Development Bank, the African Development Bank, and the Central American Bank for Economic Development should be provided with greatly expanded development funds by the United States. These channels combine a professional, non-political approach to development with a healthy stress on regional development, a combination lacking in the bilateral approach. The Mekong River development project, for example, united in a common cause Laos, Cambodia, Vietnam, and Thailand (some of whom had no diplomatic relations with each other); none of the states involved could have undertaken significant action alone, nor through a fragmented bilateral arrangement.

One possible device for generating increased support for multilateral aid would be a parliamentary forum, enabling a frank and full exchange among legislators of developed and underdeveloped nations alike of the problems and prospects of aid. Such a healthy and humbling exchange could produce support for expanded aid efforts through multilateral channels.

But the United States should take the lead in persuading other donor nations of the advantages of multilateralism through the example of its own deeds.

III. THE ADVANTAGES

The shift from bilateral to multilateral foreign aid would channel more funds into those projects which are both significant and economically viable. The selection and operation of these projects would contribute to political education and the growth of responsible democratic institutions. Meanwhile, the U.S. would not find itself a prisoner of internal political events in which it has no interest.

A gradual shift to multilateral economic aid will help to clearly distinguish development aid from military assistance, long-term aims from stop-gap security measures. The current overlapping in authorization and operation of bilateral military and economic assistance leads recipients to suspect that conditions attached to one form of aid are in reality intended to advance the purposes of the other. A requirement, written into the Mutual Security Act in the 1950's, that recipients of *economic* aid pledge to use their full resources to defend "the strength of the free world" led ten countries to refuse assistance under such confused terms. These two functions – development and military aid – should be separated to ensure the economic integrity of economic development programs both in the mind of the recipient and in the policy of the U.S. As the Republican Critical Issues Council stated in 1964, aid for short-term or military purposes "should not be confused with economic and technical assistance directed toward what we believe is foreign aid's appropriate role in achieving longer-range purposes." An end to the confusing of development and security goals is especially imperative in the wake of the Vietnam experience.

Multilateral aid also has the advantage of allowing developed nations to achieve their long-term goals in the development of the Third World without poisoning their relations with these highly sensitive states. Henry Cabot Lodge has noted that multinational organizations "can push a recipient government in a way that no sovereign government can ever push another. No international prestige is involved, nor can the cry of "imperialism" be raised when it is the gently friendly pressure of the . . . United Nations. How much better it is for us not to be the ones who cause disapproval or displeasure."

In addition, by making greater use of international and regional bodies in which the less developed countries could share the responsibility of distributing aid, an increased recognition and appreciation of the inherent problems of allocating scarce resources would follow. Professor H. G. Johnson has suggested that:

> In the process, (these nations) would have to become hardheaded and hardhearted about each other's economic policies and performances . . . the educational effects in

> the long run could be of tremendous value in improving the efficiency of the use of foreign aid and of development planning in general.

Finally, the limited amounts of aid which are now disbursed bilaterally could achieve far greater results if they were distributed on the basis of a coordinated strategy. Confusion, duplication, and the existence of pockets of neglect would become much less of a problem. Regional development would be encouraged rather than frustrated.

IV. POSSIBLE CRITICISMS

There are several possible objections which could be raised against a shift toward multilateral foreign assistance. Most of them, in fact, stem from the confusion as to our real purpose in providing such aid.

A. "It can't fight communism"

The argument that increased use of international agencies which are non-political or which encompass a variety of political ideologies would deprive the United States of political control of its aid overlooks the stark fact that past attempts to exercise such short-term control have been not only a major cause of our current difficulties but also absolutely fruitless. Economic aid *should* not be used to "buy friends" abroad; its true purpose is to promote more stable and independent regimes which will be better able to resist such pressures. Furthermore, it *cannot* be used in such ways; the use of aid to bribe or punish creates resentment and undermines the popular support of governments willing to comply with such tactics. Far from increasing our flexibility, it ties us in rigid relationships from which we cannot escape. We have programs of military assistance with which to strengthen our allies – the task of economic development should remain distinct and separate. Nations which receive our economic assistance through multi-lateral channels without political strings will, indeed, have an *increased* respect for our motives and policies.

It must be observed that this proposed shift in the emphasis in our aid program would in no way prohibit us from engaging in a massive one-shot aid program to boost an ally over the economic hump. We could always initiate another Marshall Plan or offer substantial bilateral assistance to another Taiwan.

B. "The aid will be wasted"

The argument that close Congressional and Administration scrutiny of all details of aid is necessary to prevent "waste" of assistance is deficient on two counts. First, aid distributed multilaterally is not uncontrolled; thorough surveys are made of requirements and resources and the standards enforced are based on strict economic criteria. The substitution of "businesslike" criteria for short-term political purposes will *increase* efficient utilization.

But to expect *no* unwise use of resources by less developed countries is visionary. If these countries could invest capital as efficiently, maintain machinery and equipment as well, administer enterprises as smoothly as developed nations, they would not be as poor as they are. "Waste and inefficiency should be looked on as normal companions of an accelerated development effort, not to be encouraged or placidly accepted, but as elements that can only be reduced gradually," comments John Pincus.

C. "Our balance of payments deficit will be worsened"

CHAPTER 23
NEW NATIONALISMS

This article, written by Robert Dickson Crane, a research fellow of the Hudson Institute, appeared in the Ripon FORUM for May of 1968 and helped to bring together threads which ran through Ripon analyses of both foreign and domestic issues.

– Editors

A chance is taking place within the nationalist leadership of many newly independent states that profoundly challenges the "nation-building," concepts that American experts have used for analyzing the Third World.

The first generation of Third World nationalists, who succeeded European colonial rulers, were so eager to modernize their "backward" societies that they often rejected their own traditional cultures as suitable vehicles for change. They emphasized "nation-building" and borrowed their political and economic models from the centralized governments of developed countries. Today a second generation of nationalists is trying to fill the cultural vacuum by resurrecting the best from their traditions, in particular those elements that promote discipline and honesty. Their object is not to import forms of industrialism directly from the West, but to create an independent culture that can incorporate the character traits essential to modern technological society.

The new second-generation nationalists are thus critical of rigid or magical reliance on any form of economic or political order to solve problems that often are unique to each geographical area and to each society. Instead they seek the political aggregate, the method of government, and the economic methods that can best evoke the social energies necessary to sustain modernization. The new nationalists abhor the social dislocation that occurs when the leaders of a society reject traditional values, customary law and existing social fabric without providing suitable replacements. They believe that workable replacements must come naturally from traditional cultural communities rather than artificially from outside them.

This is particularly true where the political ferment motivating the new Asian and African leaders is based on their deep belief that the natural forces of community solidarity, if given a chance, rather than the disruptive force of political centralization, are the key to the economic mobilization of people below the state level.

Thus, whereas first generation nationalists tried to maintain central governments ruling over old colonial boundaries, the new nationalists support the creation of new political units based on the binding force of ethnic and cultural identity. Inevitably, the decline of the first-generation nationalists creates pressure for the replacement of former colonial administrative units, groupings more consistent with the ethnic and cultural boundaries. This pressure may in some cases lead directly to the breakup of first-generation states which were created without reference to natural communal bonds; in other cases it may lead to the demand for confederation, regional groupings and local autonomy within existing states; in still others, to a desire for boundary changes or for supra-state regional groupings. In all cases, the unfilled desires for communal nationalism generate severe tensions.

A few current examples will illustrate some of the strains involved. In Southeast Asia many of the rising generation of minority or communal leaders are cooperating to promote ethniccultural autonomy within a decentralized framework of confederal regionalism some times larger than the existing states in the area and sometimes different from the regional orientation of the existing state leaders. For example, in the Assame portion of India, cut off from India's main South Asian land-mass, the new generation of leaders in beginning to raise its vision to the subcontinental level, anticipating the Southeast Asian subcontinent as the political matrix for its own future.

Even in the eastern portion of Southeast Asia, the new forces of communal modernizing nationalism are observable among the intellectual leaders of Central Vietnam. They believe that the dynamic forces necessary to assure both modernization and independence must come from the indigenous Vietnamese culture, based in Hue, rather than from the two exogenous cultures, the Communist based in Hanoi, and the American based in Saigon.

One of the leaders of the new generation of Vietnamese nationalists, Nguyen Chanh Thi, who is the only peasant to achieve the rank of general in the South Vietnamese army, has long proclaimed that only immediate and total land reform can win the war, and that the landlords will simply have to wait for eventual compensation until circumstances permit. General Thi urged his senior commanders to live and work two days a week in the villages, because otherwise, he asserted, they could not know what they were fighting for. This extremely popular Buddhist commander of I corps was removed from office and exiled in 1966 upon the recommendation of the U.S. embassy.

The new Vietnamese nationalists have repeatedly warned that the imperial nature of the Communist goals in Vietnam should not blind us to the essential nationalist nature of the overall conflict. The power of nationalism, they believe, explains why the call for unifying the country has such great appeal to the cadres and potential cadres of the Vietcong, and why American support for the artificial split of Vietnam into two totally separate parts has evolved no enthusiastic response. The Communist propagandists have based their entire war effort on the political goal and slogan: "Defend the north, liberate the south, unify the homeland."

The new nationalists in Vietnam, of whom General Thi and Tran Van Dinh are among the better-known spokesmen, are convinced that the peoples opposed to the Communist power in Vietnam can win only if they can adopt and pursue a similar overarching goal to liberate Vietnam from foreign influence and recreate it in a confederal union of at least three equal partners, with capitals in the central, northern, and southern regions, and perhaps one in the Montagnard region of the west, if the Montagnards should wish to join such a confederation. The union of a free Vietnam has been a key goal of all Vietnamese for more than a generation. Vietnamese nationalists have repeatedly tried to impress on American officials that the Vietnamese people will sacrifice their lives in limitless numbers if they can fight for such a nationalist goal. For proof they merely point to the indomitable courage of Vietcong cadres, who fight on against seemingly insuperable odds.

General Thi and Tran Van Dinh have long represented a large body of Vietnamese professional opinion, in their insistence that most of the work of the U.S. forces in Vietnam could be accomplished by doubling the size of the South Vietnamese army. The Americans, they insist, should be restricted by a formal treaty to the interdiction of North Vietnamese regular units in South Vietnam. This would force the non-communist Vietnamese to win or lose the revolutionary struggle by themselves, thereby giving them the only chance to win it.

Although most Vietnamese nationalists are discouraged by the disastrous outcome of the current "American" phase of the conflict in Vietnam, they firmly believe that the genuine Vietnamese nationalists in concert with the nationalists in other countries, will eventually triumph against the Communists in Southeast Asia. The potential of the new Vietnamese nationalism they believe may be suggested by the success of the liberation movement led by Tran Van Dinh, which in 1960 had succeeded in establishing secure base areas in large parts of North Vietnam extending all the way to the Chinese border. Some of Vietnam's most promising leaders were permanently alienated from Premier Diem when he reluctantly abandoned the entire operation and the new revolutionary era it was supposed to inaugurate. Upon American orders, he concentrated instead on the negative and impossible goal of enforcing order against Communist insurrection in the south.

The loss of this initiative in the middle of a profound and growing political revolution throughout Vietnam was never overcome. It may be too late for a resurgence of Vietnamese nationalism to regain the initiative. But the lessons we and others can derive from past policy failures may help prevent repetitions elsewhere in Asia and Africa.

The new forces of nationalism are equally visible in other regions of the Third World. Perhaps the most dramatic example outside of Southeast Asia has been triggered by the growing cultural and political consciousness of the black population in the southern section of Arab-dominated Sudan. In Arabic their land has long been called "The Land of Slaves," but the blacks have changed the name to "Anzania," after an ancient East African empire. The independence struggle of this predominantly Christian people has cost them an estimated half-million lives since the first bloodbath in 1955, or one-eighth their total population. Even with American aid, the Arab Sudanese are now expending more than a quarter of their total national budget to suppress the newly conscious "Anzanian" nation.

Some of these Anzanians seem to fight without hope, in accordance with Winston Churchill's dictum: "You may have to fight when there is no hope of victory, because it is better to persist than to live as slaves." Others have a vision of their future in an East African regional polity rather than in an Arab world of the Mediterranean. They maintain hope because they are convinced that some day artificial states like the Sudan and regional groupings based upon them will no longer be considered as the beginning of a new post-colonial future, but merely as an artificial projection of a colonial past.

Potentially more tragic is the military suppression of Nigeria's most talented Christian tribes by the Federal Government in Lagos. The Ibos and related tribes from Eastern Nigeria formed the mainstay of the professional and merchant classes in Northern Nigeria before pogroms were carried out against them by the Muslim inhabitants. Perhaps a million refugees fled to their homeland in Eastern Nigeria. The Eastern Region, with some 12 million inhabitants, demanded a larger measure of autonomy from Lagos and compensation for the refugees. When the Federal Government reneged on promises to grant these demands, the Easterners declared their region the independent Republic of Biafra. They have since been fighting for their survival against Federal forces armed by both the Soviets and the British. The meagerly armed Biafrans have suffered about 100,000 civilian casualties at the hands of Federal troops but have made it clear that they will continue to fight until they are assured a measure of self-determination. The attempt to crush them can only result in civilian slaughter, exhaustion of the Federal treasury, and a reputation for genocide that will severely damage the name of Nigeria.

Communal nationalism and the revolutionary regionalism that accompanies it pose a dilemma both for the United States and for the Soviet Union. This new nationalism should appeal to the United States because its basic economic goal is responsible modernization. Its basic cultural goal is evolutionary traditionalism, and its basic political goal is the self-determination of peoples. It should appeal to the Soviet Union because its basic political methodology by necessity is revolution. The combination of the above characteristics, however, has made the new nationalism unacceptable to either the United States or the Soviet Union. Americans tend to assume that revolutionary groups, of whatever nature, are influenced or controlled by Communists. The Soviets tend to assume that traditionalism, until proved otherwise, is merely a reactionary reversion to an outdated capitalist or feudal order.

The Soviet problem is particularly acute, because the Soviets themselves are intellectually akin to the first-generation nationalists. Their own state was built by the violent suppression of communal nationalism and a brutal drive toward monolithic centralized power. Although the Soviets, unlike the Chinese, are already, and perhaps rapidly, moving into the stage of second-generation nationalism, their foreign policy still retains its stake in helping first-generation colonial movements fill the vacuum left by the departing colonial powers. The Soviets see second-generation nationalism as a major threat to their efforts to remake the world in their own desired image. Only a major modification of Soviet domestic and foreign policy would permit the Soviets genuinely to support the new nationalism in Asia and Africa. By supporting existing power structures in the Third World the Soviets may be aligning themselves not with the wave of the future but with a hangover from the imperial era.

The age of empires required large political aggregates designed above all for efficient economic administration in a world economy in which each power tended toward an autarky. The shift of the basic unit of economic growth toward smaller political aggregates, if combined with the growth of economic macro-regionalism in a more cooperative world economy, works against the continued existence of any empires based on first-generation nationalism. During the present century, this development may prove decisive in destroying perhaps unworkable Third World empires, such as India, or in preventing the implementation of others, such as Nkrumah's dreamed-of African empire. Over the long run, the growth of the new communal nationalism may result in the transformation even of such Second World empires as the Soviet Union and Communist China.

For the United States, the new nationalism should present a welcome challenge, because it enables us to perceive important forces in our own society as well as in the Third World. We were more fortunate than many states in Asia and Africa, because after independence the United States did not have a major problem of integrating previously entrenched cultural groups, but had merely to integrate individual immigrants already alienated from one culture and ready for another. We therefore were able to build one of the world's model nation-states, where the state is based on a cohesive nation and the nation is coextensive with the state.

Very recently, the growing cultural and political consciousness of the blacks in our society has created a new problem of incipient communal nationalism that cannot be solved by territorial adjustments as it can in many African and Asian states. We should welcome the responsible elements of communal group loyalty among the blacks within our society, because this new communal loyalty gives us, both blacks and whites, the opportunity to demonstrate how a genuinely and deliberately pluralistic society can accept communal pride and channel it into a positive force for modernization through self-help.

The real challenge to U.S. policy, therefore, is not the existence of a new nationalism in Asia and Africa, nor its counterpart among the responsible black leaders in our own country, but the myth that such natural communal forces need pose a dilemma.

We pride ourselves on being a non-ideological, problem-solving people devoted to democratic self-determination. We should therefore be first to understand the new nationalist forces at work in the world in this revolutionary era.

CONCLUSION
THE RIPON ROLE AS RIPON SEES IT

The Ripon Society has produced a series of papers on substantive issues and political trends, most of which are collected in this volume, since its inception in Cambridge, Massachusetts in December of 1962. The group of teachers, lawyers, businessmen, law and graduate students which gathered then took its name from the birthplace of the Republican Party, Ripon, Wisconsin, and modeled its organization in part after the Bow Group, formed by young members of the Conservative Party in Great Britain.

For over a year the group met and debated; its first public statement was a declaration of moderate philosophy entitled "A Call to Excellence in Leadership" and issued in January of 1964. The title soon became the Society's motto; the wide response to the paper reinforced members' conviction that one could contribute to the American political dialogue by saying the right thing at the right time and that this did not require large numbers of famous names.

Ripon began to surface more frequently with the passing months. A civil rights study was published through the Republican Citizen's Committee in the spring of 1964. On the eve of the Republican National convention, the Society gathered in Ripon, Wisconsin to issue its "Declaration of Conscience," a statement which recalled the GOP tradition in civil rights and warned against any attempt to compromise it.

Two days after the 1964 election Ripon released a preliminary analysis of the results, based on data from a national network of correspondents. (The project has been repeated for each subsequent fall election.) Later, the complete results of this effort were printed in a 124 page *Election '64* report described by Theodore H. White as "far and away the best study of the elections made by anyone." Said retiring GOP National Chairman Dean Burch when the report and its recommendations were presented to the National Committee in January, 1965: "It's amazing to me that a group of eighty members can write a report and get so much attention."

In December, 1964, the Republican Governors Association adopted a number of recommendations from a study presented by the Ripon Society, an occasion which the London *Economist* described as Ripon's "first substantial success in Republican affairs." The next summer the Society's research paper calling for unconditional sharing of federal tax revenues with state and local governments was issued jointly with the same Republican Governors who gave it their unanimous approval. The *New York Times* later credited the paper with reviving what had seemed to be a lost cause after President Johnson had turned thumbs down on the tax sharing idea just after his reelection.

Three major changes in Ripon operations took place in 1965. First, a two room office was rented overlooking Harvard Square in Cambridge, Massachusetts and a secretary hired to help run it. Secondly, the group moved beyond its local base by establishing a chapter in Los Angeles. (New Haven and New York chapters came on a year later.) Thirdly, Ripon began to issue a regular monthly magazine, *The Forum,* which featured both research materials and political reports and was described by the *Washington Post* as presenting "some of the most thoughtful discussion in Republican circles."

Major research papers in 1966 and 1967 included proposals for greater diplomatic contact with China, the replacement of the draft with a volunteer military, greater concern for the civil rights of the mentally ill, and the adoption of a negative income tax to help the poor. A 129 page study called *Southern Republicanism and the New South* was issued jointly with Republicans for Progress in October of 1966 and the Society's first book, *From Disaster to Distinction* was published in September.

But only a part of Ripon activities are reflected in pages of print. Research teams have worked closely with GOP leaders, drafting legislation, writing speeches, and staffing campaigns at all levels of government and in all parts of the country. A contract research service was recently established. Members have testified before Congressional Committees and the party's national platform committee; they frequently travel to speak on college campuses and at political events. Ripon is represented at all major GOP gatherings and is a member of the Council of Republican Organizations. The oldest Ripon tradition, that of bringing together leaders from the world of politics and the world of ideas, has been continued at program meetings in all of its chapters.

For some time, members have realized that the organization's responsibilities and opportunities were growing faster than its resources. Major efforts to expand Ripon's organizational base were undertaken in 1967; an important step was the decision to employ a full time executive director. A founding member of the Society, Thomas E. Petri, took over than new position in June. And J. Lee Auspitz came on as full time editor of the Ripon *Forum* at the end of 1967.

Ripon growth continues. The *Forum* adds pages and readers each month; its masthead now lists correspondents in most of the fifty states. While the Society does not seek to be a mass membership organization, it is in contact with groups in a dozen major cities which are taking steps toward affiliation. Ripon affairs are directed by a National Governing Board, representing both its chapters and National Associate Members who live outside chapter areas.

Ripon's budget was only $20,000 in 1965, $32,000 in 1966, $49,000 in 1967, and $95,000 in 1968. It is spent chiefly on salaries for the director, editor, secretaries, rent and printing and mailing of publications. It is provided largely by *Forum* subscriptions and contributions from interested friends. From these resources – thanks to a considerable supply of volunteer interest – Ripon has developed a program larger and more visible than its size and budget would predict.

* * *

Because moderate Republicans traditionally organize best around individual candidates, the Ripon Society has become one of the very few organizational spokesmen for the progressive impulse in the GOP. Right wing partisans pour several millions of dollars into the Young Americans for Freedom (budgeted at $25,000 a month), the Free Society Association, the American Conservative Union, Americans for Constitutional Action, *National Review, Human Events,* and a wide range of even more extreme voices ranging from the United Republicans of America to the John Birch Society to the Christian Crusade. Such organizations work constantly to propagate a conservative ideology, a body of belief which will set right a world gone out of kilter, a dogma for which mothers will work long hours and fathers will sign large checks. Their adherents are given the sense of a movement, a cause, a crusade. As a result all of these groups have important influence in Republican politics. They help to explain why conservatives control so much of the Republican political machinery including the Young Republicans and the women's auxiliary, the House and Senate Campaign Committees, some important national committee posts, and most importantly – the machinery which selects national convention delegates in most of the non-primary states.

Republican moderates have often lacked a similar sense of mission and purpose and cause. In fact, at the present time, the only nationally oriented organization in the progressive wing of the party which operates a full time office is the Ripon Society. And the only regular publication identified with GOP moderates is the Ripon *Forum.* Members acknowledge that this is one reason for the publicity their small voice has received. "In politics, if not in physics, the reverberations in a vacuum are powerful," one early publication said.

At the same time, right wing groups speak of Ripon's symbolic role. *National Review* for example, sees the Society as the "think tank" and "incessant foghorn" of moderate Republicanism. In the fall of 1966, the American Conservative Union published a 26 page study of the Ripon Society which described the group as "the tip of the iceberg" of the moderates' designs and concluded, "We should never underestimate its influence and determination."

The Ripon Society of today seeks to retain the informal and enthusiastic air which characterized the group of sixteen who met to share their concern and their hope for the Republican Party five years ago. They met then, one member said, because they were tired of apologizing to those who represented the world of ideas for being Republicans; and they were tired of apologizing to fellow Republicans for being interested in ideas. From the outset Ripon members have seen that their most important contribution to American politics can come in bridging the gulf which has separated much of the GOP from the intellectual and professional community. This gulf first began to open when Theodore Roosevelt left party ranks to form his Bull Moose movement in 1912. It was accentuated during the 1920's and widened further during the New Deal. It was fixed most firmly by the McCarthy experience of the early 1950's. It is a gulf which, as Walter Lippmann has written, is "at the root of the Republican decline." It is a gulf which must be spanned.

This, then, is what the Ripon Society is all about. It is *not* much concerned with outmoded concepts of "liberalism" and "conservatism." It is *very* much concerned that Republicans be receptive and responsive to new ideas from every quarter. It is *not* interested in having the Republicans become either a "me too" party or a "not me" party. It *is* interested in helping the GOP become the party of initiative rather than mere response.

There are many who argue as so many independents and Democrats did during the Goldwater episode of 1964, that working in this way to save the Republican Party is a waste of energy, that the Party should be allowed to follow its death wish without impediment. The Ripon Society firmly rejects this counsel; it believes that the battle for the soul of the Republican is well worth fighting. A number of young and able Republican leaders have helped to encourage this faith.

Not only is the battle worth fighting, it is essential that it be fought well. In the first place, a nation in crisis desperately needs a second party which is strong, progressive, and responsible. The majority party needs the foil of quality opposition if it is to govern and campaign constructively. The tragedy of 1964 was that President Johnson was handed a blank check by voters who had *no choice* but to support him and no leverage for extracting from him commitments on a number of vital issues.

But more than that, we must battle for a responsible and creative GOP because sooner or later it *will* be returned to power. For better or worse, there is going to be a strong Republican Party in this country for some time to come. And, unless there is a concerted effort to make it better, things could be a lot worse for everyone.

What are the chances for making it better? Good enough to make the game well worth playing. For as a Ripon book puts it: "A new order is coming in American politics based upon a new generation and continued growth and concentration of population. By 1975, the politics of today will be almost unrecognizable – in style, in vocabulary and in substance. But few politicians have yet begun to explore the changes which lie ahead."

Will the parties also change this fast? They can. The democratic candidates for President between 1880 and 1932 were Hancock (that's right, Hancock), Cleveland, Bryan, Parker, Wilson, Cox, Davis, Smith and Roosevelt. Do we live in such a stable age that such frequent fluctuations in temperament and philosophy will not be seen again? The difference between FDR's campaign in 1932 and that of 1936 should alone be instructive as to how quickly parties *can* adjust. The intellectual community and the Negro population were identified as largely Republican fifty years ago and we were well into the New Deal before that stereotype was changed. The Goldwater takeover in the face of a two to one edge for Scranton among Republicans in the public opinion polls, testified to the malleability of party orientation. Consider how fast both parties change positions in state contests, particularly in the south, depending on which faction gains control. And remember, too, that 1967 Louis Harris polls showed that the normal Republican constituency is more "liberal" than the normal Democratic constituency on the two great issues of our time: civil rights and Vietnam.

We believe that the Republican party can speak creatively and responsibly to a troubled and bewildered world. And we believe it must. When the margin between sanity and chaos is as thin as at present, we dare wish only the maximum wisdom for any powerful institution. Some day the Republicans will win the Presidency and before they do that, they will continue to control state houses and city halls and congressional seats. They will write legislation and appear on television and they will contribute much to our political dialogue and education. The great question, a deadly serious one in our opinion, is whether that influence will be a force for evil or for good.

* * *

If the Republican Party is to be lively and influential in the future then it must actively and systematically involve those who will shape tomorrow's world. It must learn to excite intellectuals, minority groups, laborers and urban dwellers. It must win the confidence of those who are not at home in the politics of another generation, the new middle classes of our suburbs, the young who are more concerned with opportunity than security, the moderates of the New South. And it must understand that it is ideas that will make the difference in the long run.

The Ripon Society wants to help Republicans achieve these goals. For Ripon believes that the Republican party can break new ground in American politics and serve as a flexible instrument for exploring the challenges of the decades to come.

In this book and elsewhere, Ripon hopes that it can help a party and a nation articulate new approaches to complex problems, to raise questions others do not ask, and to grasp ideas "whose time is yet to come."

Other Ripon Society Publications include:

"The Republican Party and Civil Rights: A Continuing Commitment," prepared by the Ripon Society for the Critical Issues Council of the Republican Citizens Committee April, 1964

"The Republican Governors' Association: The Case for a Third Force," Ripon Society Report and Recommendations to the Republican Governors December, 1964

"The Idea for the Ripon Society" June, 1964

"A New Republican Mandate," Preliminary Analysis of the 1964 Elections November, 1964

"A Republican Civil Rights Platform for 1965" June, 1965

"A Second Mandate to Republicans," An Analysis of the 1965 Elections November, 1965

"The Potential to Govern," Ripon statement on the 1966 Elections November, 1966

"Citizenship for Cuban Refugees," a Ripon Legislative Proposal May, 1966

"Overkill at Omaha," Analysis of the Young Republican National Federation 1967 Convention at Omaha, Nebraska June, 1967

"The 'SMIC' Boondoggle," a Ripon Analysis of the Influence of the Southern Military Industrial Complex in the Johnson Administration February, 1968

"Here's the Rest of Him," A Report on Ronald Reagan June, 1968

The Ripon *Forum,* Monthly Magazine of the Ripon Society Monthly, beginning in 1965

Information on receiving any of the above publications, or copies of other Ripon books on subscribing to the Ripon *Forum* and future publications of the Ripon Society may be obtained by writing to:

The Ripon Society,
14a Eliot Street
Cambridge, Mass. 02138
Tel. 617-491-4180